Ira Hayes

Also by Tom Holm

Nonfiction

Indian Leaders: Oklahoma's First Statesmen
with H. Glenn Jordan

*Strong Hearts, Wounded Souls: Native American Veterans of
the Vietnam War*

*The Great Confusion in Indian Affairs: Native Americans
and Whites in the Progressive Era*

Code Talkers and Warriors: Native Americans and World War II

Native Apparitions: Critical Perspectives on Hollywood's Indians
with Steve Pavlik and M. Elise Marubbio

Fiction

The Osage Rose: An Osage Country Mystery

Anadarko: A Kiowa Country Mystery

Ira Hayes

The Akimel O'odham Warrior, World War II, and the Price of Heroism

Tom Holm

12

TWELVE

NEW YORK BOSTON

Twelve
Hachette Book Group
1290 Avenue of the Americas, New York, NY 10104
twelvebooks.com
twitter.com/twelvebooks

First Edition: August 2023

Twelve is an imprint of Grand Central Publishing. The Twelve name and logo are trademarks of Hachette Book Group, Inc.

The publisher is not responsible for websites (or their content) that are not owned by the publisher.

The Hachette Speakers Bureau provides a wide range of authors for speaking events. To find out more, go to hachettespeakersbureau.com or email HachetteSpeakers@hbgusa.com.

Twelve books may be purchased in bulk for business, educational, or promotional use. For information, please contact your local bookseller or the Hachette Book Group Special Markets Department at special.markets@hbgusa.com.

Additional copyright/credits information is on page 301.

LCCN: 2022039515

ISBNs: 9781538709504 (hardcover), 9781538709528 (ebook), 9781668626542 (audio download)

Printed in Canada

MRQ-T

10 9 8 7 6 5 4 3 2 1

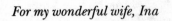

For my wonderful wife, Ina

Contents

Introduction

Ira Hamilton Hayes was easily one of the most written about, photographed, venerated, and exploited young Native men in American history. He received more press than Geronimo, Sitting Bull, Crazy Horse, Cochise, and Tecumseh combined. And he fought not against the white people but shoulder to shoulder with them against the enemies of the United States. He was also in perhaps one of the most seen photographs in American history. The interest in his life was sustained even long after his death. Movies and television programs were made with Ira as the subject or as a principal character.

The use of stereotypes in storytelling is universal and a way of taking a shortcut to the moral of a narrative. Ira was "the Indian" who fought for America and who lifted the Stars and Stripes on Mount Suribachi. As such, he personified the ideal of American racial unity against Nazi racism and Japanese imperialism. He, along with a large number of Native people—disproportional to their population in American society by far—somehow made the American involvement in World War II a righteous crusade. Specifically, he was the hero who personified the United States motto of *E pluribus unum.*

But then Ira became an object of pity. His battle with the Japanese over, he began a struggle with alcohol addiction. Since the late 1940s, Ira's life has been seen as a Shakespearean tragedy. He had become a national hero because he participated in the second flag raising on Mount Suribachi during the terrible battle for the island of Iwo Jima. The picture of that flag raising is easily the most memorable photograph of World War II. However, soon after his return from the war, the newspapers began to hint that, like Shakespeare's tragic heroes, Ira possessed a fatal flaw that led to his descent from heroic status to degradation and a lonely death in the desert. In the tale of his melancholy life story, Ira's lethal weakness was alcoholism. The newspapers and magazines of the period fell into using, perhaps unintentionally, the old trope of the "drunken Indian" to describe Ira's supposed fall from grace.

The problem with this inevitable narrative about Ira's life is that it is too linear and based on a few ideas that stem from larger American cultural references. The heart of Ira's story, taken from the perspective of American culture, is that he was a shy young man who joined the Marines to better serve the nation. He went to war, saw the horrors of the battlefield, and turned to whiskey to remove himself from the reality of life. The poverty of the reservation, both before his military service and after, exacerbated his drinking. It is "very American" to think in these linear terms and put the blame on a perceived lack of individual responsibility on Ira's part. In this narrative, Ira was unable to cope with life in mainstream America and on his reservation. In short, he had neither the drive nor the fair chance to live the American dream. Try as he might, Ira could not avoid the liquor. This is the essence of the "drunken Indian" imagery. Alcohol consumption is, unfortunately, pervasive among Native American veterans, and Ira was saddled with the brand of being an alcoholic for at least ten years prior to his death. Alcoholism was even listed as a cause of his death.

INTRODUCTION

This book is an examination of Ira's life from a different perspective. His life was much more complex than the simplistic story of the fallen hero lost in his addiction. His people have a tradition of depicting the one they call Elder Brother as a man entering a circular maze. Many Akimel O'odham people interpret the illustration as the twists and turns and roadblocks a person encounters in a lifetime. This volume begins with the notion that Ira's life was a complicated journey from his birth to his passing. There were many twists and turns in his life, most of which were *not* of his own making. Circumstance certainly played a part, but the debilitation caused by post-traumatic stress disorder (PTSD) lies in the center of the maze that was Ira's story.

This book is equally about the price of warfare. Ira's people knew war before the white man came. They knew war but also knew how to handle it. They limited it, because they realized that its cost in lives and spiritual anguish could become too high. As one elder put it to me, the ceremonies "put the armor on and take it off again." In the mid-1990s, owing to a more conservative tilt in academic research, historians, pundits, anthropologists, archaeologists, and writers began to dredge up the ideas of seventeenth-century political philosopher Thomas Hobbes. Hobbes had the idea that so-called primitive peoples engaged in "war of all against all." This notion not only revived the "ignoble savage" stereotype of Native Americans but also cast them as more violent than modern non-Native human beings. Somehow violent death was presumably more prevalent among pre-state peoples than those in modern, supposedly civilized nation-states. If any battle could stand as a refutation of the notion that humans have become less violent through time, it was the campaign that Ira Hayes survived on Iwo Jima.

In both of his major combat experiences, on Bougainville

and Iwo Jima, all of his senses were assaulted. He remembered the sound of bursting shells, the crack of gunfire, the screams of the wounded, and the sight of maimed and dead human beings in flashbacks, dreams, and every time he was asked to appear at a public event. Even his sense of smell was affected by the miasma of sulfur fumes, the dankness of the jungle, the stench of decay and bodily odors, and the stink of gunfire. Often times, speech was simply reduced to grunts, sobs, yells, and monosyllable words like "Duck," "Fire," "Move," and, of course, screamed and whispered obscenities.

Although one can deduce that Ira did suffer from PTSD, he did not leave much behind for researchers to confirm his exact symptoms. Two of his biographers, William Bradford Huie and Albert Hemingway, relied on Ira's letters to his family and interviews with those who knew him in life. These were sound approaches to a biography, but they do not delve deeply into the reasons underlying Ira's postwar problems. Ira Hayes had a place in American popular culture, and his story was fully in line with the plots of hundreds of legendary tragedies in the western literary tradition. And so his biography both suited a cultural preconception about Native Americans and fit into a particular literary convention. Because Ira's story fit so well into this tradition, it has been more or less accepted without question.

As mentioned above, a predominant feature of this tradition is the trope of the "drunken Indian." The focus of most newspaper stories, the work of his biographers, and the motion pictures featuring Ira was his struggle with alcohol addiction. In most of these stories, alcoholism is the main feature eclipsing Ira's mental health. The "drunken Indian" stereotype remains even today a way of denigrating Native peoples in order to promote a particular ideology. The idea of Native Americans as being prone to drunkenness and dependent on the largesse of white Americans continues to appear every so often in newspapers and on cable news channels. In October 2021, Fox News personality Rachel Campos-Duffy asserted that the problems of Native Americans have "everything to do with government dependency" and "alcoholism." She also asserted that "Christopher Columbus...is the first victim of cancel culture." She conjured Native American relatives to prove what she avowed was true. How her logic worked was unclear. It seems as if she was suggesting that her Native relatives were alcoholics and dependent on government charity. The unvarnished truth is, of course, that the philosophy of eugenics and the trope of the drunken Indian are alive and well at Fox News. Apparently, the only person to call out Campos-Duffy for her glaringly racist and bigoted words was Justin Baragona, the media reporter for the *Daily Beast*. [1] Hopefully, revealing the real reasons underlying Ira's battle with drinking will help quell this misleading and misanthropic view of Indigenous people.

Nevertheless, the idea of Ira as a tragic figure has sunk into the fiber of American culture. But in the final analysis, that image does not put the story of Ira's life into the context of the times in which he lived, his obvious symptoms of post-traumatic stress disorder, and the intergenerational, historical trauma of the Akimel O'odham. His life took twists and turns as depicted in the O'odham "man in the maze" and was far more complex in actuality than the standard narrative of his life. He might have been a tragic figure to many, but he was a product of the conditions of war. He was also the archetype of the modern Native American veteran. Ultimately, this account of Ira's life is also a history of his times and how he attempted to navigate his way through the maze of poverty, emotional trauma, media scrutiny, racism, and addiction. His story is the story of Native Americans.

Ira consistently denied being a heroic figure. Even today, few combat veterans enjoy being called heroes. In fact, it is sometimes galling. From the perspective of a combat veteran, the true heroes, as Ira always acknowledged, had been killed in the most appalling ways. Survivors of those horrors are, again like Ira, reluctant to talk about them because noncombatants could not possibly understand what seeing those kinds of deaths was like. An aspect of PTSD is known as "survivors' guilt" and is the recognition that these heroes sacrificed their lives for the survival of others. Nationhood and patriotism mattered little; the guy in the foxhole with you was far more important. In short, the way Ira understood it, the deaths of the men with him during the battles he fought made it possible for him to live. Ira was unwilling to accept himself as a true hero, to ensure those who died for others had not died in vain. From the perspective of the combat veteran that he was, Ira owed them the tribute of being the real heroes. He mentioned several times during his life that there were only twenty-seven survivors out of his company of around two hundred Marines. That casualty rate was perhaps the highest of any Marine battle of the war. He carried the burden of their sacrifices for the rest of his life.

Terminology is often a problem in any book about Native people and a Native person in particular. In this book, I have attempted to use *Akimel O'odham* rather than *Pima* for Ira's people. For their friends and allies, I have used *Piipaash* instead of *Maricopa*. I also use *Native, Native American,* and *American Indian* interchangeably. Although many American-born whites sometimes call themselves natives of the United States or whichever state from which they hail, *Native* and *Native American* might be misnomers as well. *Indian* is the term I grew up with, and it was the term for a Native American in Ira Hayes' time. I tend to think of the term *indigenous* in lowercase. That is to say that something is local or perhaps native to a particular place. *Indigenous American* is perfectly acceptable. *Aboriginal* is synonymous with *indigenous*, but few Native people use it. In Canada, *First Nations* is the term very often used for the indigenous people there. I am often asked why there are so many terms for Native Americans. The answer I believe, rather than know, has to do with a search for ownership of a specific term that not only describes who we are but also is distinctive and cannot be used in a derogatory sense.

Many Native veterans have complained about the use of inappropriate terminology when applied to indigenous people in general and to Native individuals in particular. Nearly every Native veteran has been called "chief." Ira was called chief by his friends, who thought of it as an honorific. As a result of his parachute training, he was called Chief Falling Cloud. He, like most Native servicemen, usually took these names, or misnomers, with humor, but would later point out that they were, at minimum, mildly irritating. One of the worst problems was stereotyping. One Vietnam veteran related that his company gunnery sergeant gave a speech to him and other incoming replacements saying, "This is Fort Apache...and out there is Indian country" in reference to the Viet Cong or the North Vietnam Army. Referencing Native Americans as "the enemy" is an old practice that was part of Ira's experience as well. Still, he made friends and was part of the unit in which he served. His fellow Marines accepted him as such because he, like them, went through the rigors of boot camp, parachute training, and combat. The military unfortunately still uses so-called Indian terms and names to project upon an enemy. The special operations team that killed Osama bin Laden, for example, used the name Geronimo as code for the targeted terrorist. Given the use of this type of terminology for Native people in general, I have avoided using it in this volume.

Ira's heroism was undeniable. But the causes of his postwar problems were very different than what the general public has been led to believe. If there is a true line of progression in his misfortunes, it has to begin with PTSD. His battle with the symptoms of post-traumatic stress disorder is more difficult to understand given his life's narrative. During his life this complex emotional problem was either ignored or treated as a predicament that would simply go away if the correct words were said to its victims. "Get over it," "You're a hero," "Just relax," and "Have a drink" were phrases in use at the time, and they are still used even today. No one understood PTSD in Ira's day, and few know it to be a disorder that is ongoing, cumulative, and undying. It can be mitigated but not completely cured. Consuming alcohol, in Ira's day, was equated with relaxation, entertainment, and forgetting one's troubles. While in the military, Ira drank with his fellow Marines while on liberty. Few Marines passed up an evening of libation, as it was called then, and at his young age, he likely thought of it as a convivial pastime. After the horrors of the battlefield, it might have been considered a kind of alleviation of the problems associated with "battle fatigue," as it was referred to in the 1940s, but it was certainly no remedy. His problem was not necessarily an addiction to alcohol as much as it was a symptom of his PTSD.

Immediately after his death, one reporter wrote that war itself was the cause of Ira's demise. Indeed, it was the central experience in his life. The press, before and after he died, presented him as a flawed hero. His being was much more than that. He was a true warrior in his heart. And his short life reflected that view.

Chapter 1

Mount Suribachi and the Price of Combat

General William Tecumseh Sherman of Civil War fame has been credited numerous times for coining the phrase "War is hell." He may or may not have actually said those exact words, but the phrase has become part of American lore. Marines in Vietnam would often use the quote "War is hell" and add the corollary "but combat is a mother******." This profoundly vulgar Marine Corps axiom was intended to convey the idea that the first phrase, "War is hell," is an abstraction. The second part is, on the other hand, a personalized reality.

Ira Hamilton Hayes probably would not have uttered those words, to use the jargon of the time, "in mixed company." He had been brought up in a solid Presbyterian household on the Gila River Reservation in Arizona. His people, the Akimel O'odham, had syncretized Christianity and their traditional spiritual beliefs into an ethos emphasizing humility, courtesy, and generosity. Moreover, Hayes was said to be a thoughtful and modest young man. But he likely used profanity among his Marine buddies, who notably used vulgar language frequently, and he certainly would have understood what those words were intended to

1

express. Hayes had been through the crucible of battle in other campaigns, but on Iwo Jima he would see the horrors of modern warfare in their most gut-wrenching reality. He also experienced perhaps the most inspiring and iconic moments in all of human conflict. His survival, as with those others who made it off Iwo Jima alive, was in many ways miraculous.

What Hayes and the rest of the invasion force faced were the most formidable island defenses ever planned and built. Lieutenant General Holland M. Smith, who was the commanding general of the Fleet Marine Force, Pacific, wrote: "Iwo Jima, when we got to it, was the most heavily fortified island in the world." [1] Fleet Admiral Chester W. Nimitz, Commander in Chief, U.S. Pacific Fleet, not only echoed Smith's appraisal of the Iwo Jima defenses, but also added a grudging tribute to the cunning expertise of the Japanese planners. He also acknowledged that the nature of the island itself favored the Japanese defenders. Nimitz wrote that Iwo Jima possessed "the most difficult defenses that skill and ingenuity could construct on a small island that nature herself had already made strong for military defense." [2]

The mastermind of Iwo Jima's defenses was Lieutenant General Tadamichi Kuribayashi. Not only was Kuribayashi an old-time cavalry officer, but he was also a meticulous student of military history, including the art and science of war. Like another flag officer of his era, Admiral Isoroku Yamamoto, he had spent time in the United States and was leery of taking on the industrial strength of the Americans. Nevertheless, as did Yamamoto, Kuribayashi received his marching orders and attempted to fight as best he could, utilizing modern and ancient military tactical and strategic precepts. He no doubt had studied the writings of Sun Tzu, Carl von Clausewitz, and Antoine-Henri,

Baron de Jomini, for he used nearly every conceivable method of slowing down and grinding away at the forces of his enemy. The ancient Chinese philosopher of warfare Sun Tzu admitted that while the offensive in war attained victory, he also said that "invincibility lies in the defense." Kuribayashi knew that he did not have the numbers, in terms of combatants and munitions, on his side, so he followed Sun Tzu's admonition that "one defends when his strength is inadequate." Kuribayashi took the ancient philosopher's idea that "experts in defense conceal themselves as under the ninefold earth." [3] The "ninefold earth" was on Kuribayashi's side.

After the American capture of Tinian, Saipan, and Guam in 1944, both the Japanese and American higher commands knew that the battle for Iwo Jima was inevitable. The Americans needed a base to launch fighter cover for the long-range B-29s flying from Saipan and Guam to bomb Japan. Iwo Jima would also serve as a base from which the Americans could provide fighter escorts for the bombers and, if the need arose, a safe and close refuge for crippled B-29s. The Japanese admirals and generals viewed Iwo Jima not only as Japanese soil but as a strategic necessity. From its two landing strips, and with a third one under construction, the Japanese could launch interceptors to bring down the marauding American bombers. [4]

First, Kuribayashi evacuated all Japanese sulfur miners and their families from the island. Not only would that save Japanese lives, but it allowed Kuribayashi free rein to build fortifications without civilian interference or complaint. The sulfur mines were also used as living quarters for Japanese troops. Kuribayashi set his soldiers and Korean slave laborers to work digging more tunnels and installing pillboxes, gun emplacements, revetments, bunkers, and blockhouses. One of the more interesting things about the tunnel system is that the soldiers chiseled ninety-degree turns so that none of the tunnels ran in a straight line. This idea came from trench warfare in the First World War. Trenches were dug with these zigzag bends and turns, called traverses, so that if a shell exploded in one part of the trench the blast could not travel the whole length of the line. From the tunnels, Japanese gunners would be able to move and concentrate their weapons on the beaches with overlapping fields of fire. The tunnels allowed Kuribayashi's riflemen and gunners to maneuver within these strongpoints on relatively safe interior lines. The Japanese even dug mortar pits with domed roofs so that the crews would have some degree of concealment and cover. Mortar shells were lobbed through holes in these mortar pit ceilings.

On the southern narrow tip of the island stood a dormant volcano, Suribachiyama, or Mount Suribachi. As one moves northward from Suribachi, the island fans out and looks on a map somewhat like the outline of a pork chop. It had very little foliage. The three landing strips were to be defended at all costs. They were interspersed with rocks, sand, crags, and jagged hills. A number of lifeless-looking trees and bushes lay around the island, especially at the foot of Suribachi. Another strange obstacle that the Marines would face was the way in which the wind, storms, and sea changes had formed a terraced, steplike terrain instead of easily traversed sloping beaches. The beaches themselves were loosely packed, black volcanic ash and debris. Foxholes seemed to fill themselves in, and vehicles could become mired in the sand. It was not exactly a South Seas island paradise; it was more like an ugly, smelly (from the sulfur), desolate place with no redeeming qualities, except for the airstrips. Fighting and dying for a place such as Iwo Jima would have appeared to most Marines to be insane. Typically for Marine commanders and even the combat troops themselves, they felt that if there had to be a fight, better to have it now than to put it off.

Kuribayashi badgered his superiors for better weapons and more troops. He even suggested that a new infantry rifle be produced like the semiautomatic American M1 Garand. He received more troops so that by the time of the American invasion, he had between twenty-two and twenty-three thousand army and navy personnel under his command. But most importantly, Kuribayashi had created a series of tunnels in the hills of the central and northern parts of the island, as had been done within Suribachi, that would enable his troops to sit out the coming American bombardment from the sea and air. [5]

His troops were armed with artillery field pieces, tanks, rockets, mortars—one of which was a 320-millimeter giant—grenades, and light and heavy machine guns. Kuribayashi planned that the artillery, high explosives, and shrapnel would go to work after the greater part of the invasion force landed. Artillery and mortar rounds could either tear a victim apart or produce a primary blast wave that could kill by concussion without leaving a mark on the victim. Shrapnel wounds could be far more insidious. Even expert surgeons often found it difficult to locate these tiny pieces of metal lodged among a victim's internal organs. X-ray machines, large and cumbersome in those days, were located aboard the hospital ships that were to lie some distance offshore, out of range of Japanese guns. When it came to that, the evacuation of the wounded had to be done on amphibious tractors and other landing craft, themselves under artillery and mortar fire. Until the hospital ships arrived, the wounded had to be ferried to specially equipped, organized, and manned tank landing ships (LSTs.) [6]

Other Japanese commanders depended in large part on the

individual soldier's supposed fighting spirit and devotion to the emperor. Kuribayashi viewed the mass banzai charges carried out on other islands as wasteful and notoriously unsuccessful. Still, he went along with the message in his first set of instructions. He asked his troops to take as many American lives as possible before their own deaths. He also knew, by the weight of historical evidence, that the Americans would come at him with at least three times as many troops as he had under his command. They would come with greater fire power as well. [7]

The individual Japanese soldier carried the Model 38, 6.5-millimeter, bolt-action rifle. It had a slower rate of fire than the M1 Garand the Marines carried, but it produced a particularly nasty wound. The bullet itself had a lead core within a copper-and-zinc jacket. The jacket was relatively thin in the first place, but its back wall was even thinner, causing part of the lead core to exit backward upon impact. It appeared to explode when it hit a victim. Another noteworthy aspect of the Japanese bullet was that its metal jacket was weak. The thin jacket struck and stayed in the wound while part of the bullet broke into pieces and traveled deep into the victim's body. According to those who studied the wounds from World War II, the Model 38 round often made one entrance wound and exited in several places. Also, as a kind of by-product of heavy use, the rifling of the Model 38 became worn and left the round it fired exceedingly unstable in flight. The bullet would yaw in the air and cause "keyhole" or elongated entrance wounds.

By 1945 Japanese infantrymen began receiving the newer Model 99 7.7-millimeter rifle, which boasted a larger-caliber round and an increased muzzle velocity. The same bullet was used in machine guns as well. A bullet with a higher muzzle velocity and a sturdier jacket causes what are called cavitation wounds. What this means is that when a bullet of this type enters the body of a victim, it can yaw, tumble, splinter bone, or keep on moving. The bullet drives the tissue and fluids away from its track and, when it passes through, creates a wave that collapses behind the projectile, creating a vacuum that can drag tissue along with the bullet. This kind of projectile leaves behind small entrance wounds and much larger exit wounds. [8]

Casualties in battle occur in what are known as killing or beaten zones. Beaten zones are more often fairly narrow and determined by the effective range of the weapons used at the time. Since Iwo Jima was small to begin with, Kuribayashi could, in fact, make the entire island into a killing zone. The general could train his artillery pieces from their hidden lairs onto either the western or the eastern beaches or even out to sea.

Ultimately, Kuribayashi's strategy was meticulously designed to create as many casualties as possible among the invading Americans. It would be a battle of attrition. In the final analysis, Kuribayashi's weaponry—as well as that of the Marines—was intended to overwhelm the ability of a military force to deal with casualties. Military weapons are not always used to kill, although that would be the ideal circumstance. Severe wounds, like those produced by modern weapons, require immediate and intensive care.

American planners knew that Iwo Jima was going to be a tough fight. After the Americans pummeled the island with naval gunfire and attacks from carrier-based airplanes for months, the landing force was to assault the eastern beaches along the southern part of the island. Ira Hayes' fight began on February 19, 1945. It would last for nearly a month of assaults, continuous patrolling, digging in, firefights, and seeking cover from Japanese artillery and mortar barrages. It would also include a memorial service for those who died. If it were not for a single snap of a camera shutter, Hayes would have completed his service in the Marine Corps and gone home to his family in Bapchule on the Gila River Reservation without further ado. He would still have suffered from PTSD, but the attention the photograph generated exacerbated his pain.

Years later, a man named Milo Fisher, a mail carrier in Knoxville, Tennessee, and a Marine Corps veteran, gave the local newspaper an account of Ira Hayes' landing on Iwo Jima and the flag-raising on Mount Suribachi. Fisher was on the same troop transport as Hayes and several other Marines who had survived the fighting. According to Fisher, he asked a number of them aboard the ship to write down their personal experiences on the island. Fisher said that he kept Hayes' statement "as a memento of the war." Although there are questionable aspects of the account, it nevertheless presents a picture of what was going on in the mind of a young man about to enter the maelstrom of combat. [9]

Hayes' account was short and to the point. He was a member of Easy Company, 2nd Battalion, 28th Marines, and went ashore in the third wave of the attack on Green Beach, the sector closest to Mount Suribachi. All was relatively quiet when Hayes and his platoon climbed down the "wet nets" and into the landing craft. As they approached shore, Kuribayashi's guns erupted. The first and second waves of the 4th and 5th Marine Divisions were on the beach and a few yards inland when they came under fire from at least three directions. The Japanese gunners also began to score hits on the approaching landing craft, infantry (LCIs) and landing craft, vehicle and personnel (LCVPs). Hayes wrote that a boat near his was hit with a shell from Suribachi. About a thousand yards out, Hayes noted that he "couldn't see much except men strung all along the beach on their bellies. Men would get up and run for a distance and flop down. I knew then that things on the beach were rough." He was amazed and "scared" because it was difficult to understand how the Japanese artillery was still in operation despite "a lively pasting" the mountain was receiving from the air and the sea. As Hayes' boat approached shore, the shelling became more intense, and rifle and machine-gun fire joined the tumult. Bullets from Suribachi were coming close, and the Marines were "ordered down close to the deck." He admitted once again that he was a "scared son-of-a-gun."

After running a gauntlet of artillery, mortar, and gunfire, Hayes' boat finally touched shore. He "jumped clear of the ramp and about three yards ahead laid a dead Marine right on the water's edge shot through the head." Easy Company struggled up the black ash beach. The gunfire on the beach was so heavy that the only way to avoid getting blown up or shot was to keep moving. But even then, movement was next to impossible. The black volcanic ash, according to Hayes, "was a menace to our running and to our weapons." It took, he wrote, "two hours to get 75 yards."

At one point, Hayes looked back and watched the various types of landing craft shuttling in more troops, supplies, tanks, tracked vehicles, and even bulldozers. When the boats went back out to the ships, they carried the wounded. It was constant back-and-forth movement. The "dead and wounded were lying all around," he wrote. He could smell the "powder, smoke, and blood in the air."

Marine and Navy planners knew that cutting off Suribachi would be the first major step in securing the island. A communication cable connected the mountain fortress to the northern defenses and to Kuribayashi himself. It had to be cut. The 28th

Marines, because of their proximity to the mountain, were to cross the island from east to west. The 28th Marines "did a left flank" movement, according to Hayes. This left their backs to the north. They now faced Suribachi from its most dangerous side. Hayes' regiment was spread across the narrow southern tip of the island.

The rest of the invasion force turned northward to take the airfields and clear the rest of the island. If the 28th Marines could take Suribachi, its guns would be silenced. The 4th, the rest of the 5th, and soon the 3rd Divisions would not have enemy artillery at their backs. Easy Company dug in and waited for the assault on Suribachi to commence the next morning.

General Kuribayashi, in his northern command post, sent his last message to the troops manning the defensive ring around Suribachi. He urged them to give and take no quarter. Although there were actually few Japanese soldiers at the southern tip of the island compared to the number of Marines, their position was, according to a later navy assessment of the operation, "notable for its economy of force." [10]

Ira, in his foxhole, knew Suribachi would be costly. The Marines were approximately 1,300 yards from the base of the mountain and had to get close enough to throw grenades and high-explosive satchel charges into the Japanese positions between them and the base of Suribachi. At that point in the assault, they could use flamethrowers to mop up the pillboxes, spider holes, and bunkers. Horrific weapons that they were, flame-throwing tanks and individually operated flamethrowers became essential to taking Suribachi—indeed, all of Iwo Jima. One of the problems was that the tanks were essentially stuck on the congested beach. Gas was difficult to come by, and the tanks did not arrive for the attack on Suribachi until after it had already begun.

The use of fire, especially when propelled by compressed air, could burn, and asphyxiate—by sucking all the oxygen out of a confined space—the occupants of a bunker or cave. The trouble with flamethrowers was that they were often as deadly for the operators as they were for the enemy. The Japanese specifically targeted the men carrying the two fuel canisters on their backs. Someone once said that the life expectancy for an operator of a flamethrower in the Pacific was about four minutes. The Marines gave nicknames to their flamethrower tanks, after brands of cigarette lighters. One type blew flames from its turret barrel and was known as "Ronson." The other, called "Zippo," mounted its flamethrower just below the turret.

Another essential weapon was the satchel charge. Marine engineers with training in demolitions carried these bags filled with high explosives that could be triggered and thrown into or around a cave opening either to kill all those inside or possibly seal off an entrance or exit dug into the mountain. Infantrymen carried hand grenades to do the same, only on a less explosive level. The antipersonnel grenades were generally fragmentation or "pineapple" types. Marines also carried white phosphorous grenades to both mark targets and use as antipersonnel weapons. [11]

Strategically, isolating Suribachi was correct. The Marines would be able to concentrate force northward to take the three airstrips. The mountain and its surrounding defensive system, on the other hand, looked like a tactical nightmare. In today's jargon, Whac-A-Mole would perfectly describe the tactical difficulty in capturing Suribachiyama. The Marines could, in theory, clear one bunker only to have a machine-gun position appear in another place behind them, to their front, or on their flank. In fact, the only tactical solution to Suribachi was fire and movement and fire team rushes combined with an old-time assault—with help, of course, from the artillery of the 13th Marines and carrier-based airplanes dropping high explosives and the newly developed napalm. The fire-breathing Ronsons and Zippos, despite having trouble getting fuel and negotiating the congestion and volcanic ash on the beaches, would become the main support for the infantry.

That first night on the island offered no peace. Flares went up and floated, swinging downward and causing ghostly shadows to move over the eerie landscape. Once the Marine artillery batteries and the naval gunners offshore got the mountain's coordinates, the guns pounded Suribachi throughout the day and well into the night. The Japanese continued to concentrate fire on the beaches from the north and from Suribachi. Two Japanese attacks took place that night. The first was a battalion-sized assault on the 27th Marines at the first airstrip. The second was a barge of Japanese soldiers either trying to make an escape to the north by the sea or to counterattack the 1st Battalion, 28th Marines (1/28). Of that group of Japanese soldiers, 1/28 killed twenty-five in the early morning hours. As darkness wore on, the air chilled and Hayes' platoon huddled in their foxholes, trying to get some sleep between watches. In a way, Hayes and the members of his platoon probably hoped for one of the seemingly insane banzai charges. They had the firepower to halt one dead in its tracks. Instead, the Japanese used a kind of guerilla tactic during the night. Two to four Japanese soldiers, operating independently as hit-and-run cells, targeted the Marines in their foxholes. Another weapon that was used more to harass the dug-in Marines was the giant, 675-pound, 320-millimeter spigot mortar, which was not only loud, leaving a trail of fire in the sky, but wildly inaccurate. The weapon kept the Marines guessing and praying. [12]

The attack on Suribachi promptly began on the morning of the second day of the Iwo Jima ground campaign. The Marines of Hayes' battalion, though tired, fought the entire day without rest. When they left their foxholes, they were met with a hail of fire. From their bunkers and pillboxes, the Japanese poured rifle and machine-gun rounds at the advancing Americans. Japanese mortars of all types were used very effectively against the Americans on Iwo Jima. Small "grenade dischargers" could be carried by one man and moved from place to place easily and quickly. The more static mortars ranged in size from 50 to 320 millimeters. The main infantry mortars were the 81-millimeter types 97 and 99. The Japanese used their mortars cleverly. Sometimes they would time their salvoes with American artillery barrages in order to make the Americans think that they were being hit by their own batteries. One of the names the Marines coined for Suribachi was "Mortar Mountain." That morning two mortar rounds hit the regimental command post, killing and wounding six people. Mortar Mountain had earned its nickname. [13]

The 28th Marines had to assault particular targets in their general advance across the space between their lines and the base of Suribachi. The pillboxes, bunkers, mortar pits, trenches, tunnels, and spider traps were located so that each of these positions covered one another. They were not placed directly on an observable line as in trench warfare. As a consequence, the Americans would have to attack these positions individually while simultaneously suppressing the fire from other gun emplacements or infantry foxholes. The tanks finally arrived at around eleven a.m. to offer military support. They supplied the much-needed literal firepower to turn the Japanese pillboxes into concrete ovens. In the afternoon of the first assault on

Suribachi it began to rain, making the footing even worse and causing jamming, particularly in the Browning Automatic Rifles (BAR). At the time, Ira Hayes was the BAR man on his fire team. By the time of the flag raising, he had exchanged the BAR for the M1 carbine, much lighter and less prone to jamming than the one he carried on Bougainville.

Hayes' battalion shut down forty-odd pillboxes, tunnel openings, and bunkers that day. Casualties were high, and fighting hand-to-hand was typical. Members of the 5th Engineer Battalion found and cut the communications cable connecting the Suribachi defense to the northern command center. Suribachi was isolated but still dangerous. [14]

It had been the plan of the 28th Marines' commander, Colonel Harry Liversedge, to surround Suribachi and then find pathways up the mountainside, sealing the tunnels as his regiment went. On the second day of the assault, Liversedge brought his 1st Battalion out of reserve and committed it to the battle. Hayes' 2nd Battalion, although it lost a great deal of its strength the first day, was nevertheless ordered forward once again. The assault began with a rocket attack. When the Marines left their foxholes, the fighting, unfortunately, was much like it had been the day before, except that naval gunfire and the air campaign had taken out most of the Japanese big guns. The Japanese casualties were heavy. The second day of the battle was different in that a member of Easy Company became the first to be awarded the Medal of Honor of the Iwo Jima campaign, albeit posthumously. A Japanese soldier hurled a hand grenade that landed close to Ira's platoon sergeant, Henry Hansen. Private First Class Donald J. Ruhl pushed Hansen out of the way and covered the grenade with his own body. Ruhl was the first of twenty-seven men to be awarded the Medal of Honor on Iwo. Hansen was also a Bougainville veteran and one of Ira's fellow parachutists. He would take part in hoisting the first flag on Suribachi and would be misidentified as a subject in Rosenthal's iconic photograph of the second flag raising. He was killed six days after the flag raising. [15]

Ruhl's self-sacrifice was the rule of the day, especially on the part of the 2nd Battalion. The Marines were still advancing across the last few yards in fire-team rushes while the flame-thrower operators and the men with the satchel charges were running toward the pillboxes, bunkers, and tunnels to pour fire into them and seal them off. Mike Strank, Hayes' squad leader, led a final charge that reached the base of Suribachi. When the assault ended on February 21, Lieutenant Colonel Chandler W. Johnson's 2nd Battalion ended up on the southeast side of Mortar Mountain without support on either flank. As darkness approached, Easy Company set in. The 13th Marine artillerymen continued to pour fire into Suribachi. In many places along the line, the shells were landing "danger-close" to the Marines in their foxholes.

Undermanned and undersupplied, the 2nd Battalion was placed in reserve to regroup. Meanwhile the rest of the 28th Regiment was focused on gaining a full encirclement of the volcano on February 22. The artillery, tank shells, naval gunfire, and air strikes had obliterated the paths up Suribachi. The Japanese troop level on Suribachi had shrunk to about 300 men, a number of whom were wounded. Consequently, some of these soldiers decided to make a quiet escape to the north. Few survived this clandestine attempt to reach the northern Japanese command center. Except for a few sporadic Japanese attempts to beat back the Americans, Suribachi, which earned itself two more nicknames—Hot Rock and Plasma Mountain—was finished. A number of the Japanese soldiers committed suicide.

General Kuribayashi had hoped for the mountain defenses to hold out for at least ten days. Unfortunately for his strategic planning, the mountain's big guns had been silenced and its garrison crushed in less than four. Securing Suribachi gave the Marines the advantage of driving northward on a broad front, thus eliminating Kuribayashi's ability to concentrate his forces both tactically and strategically. [16]

The next day, Easy Company was called upon to reconnoiter the mountain. The company commander, Captain David Severance, ordered the 3rd Platoon to climb Suribachi on a combat patrol. After the patrol left to ascend Mortar Mountain, Severance decided to follow up with a second. According to Hayes, "Our CO then picked our platoon to send twenty men to go on the same mission." Hayes' patrol, under the guidance of Sergeant Mike Strank, climbed the volcano and "were very lucky not to meet any kind of resistance as we had expected." About halfway up, Ira saw the first flag being raised. "It was pretty small, and I couldn't hardly make it out." In his account, Hayes was happy because the flag sent the message that "the 3rd Platoon had made it to the top after engaging a small group of Japs on the way up." [17]

Ira's patrol came back down the mountain to the company bivouac. They rested for some five minutes before Strank picked Frank Sousley, Harlon Block, and Hayes to go back up the mountain on what Hayes guessed was another reconnaissance patrol. Hayes also identified Henry Hansen as being part of this second ascent. He was not. Hansen, in fact, had taken part in the first flag raising. Along the way they picked up the battalion runner, Rene Gagnon. Gagnon was carrying another, larger flag. Hayes wrote that Strank told the patrol that it was to take the "place of the little one so the whole island could know that the 28th had secured Suribachi."

When the Strank patrol reached the summit, Hayes and Sousley were ordered to find something that they could use for another flagpole. "Much to my luck," wrote Hayes, "I found an old rusty Jap water pipe." Hayes and Sousley dug the pipe out and attached the flag to it. Six men raised the new flag while several others lowered the first one. As they brought the rusty water pipe with the larger flag attached to an upright position, Joe Rosenthal, an Associated Press correspondent, snapped a picture. Sergeant Bill Genaust, a Marine motion picture photographer, also filmed the flag raising. According to Hayes, "We didn't know they were taking our picture."

Rosenthal's photograph ended up on President Franklin D. Roosevelt's desk. Roosevelt saw the picture as an almost perfect piece of war messaging and ordered the commandant of the Marine Corps to bring the six men in the picture home to sell war bonds. The true identities of the Marines in the photograph were not sorted out for more than seventy years. As it turned out, three of the flag raisers were killed in action later in the campaign, and three were misidentified. Two of the men who were sent back to the United States to sell war bonds were actually not in the picture. Two more Marines who were in the photograph were not identified until many years later. Hayes, who was in the picture, did not want to leave his unit; nor did he want to sell war bonds. He even threatened Rene Gagnon with physical harm if the battalion runner revealed Hayes as one of the flag raisers.

Hayes' participation in the flag raising on Iwo Jima did not end his combat experience. The fight for Iwo Jima dragged on another twenty-two horrific days, and Hayes was there from its beginning to the end. He was on his way back to the United States when Gagnon broke down and divulged Hayes' secret.

Ira Hayes had experienced combat as few others had, save,

of course, for his fellow Marines on Iwo Jima. Although many others who served in the American armed forces had been in combat in many different places all over the world, Iwo Jima was unlike all other battlefields of World War II. There were certainly larger and more costly battles. And they had been fought under the most adverse of circumstances. Soldiers fought in freezing conditions and in hot, humid jungles. But Iwo Jima stands out as a truly horrific battlefield. Nearly ninety thousand human beings were crammed on or inside of an island that was, simply put, an eight-mile-square killing zone above- and belowground. There were air battles above it, and the island itself was continually rocked by naval gunfire. Ira Hayes had to move from place to place during the advance on Suribachi, firing into spider holes, throwing grenades into bunkers, heaving satchel charges into cave entrances, and hearing the sound of explosions deep within the mountain as Japanese soldiers committed suicide by holding grenades against their chests and pulling the pins. Hayes would see the result of these suicides when he and his fellow Marines looked inside Suribachi's defenses.

Both the Japanese and American troops were assailed by the same battering of the senses. In addition to seeing the carnage and what various kinds of weaponry can do to a human body, they saw explosions and various kinds of human-made structures incinerated. They heard the cries and groans of the wounded, the roar of flamethrowers, the rattle of machine guns, the snap of rifle fire, the scream of rockets, the whine of mortar rounds, and the buzzing sound bullets make when they have lost velocity. They smelled the rotten-egg scent of sulfur, the stench of rotting or immolated flesh, human waste, and the reek of themselves after days and weeks without a change of clothing. And they felt the weight of their packs, helmets, weapons, and ammunition after being soaked with rain. They tasted sand, dirt, ash, and the almost tasteless meals in C or K rations.

Combat is, and probably always has been, a singular and most profound event in a person's life. It means putting absolutely normal men and women into circumstances that are anything but normal. It is at once frightening, enraging, exhilarating, wretched, and even poignant. It ennobles and, more often than not, demoralizes the spirit at the same time. As such, it outweighs nearly every other event in life. For most of those who have been in battle, it cannot be forgotten. It is a burden, a taint, and a source of pride.

But at the same time, Hayes' life mimicked Rosenthal's picture in a way that some Native people have just begun to notice. Hayes is the last man in the picture. He did the heavy lifting to get the flag raised to an upright position. In Rosenthal's photograph, Hayes is not holding on to or even touching the flagpole; it has been taken out of his hands. In a way it is symbolic of the Native servicemember in that era—and today. In the picture, Hayes appears to be futilely reaching for the flag. Native veterans served the nation, but American justice has not been within their reach. It certainly was not within Ira Hayes' grasp. And so he sought solace with his own people and within his own culture.

Chapter 2

Ira Hayes' People: War, Water, and the Collective Ordeal of the Akimel O'odham

Ira Hayes' combat experience was extensive and emotionally painful. Before and after, he was the son of the Akimel O'odham—a people that collectively suffered the oppressive trauma of colonialism. Over the period of three hundred years the Akimel O'odham were pushed to the brink of cultural, political, and economic destruction. Ira, born in 1923, inherited a history of psychological pain.

Ira's people, living on the Gila River Reservation, knew warfare, betrayal, and hardship very well indeed and what they could do to the human spirit, even down through generations. They had endured long bouts of warfare and the theft of their land and the water that sustained their lives. Only a few years before Ira's birth, Owl Ear, an Akimel O'odham elder, told an anthropologist that his people had fought "the bloodiest fight known." [1] The Akimel O'odham had devised ceremonies that dealt with warfare—how to prepare warriors for battle and how to take care of them after a battle was fought. They had also endured a devastating famine brought on by the whites who siphoned off the waters of the Gila River for their own crops. There were no corresponding ceremonies that dealt with the betrayal they experienced at the hands of their supposed friends.

Warfare is a singularly traumatic experience on both the personal and societal levels. A few studies have indicated that Native American ceremonies and concomitant family and community support systems have aided in the return and adjustment of their veterans. Many Native peoples long ago formulated—or, in many cases, were given by way of dreams, visions, or revelations—ceremonies that aided returning warriors. Some of these rites, like the Southern Plains Gourd Dance, the Navajo Enemy Way, or the Cherokee Going to Water, were designed either to honor the warrior or to cleanse the warrior of the spiritual suffering contracted in battle or from being in close contact with death. The ceremonies, usually arranged by the warrior's family, were performed by an entire community in an attempt to relieve the warrior's pain or honor the warrior's bravery. [2] And the Akimel O'odham were no exceptions.

The Akimel O'odham are generally a peaceful people. They were a sedentary, agricultural people who built irrigation systems to water their crops. The fact that the people irrigated crops and lived in permanent settlements has been viewed as indicative of a group that is progressive or civilized in the Western European tradition. Additionally, when the Americans came to their land, the Akimel O'odham welcomed them, traded with them, and provided them with food and the knowledge to survive in a desert environment. Following the axiom of "The enemy of my enemy is my friend," the Akimel O'odham and their allies, the Piipaash, joined and even led American military expeditions against the Apaches. To the Americans, Akimel O'odham and Piipaash friendship was equated with being peaceful.

But perhaps the most indelible image of Native Americans in the larger American culture is that of the Indian savage bent on halting the spread of civilization across the vast continent of North America. In American folklore Indians have attacked peaceful wagon trains, dashed out the brains of white children, toasted hapless frontiersmen at the stake, raped hundreds of beautiful white women, scalped innocent pioneers, and treacherously murdered and mutilated thousands of gallant soldiers in unprovoked ambushes. These old and tired images have been permanent features of hundreds of books, stage plays, television programs, and motion pictures. [3]

Most colonizing groups seem compelled to celebrate their often violent and nefarious deeds in bringing "civilization" and their religion to an untamed and savage wilderness. [4] The creation of the vicious as well as the noble savage was necessary to the epic of settling (as opposed to "appropriating") whatever lands the colonizers coveted for themselves. Without a contrasting foe, the colonizer-settler could not lay claim to a unique identity. Without a struggle for survival or supremacy against a bloodthirsty, barbaric, and maniacal opposing force, the colonizer's sacrifices and martyrdom would have no great meaning. Native Americans were characterized as being subhuman, superhuman, and inhumane all at the same time—the classic definition of "the enemy." The colonizers' moral (as opposed to legal) claim to a new land rests on a glorious blood sacrifice that transforms the place in which they died or in which they killed its original inhabitants into a kind of hallowed ground. The bloodletting confirms proprietorship. The carnage also sanctions a kind of secular sacredness of battlegrounds and cemeteries. If seen from that perspective, the whole of the United States is a single, vast battleground.

The idea of a peace-loving, progressive, and friendly indigenous group is an idea that is difficult to swallow for many white Americans. The stereotype of the vicious savage is too ingrained for it to be swept away even within a span of two hundred years. On the other hand, there exists in American culture the image of the noble savage who helps the Pilgrim and the Patriot get along in the American wilderness and even takes up arms to aid the white man as he settles the country and plants the American flag from coast to coast. This concept is part of the legend of the first Thanksgiving, the Leatherstocking tales, the all-knowing Indian scout legend, and the Indian companion imagery as depicted in American popular culture.

The Akimel O'odham maintained a common philosophy or ethos known as Himdag. The term is loosely translated as "the way" and is a complex understanding of the interaction of religion, history, the human relationship with place, the flora and fauna of a given territory, the spirit world, and the cosmos as viewed from Akimel O'odham national territory. Equally, it is the accumulated knowledge of the Akimel O'odham of how and why the earth and the heavens sustain a universal order. Himdag is also the comprehension of human relations, in terms of kinship and with other peoples. This all-encompassing idea of order and justice includes warfare and how it is conducted. If seen from the perspective of Himdag, the Akimel O'odham have always been a peaceful people. Warfare had to be defensive, restrained, and limited in scope because it was thrust upon them against the universal order as perceived through Himdag, the idea being to restore natural order out of the chaos of conflict. There are two aspects of the story of Elder Brother in the maze that have been sustained over the years. The maze has been seen as Elder Brother's ki, or house in the Sacred Mountain. Long ago a group of enemy warriors came to raid Elder Brother's house. He retreated inside, and the enemy warriors went in only to get lost and die in the labyrinth. O'odham scholar David Martinez has argued that Elder Brother represents Himdag, in that he is always there and he emerges when the people need direction in the way of peace and orderliness. The irony was that the Akimel O'odham became embroiled in some level of conflict—from warfare to the struggles for water and voting rights—almost constantly from the 1700s until the present. [5]

Himdag entered into the ideas behind and the practice of warfare. The line between war and peace had to be crossed back and forth to ensure that the chaos of war would not become all-encompassing or an everyday part of life. The Akimel O'odham way of war was a complex amalgamation of preparatory rituals, limited aggression, the ceremonial expungement of the pollution of death, healing, and the celebration of the return of the relatives who took part in the conflict. Combat, in fact, was a phase in the entire rite and even sacrament of warfare. There might also be a period of mourning should a death occur in a raid or pitched battle.

The preparations for war were highly formalized. If a headman from one of the villages "felt in his heart" that a raid was necessary to punish an enemy for killing a person's relatives, he would go from village to village inviting warriors to follow him in seeking justice. When the volunteers were gathered at the headman's village, four nights of preparations began. While food for the journey was prepared, every night a speech was made extolling the virtues of the Akimel O'odham. Elders called upon the spirits of various entities to protect the warriors and also to blunt the spiritual powers of the enemy.

After the battle or raid, the warriors who had killed an

enemy warrior were expected to go into seclusion for a period of sixteen days. Each was accompanied by an elder who said the prayers, occasionally broke the warrior's fast, served him water at specific times, and went with the warrior to the river to wash away what one man called "blood guilt." A victory dance was held, and a feast was served. Captive children were adopted by grieving women, and goods taken in the raid were distributed to the needy. [6]

Akimel O'odham traditional enemies were the Apaches, and their raiding and warfare tactics are well documented. Raiding might well have been an economic necessity or possibly done to take captives, in particular women and children to expand the tribal population. There could have been a revenge factor involved, which would have led to back-and-forth raiding and out-and-out murder. Male desire for valued status in society was undoubtedly part of the Apache raiding motivation. To be a man and called "lazy" in Apache society was a terrible insult. Taking part in raiding demonstrated a man's willingness to contribute economically to society and care for his family. [7]

Since the Akimel O'odham were primarily an agricultural society, living in permanent villages, they were a target not only of Apache raids but also of Quechan, Yavapai, and Mohave war parties. Akimel O'odham warfare escalated over time from the purely defensive to revenge raiding. Militarization generally increased, and all young Akimel O'odham men were expected to train for combat. Still, these raids were not as costly in human terms as they could have been. Often, there were self-imposed limits on raiding.

The first Europeans to make their way into Akimel O'odham territory, part of which came to be called Pimería Alta (Upper Pima Territory), were the Spanish. At first, the relations between the two peoples were affable. Father Eusebio Kino was on a mission to convert all of the Natives of Pimería Alta. Kino made only two trips to the Akimel O'odham proper. But for the most part, Ira Hayes' ancestors were left alone in their distant villages. Their cousins to the south, however, were recruited to serve as auxiliaries with the Spanish garrisons to stave off Apache and Seri attacks. [8]

By the mid-1700s "tensions" arose within the diverse Spanish colonials. The "gente de razón," or "people of reason," or the Spanish, were at odds with one another as to what to do with the Native people of the region. The Native peoples were referred to as "gente de costumbre," or "customary people," meaning that they were without reason and thus only acting in a traditional manner. [9]

Two centuries before, the Spanish had essentially laid out the legal and moral justification for colonizing the lands of Indigenous peoples. Between 1537 and 1539, Fray Francisco de Vitoria, of Salamanca University in Spain, delivered a series of lectures on the justification for claiming land in the New World. In the first of these "Relectios," Vitoria outlined the idea that land could be taken if there were no humans occupying it or if indigenous peoples were there and they had not improved or cultivated the land. The land was therefore open for settlement. These notions became known as the "Doctrine of Discovery." In the second Relectio he laid out the idea of the "Right of Conquest in a Just War." Essentially, this so-called right was based on the notion that if an indigenous group of people refused or even ignored diplomatic overtures, including establishing missions, they could be subject to a just war and conquest. [10]

In 1550, two Dominican friars, Juan Ginés de Sepúlveda and Bartolomé de las Casas, formally debated the question of what

27

to do with the indigenous peoples of the newly "discovered" land across the sea. Known as the Vallodolid debates, the priests held two very different views of the Spanish conquest. Las Casas argued that no matter how indigenous peoples used the land, or if they were pagans, they were nonetheless human and could therefore own property. Land had to be purchased or ceded by way of treaty or convention. Las Casas had witnessed the brutality of the Spanish conquistadors in their merciless acts of genocide that enabled them to confiscate land and steal precious cultural items. They had enslaved Native Americans to work in their mines and be used as a free agricultural labor force.

Sepúlveda was a Renaissance scholar who based his arguments regarding Native humanity on liberal interpretations of both the Bible and Aristotelian thought. In the debate he presented the idea that there were two types of human societies. The first type followed "natural law" in the construction of civil societies, sanctioning friendly commerce and viewing violence as an unnatural human activity. The second type was the barbaric society that was devoid of culture, waged brutal warfare, practiced idol worship and human sacrifice, and participated in a simple, subsistence-level economy, only rudimentary horticulture, with no markets or free trade. Moreover, the laws and public institutions of these barbaric societies sanctioned these "uncivilized" behaviors and practices. According to Sepúlveda, Native Americans were subhuman barbarians whose labor could be exploited, whose lands could be appropriated, and whose beliefs and customs could be wiped out. [11]

The tensions that developed among the Spanish in and bordering on Pimería Alta were the result of the two-hundred-odd-year-old ideas of Vitoria, Las Casas, and Sepúlveda. The debate over what to do with Native Americans had not exactly been decided. In consequence, Spanish policy in Pimería Alta was a mixed bag of local church regulations, land seizures, enslavement, and conscription of Native warriors. The opinions like those expressed in the Vallodolid debates created a break between the different factions involved in Spanish colonization. The governor and the church maintained that peace, by way of converting the indigenous population to Catholicism and forming military alliances, was the proper position of the Spanish regime. The land-hungry Spanish citizens who were attempting either to steal Native lands or enslave the indigenous peoples to work their mines and fields were following the arguments that Sepúlveda made in 1550.

In large part, the Akimel O'odham were out of reach of the Spanish slavers and the military. A few priests, like Kino, ventured into the Gila and Salt River villages. Not that they were insulated from attack or the news that their southern cousins had initiated a revolt against the Spanish in 1751. The revolt was quickly quelled and its leader, Luis Oacpicagigua, was put in prison, where he subsequently died. [12]

After the revolt, the Gila River people reached a stable relationship with the Spanish. The Akimel O'odham acquired wheat seed from the Spanish in 1775 and began growing a winter crop. Akimel O'odham wheat, in fact, supplied the newly established Spanish garrison in Tucson. They also began raising cattle and horses. Unfortunately, this newly acquired foodstuff and livestock made the Akimel O'odham villages prime targets for raids by the Apache and Quechan peoples. [13]

Warfare between the Spanish colonials and the Quechan and Mohave began in earnest in 1781. Quechan warriors destroyed two Spanish settlements and cut off the Yuma crossing and thus access to Spanish California. The Colorado River

peoples established themselves as the blood enemies of the
Spanish and anyone else who cooperated with them. Smaller
tribes, like the Cocomaricopa, bore the brunt of their wrath.
Later, the Quechan and Mohave warriors ran roughshod over
the Halchidhoma and Kavekchadom peoples and made slaves of
the Kahwan and Hayikwamai. Those who escaped the Quechan
and Mohave fled to the Gila and Salt Rivers and joined together
to form what came to be called the Maricopa or the Piipaash
people. The Piipaash also suffered population loss as a result of
European-introduced disease. They joined in an alliance with
the Akimel O'odham in which the Piipaash moved into Akimel
land and agreed to hunt less and farm more. [14] At the time,
the Gila River Valley was a fruitful place to live and, between the
converging Gila and Salt Rivers, one of the best places for growing crops in what became Arizona.

The Piipaash and Akimel O'odham alliance was able to fend
off Apache raids and, importantly, build a substantial military
force. The militarization of Akimel and Piipaash societies coin-
cided with increased agricultural productivity. Trade with the
whites picked up. There also developed a market for Akimel
O'odham baskets and pots, particularly ollas, or large water jugs
used to keep a supply of water in the home and to cool the house
as well.

The principal enemies of Ira Hayes' relatives, the Apaches,
made a clear distinction between raiding and warfare. Translated from the Indé (Apache) language, raiding was "to search
out enemy property," and warfare was "to take death from an
enemy." Apaches did not think in terms of acquisition of territory, conquest, or extermination of their enemies. The Akimel
O'odham and the Piipaash were valuable resources for horses,
some foodstuffs, various goods and weapons, and captives. Very

often captives, especially children, were divided among women who had lost relatives. The captive children replaced loved ones both spiritually and physically and, according to Apaches, made the women happy once more. [15] The act of taking and adopting captives in Apache warfare is referred to as "mourning war," and practiced by tribes of the Great Plains and those located east of the Mississippi River. Victory and taking prisoners to replace spiritually and physically deceased relatives was intended to "dry the tears" of the bereaved.

The Quechan and Mohave enemies of the Akimel O'odham and Piipaash made war for many of the same reasons. It appears that the Piipaash were still the primary targets of Quechan and Mohave ire. The Quechan called a tribal war party "going to the enemy" and the small village raiding party "waking the enemy." The Quechan and the Mohave raided by way of a surprise attack to take horses or captives, and it was carried out by young men to prove their mettle in combat. To these Colorado River peoples, large military engagements were far more formal. The combatants drew up in formation, warriors carrying shields and clubs in the forefront and bowmen to the rear. Battles were often prearranged and even staged to take revenge for losses in previous conflicts. The battle would start with a warrior striding forward to shout insults and engage in single combat with a warrior from the other side. Others would come into the "no-man's-land" between the lines of warriors and fight. These single engagements then led to an arrow flight, and finally an attack that would turn into a general melee until one side or the other decided that its losses were too great to continue the contest. The losing side would make an uncontested retreat. The ritualistic battles have been described as bloody games rather than total war. [16]

Akimel O'odham and Piipaash warfare was carried out much

the same as that of the Quechan. When pitched battles occurred, they were highly ritualized and restrained. On the other hand, as the raiding by both the Apaches and the Quechan-Mohave coalition became more frequent, the Akimel O'odham, the Piipaash, and the Tohono O'odham in the south began to retaliate. Akimel and Piipaash youths were trained in wielding the war club and shield. They were also trained to hunt with the bow and fashion a separate war bow and arrows.

Historically, weapons have fallen into two basic categories: shock and missile. [17] The Akimel O'odham were highly proficient in using both. Missile weapons include thrown spears, arrows, bullets, mortars, artillery rounds, and rockets. Akimel warriors used their specialized war bows, made of mulberry branches and backed with sinew, to sow disorder among the enemy ranks, so that the special shield and club fighters could deliver the shock of close-quarter combat. As in most battles, projectiles might weaken a foe, even to the point of retreat or surrender, but taking ground depends on the foot soldier. And the Akimel O'odham foot soldier was the warrior who wielded the war club and the shield. [18]

Ultimately, the shield warriors were the focus of battle. They were the first to start the fight and call out the enemy combatants in one-on-one duels. Boys were trained to use the shield to deflect arrows and blows from clubs, spears, or knives. They also were taught that the shield could be used to divert the enemy's attention. Moving forward in a crouched position on an enemy, the Akimel O'odham warrior could dodge, duck, dart here and there, swiftly sidestepping any missile thrown at him, and avoid being hit. The warrior's shield was about twenty inches in diameter, made of thick, stiffened rawhide and painted with various designs, primarily to intimidate the enemy with their special spiritual powers. Interestingly, the designs often were swirls, circles, and curving lines that generally resembled sun symbols and, when rotated back and forth or slanted one way or another, could distract the enemy warrior from focusing on the lethal Akimel O'odham war club. [19]

The war club was of a singular design. It ranged from sixteen to eighteen inches in length and was made of either mesquite or ironwood. Shaped like a German "potato-masher" grenade of World War II, its cylindrical-shaped head was approximately four inches long and three and a half inches in diameter. The club handle was carved down to a sharp point for use as a kind of dagger. A leather lanyard was threaded through a hole bored in the handle of the club and was wrapped around the club wielder's wrist so that it would not be lost in close combat. [20]

There is a famous Akimel O'odham story about the shield warrior's prowess with his weapons. During the period when the Akimel O'odham and the Americans were allies against the Apaches, an Akimel O'odham warrior came to show the American soldiers his shield and club. The soldiers ridiculed his weapons, essentially saying that his club and shield were no match for an American firearm. The warrior decided to challenge the soldiers. He picked one of them and told him to stand and draw his pistol. He then said that he would walk ten paces away, turn, and come toward the soldier as if he were an enemy. The warrior stated that if the soldier saw any part of him outside the shield the soldier was to shoot him. The Akimel O'odham warrior came at the soldier, but the soldier saw no chance to fire. Finally, the shield bearer came within a foot of the man and knocked the gun out of his hand with the edge of the shield. The warrior raised his club, but the soldier fled. [21]

By and large, the Akimel O'odham and their allies, the

Piipaash, did not clash with the European colonists and sojourn-ers through their country. Spanish and Mexican explorers and settlers, after their independence from Spain in 1821, either trav-eled to the west to California or to the east toward New Mexico and Texas. If they came into the Gila River Valley, it was to trade.

In the mid-1800s several events spurred Akimel-Piipaash mil-itarism. First, the Apache clans kept migrating a bit farther west, making the Gila and Salt River peoples even more vulnerable to raids. Soon, Akimel and Piipaash men began to spend less time in the fields helping the women with the crops and more time standing guard over the fields and assuming picket duty during the night. The militarization led to military specialization. The already overburdened women began working the crops almost by themselves, tended children, and continued to produce utilitar-ian goods, like baskets and pots. The men stood guard and took care of the livestock and stepped up their retaliatory raiding. Horses became essential to Akimel warfare as a kind of light cav-alry. The horsemen joined the formations of archers and shield carriers. Despite the additional Akimel military buildup, the Quechan-Mohave-Yavapai raids also increased, especially against the western end of the Gila River Piipaash. The Apache raids continued, and the Apache movement south and west might very well have been the result of the increased American presence in the area during and after the Mexican War. Many Americans began to use a trail to the west coast through the Gila River Valley and received aid from the Akimel-Piipaash alliance. The Ameri-can army came first to invade Mexican California. Then came the gold seekers, traveling with livestock, guns, and trade goods, who became Apache targets while trespassing on their land. The Akimel O'odham and the Americans had a strong mutual inter-est in attempting to keep the Apache in their mountains and curb their attacks on the Akimel-Piipaash alliance. Frank Russell, an ethnologist studying the Akimel O'odham in the early twentieth century, observed that the Apache "paid dearly in blood" for their raids on the highly militarized Gila River Native communities. [22]

In 1846, the first year of the American war against Mexico, Brigadier General Stephen W. Kearny led his Army of the West through Akimel O'odham–Piipaash lands. His mission was to take California for the United States. Regardless of Kearny's mission, his importance in Akimel-Piipaash history was opening the southern Gila River Trail to California. Kearny's safe passage through what Mexican officials considered sovereign national territory provoked a response from the Mexican commander of the Tucson garrison. Kearny had left a number of army mules in the care of the Akimel-Piipaash leader, General Juan Antonio Llunas. Although Captain Antonio Comadurán thought that his small command could not oppose Kearny's forces, he felt that he could, at minimum, intimidate General Llunas into surrendering the mules to his authority. The Akimel-Piipaash general replied to Comadurán in no uncertain terms: if the Tucson garrison invaded the Gila Valley, it would be met with force. Comadurán let the matter drop. The Akimel-Piipaash alliance had taken a side in the American war against Mexico. [23]

The official journalist for Kearny's Army of the West, Lieutenant William H. Emory, wrote a detailed report of the Gila River route from New Mexico to the west coast. Less than two years after Kearny's expedition, the discovery of gold at Sutter's Fort in California began a gold rush that brought an estimated three hundred thousand adventurers to the far west. Of that number, easily twenty thousand of the gold seekers came via Kearny's southern route, many of them bearing Lieutenant

Emory's report. By that time, the solidly independent Akimel-Piipaash alliance was raising an abundance of wheat, corn, and other staples, all the while fighting their traditional Native enemies. The forty-niners were not disappointed in Emory's report. The Akimel-Piipaash alliance greeted each band of gold seekers with provisions, water, and shouts of "Amigos." [24]

The Gila River Valley provided both a respite and resupply station for the gold seekers and the later group of Americans who came to live in what was then the Territory of New Mexico. The valley also provided the military might of the Akimel-Piipaash alliance that protected the Americans from the Apaches. In 1848, the U.S. war against Mexico ended with the Treaty of Guadalupe Hidalgo, which resulted in the Mexican Cession of all of California, New Mexico, and most of what became Arizona. In 1854, the U.S. finalized the Gadsden Purchase with Mexican president General Antonio López de Santa Anna, of Alamo fame—or infamy, depending on which side one was on—primarily to safeguard the Gila River route to California. [25] It was not until 1863 that Arizona was separated from New Mexico to become its own territory. The American army did not establish itself in the area until 1856, which meant that the U.S. was completely dependent upon the Akimel-Piipaash alliance to protect American travelers. The Gila River alliance was even asked to guard the mail route between San Antonio, Texas, and San Diego, California. The alliance agreed to the task of guarding the mail route and, later, the stagecoaches along the Gila Valley route and asked for five hundred guns from the federal government to do so. After going through channels, the request for firearms was ultimately turned down. [26]

Despite the denial of the requested weaponry, the Akimel-Piipaash alliance demonstrated its military might in the 1857

Battle of Maricopa Wells or Pima Butte. In late August of that year, a Quechan, Mohave, Yavapai, and Tonto Apache coalition sent an extremely large war party to destroy Piipaash villages located near Maricopa Wells. The war party spent the night of August 31 near the location and attacked at dawn the next morning. The vanguard of the Quechan expedition encountered a group of Piipaash women together with a single warrior out gathering mesquite pods. The women were all murdered, but the man, a fast runner, escaped. He ran to the village to warn the people there who, in turn, fled toward the Akimel O'odham villages.

The Quechan warriors entered the village and set it on fire. They moved on to a second village to put it to the torch. Meanwhile, Piipaash runners had gone to get help from their Akimel allies. The women and children generally fled toward the Akimel O'odham towns of Sacaton and Blackwater. They tried to take refuge at two rocky hills known as Pima Butte. When the runners spread the word that the Quechan, Mohave, Yavapai, and Tonto Apache raiders were heading eastward, the Akimel O'odham assembled. There was no time for the preliminary prayers, speeches, and ceremonies. Warriors took up their bows, shields, and war clubs and headed toward the oncoming enemy. A number of the Akimel O'odham were mounted.

The Quechan-led war party was losing manpower rapidly. Before they set fire to the second village, they filled their empty stomachs with Piipaash corn and beans. That afternoon they were ready to push forward again. On the way toward Pima Butte two bad omens halted their progress. First, a deer fell dead without a wound but with blood seeping from its nose. Second, a hawk fell dead from the sky. A number of members of the war party, especially the Mohave, Tonto Apache, and Yavapai, began to turn in their tracks and return home. Swallow Hawk, the

Quechan leader, urged what was left of the war party onward until they finally met the line of Piipaash and Akimel O'odham warriors on an open plain next to Pima Butte.

The Piipaash and Akimel O'odham were arrayed in a semicircle with bowmen and clubmen standing in a traditional formation. After a ritual exchange of insults, the fight began. The Akimel-Piipaash bowmen let loose their arrows from three points on the line. One witness later testified that some of the Akimel O'odham warriors had guns. If so, they were likely old Indian trade guns, single-shot musket-carbines that were slow to load but carried a .45 to .50 caliber punch. But the group that caused the most fear among the Quechan were the mounted Akimel O'odham and Piipaash warriors. Their presence caused a number of the Quechan warriors to take flight. The arrow flights did a great deal of damage as well.

Unlike in most Native American ritualized pitched battles, when the Quechan warriors began to break and run, the Akimel O'odham and Piipaash horsemen went in pursuit, using lances and clubs. They rode the fleeing Quechans down and left a trail of dead bodies behind. While the mounted pursuit was carried out, the Akimel-Piipaash shield bearers attacked and slaughtered what was left of the Quechan formation. Because of the spiritual taint of killing and handling the dead, only a few scalps were taken, and the bodies of the dead Quechan and Mohave warriors were left to mummify in the dry desert air or be scavenged by buzzards, crows, and coyotes. [27]

The massacre at Pima Butte was a demonstration of the amplified militarization of Akimel O'odham, Piipaash, and Quechan and Mohave societies. The Quechan force came in large numbers, perhaps as many as four hundred warriors, to slaughter and lay waste to Piipaash and Akimel O'odham villages.

The Akimel-Piipaash maneuvered quickly to meet the challenge with a concentration of force, as would any well-led army. The defense was a diversified force with an extended missile range, shock troops, and a mounted force with the ability to envelop the enemy or to pursue a broken formation. This was only a ritualized battle to the extent that the aggressors and defenders shouted preparatory posturing insults at one another. The battle of Pima Butte was all-out, high-casualty warfare that omitted the restraint of previous battles.

More than anything else, the battle marked a departure from traditional Native warfare, especially in terms of numbers of combatants. The drawn-out hunt for survivors and the massacre itself also marked a change in the limited nature of Akimel O'odham combat. Except for raiding, the Gila River people rarely practiced offensive war. Because the Quechan-led war party was so large, numbering between two hundred and four hundred warriors, there had to be a massive defensive response.

Afterward, the victors came from the battlefield and took part in the ceremonies that crossed the line from the chaos of war to a return to the search for peace. Those who had killed an enemy went into the sixteen-day seclusion and were purified once again. After the battle of Pima Butte, the Quechan were no longer a threat. The Akimel O'odham and Piipaash gained a kind of peace as a result of a decisive battle. Any one of the well-known philosophers of warfare, from Sun Tzu to Machiavelli to Jomini to Clausewitz, would have recognized the Battle of Pima Butte as "true war" rather than just a "primitive" skirmish.

The U.S. Army certainly recognized the value of the Akimel O'odham–Piipaash armed forces. Generally, colonial-settler states like the U.S. recruit indigenous people to aid in the extension of state sovereignty over acquired territory, no matter how dubious or violent that acquisition may have been. In recruiting marginalized, ethnic, or colonized groups, two stereotypes appear to be in play. Military elites recruited indigenous peoples for service on the basis of whether or not they had martial tendencies and were reliable allies. The stereotype of Native Americans as a martial race already existed in the nineteenth century. The question was over Native American political reliability. American political and military elites did not consider the Apache people to be politically reliable. The Akimel O'odham and the Piipaash were. [28]

Consequently, the Akimel-Piipaash generosity toward the Americans, their taking the American side during the Mexican War, and their crushing defeat of the Quechan, Mohave, Yavapai, and Tonto Apache at the Battle of Pima Butte affirmatively answered the question of their political reliability and their status as a militarized society. Akimel-Piipaash warriors became exceptionally important to the American army in its continuing war against the Apache people.

During the Civil War the U.S. continued its war with the Apache people, but many of the Union troops were withdrawn from service in the West to fight elsewhere. The Akimel O'odham and Piipaash alliance was once again left with the job of protecting their homes and the Gila River Valley in general. When the rebellion began, the Confederate military command declared that below the thirty-fourth parallel New Mexico was organized Southern territory. The Union state of California reacted and sent a volunteer force into New Mexico territory by way of the Gila Valley route. The force, known as the California Column, came into the Akimel O'odham and Piipaash lands and were greeted as allies. The California troops purchased more than one hundred forty thousand pounds of wheat on credit from the alliance and were able to march into New Mexico. The alliance was in a position to protect the supply line of the Union forces from California across the Gila Valley trail. [29]

In 1863, Arizona was detached from New Mexico and incorporated as a United States territory. The new governor, John N. Goodwin, created the Arizona Volunteers to fight Confederates, should they reappear, and the Apaches and the Yavapais, on whose land a contingent of miners was camped. The miners and the Akimel-Piipaash alliance joined forces against the Yavapai and the Apaches to the east. Goodwin formed two Native companies under the Arizona Volunteers. A sage and war captain named Juan Chevería commanded the Piipaash Company (Company B), and a white man named John D. Walker led the Akimel O'odham (Company C). Walker, who was a California Volunteer, had been left in the Gila River Valley to help speed up supplies. He married into the tribe and became fully assimilated into Akimel O'odham society. The real leader of the Akimel O'odham company was Antonio Azul. Walker rode into battle wearing Native clothing and, at one time, had nearly four hundred warriors with him and Azul. [30]

The Arizona Volunteer companies were primarily sent against the Apache villages until the regular army troops were reassigned to Arizona after the Civil War. In July of 1866, Congress passed a resolution establishing the Indian Scouting Service. The Akimel-Piipaash alliance was called into service and led the regular U.S. soldiers into battle on numerous occasions in the years 1866 and 1867. In 1871, General George Crook took command of the campaign against the Apaches. Crook used the Akimel-Piipaash scouts intermittently until the final Apache war leader, Geronimo, surrendered in 1886.

The Akimel O'odham and Piipaash were highly effective scouts and fighters. Culturally, they were still performing many of the rituals that had to do with warfare. Several American commanders in the field did not consider them wholly reliable except, perhaps, when actually engaged in battle. These commanders complained that the ritual purification rites for those warriors who had taken lives lasted for sixteen days, making them unavailable for combat for a considerable length of time. Some officers did not approve of the "pagan" ceremonies and customs because they were not in line with conventional army doctrine on war-making. [31]

U.S. Indian policy following the Civil War was mixed bag of suppressing Native American cultural and political freedom, an effort to make peace with a number of tribes, an attempt to "Americanize" Native Americans, and a program designed to individualize land holdings and redistribute "surplus" property to non-Indians. It is impossible historically to determine which Native nation suffered the most from U.S. duplicity and encroachment. But Ira Hayes' people were among the most betrayed and trespassed upon, even after they fought beside the Americans in war and fed them in peacetime.

Simply put, the Americans wanted what the Akimel O'odham possessed: land and water. The white people began to siphon off Gila and Salt River water and encroach on Akimel O'odham land as early as 1866, despite the generosity and military support of the Akimel-Piipaash alliance. This incursion on land and water rights, on top of the continual state of war from the 1750s onward, created a historical, collective trauma that has been a part of Akimel O'odham and Piipaash life until this day.

Hayes spoke of the historical damage done to his people on numerous occasions. One Marine of Easy Company, Arthur Stanton, recalled to historian Albert Hemingway that he and Hayes, like all Marines overseas, used to have talks about home and

Hayes' reservation and people. "The Chief," Stanton recollected, "always longed for the days of his ancestors." Hayes "wished he had lived in the days when his Tribe was something more than beggars." Stanton heard about the days when Hayes' people "lived in peace and prosperity" until the white man began to siphon off the water and encroach upon their reservation and left them among the poorest of the poor. Hayes also told Stanton that his people were still trying to regain their water rights, land, and economic independence. [32]

The Gila River Valley in the late nineteenth century was prime real estate. In fact, the Akimel O'odham had proven its value in terms of wheat, cotton, bean, and corn production since the 1700s. Livestock grazed its fields and grew fat on the fodder gleaned from Akimel O'odham lands. It was also an easy route to California and its riches. The stagecoach and the mail traveled the route. Trade for Akimel O'odham pots, baskets, livestock, cotton, and foodstuffs along the trail was substantial. Additionally, the Akimel-Piipaash alliance entered into a treaty with the Mohave, Quechan, Chemehuevi, and Yavapai to continue war on the Apache and to protect the Americans. The treaty was brokered at Fort Yuma in April 1863. [33]

But in 1863, even before it became an organized territory, Arizona was opened to American settlement and exploitation. From that point in time, the federal government proactively made policies that encouraged white settlement in the West. The image that Americans held of the Akimel O'odham and the Piipaash was more than positive. One white observer said that the confederation of the two tribes "surpassed many of the Christian nations in agriculture." [34] Moreover, they were regarded as being well on the road to being "civilized" in the Western sense of the word. They were friends and helpmeets of the Americans.

No less a personage than cartographer, explorer, diplomat, and army major general William H. Emory had assured the Akimel-Piipaash alliance that all the guarantees of land the Mexican government made to them would be sacrosanct. Despite this assurance, miners from California came to the Gila River Valley, and close on their heels came American farmers and ranchers. These parties used Gila River water in far greater amounts than the Akimel O'odham. The Native peoples could perhaps have survived the American farmers, but the mining industry was an additional burden not only on the river but also on the water table belowground. The Akimel-Piipaash alliance soon began to butt heads with the whites. And white attitudes turned against the Native people of the Gila and Salt River Valleys. The American hatred of the Akimel O'odham grew to the point that the town of Florence deliberately diverted and wasted water specifically to deprive the Akimel O'odham of the much-needed and, in fact, sacred water supply. Ultimately, the cost of protecting, feeding, and fighting alongside the Americans was much too high. [35]

The federal government was working at cross purposes regarding the Akimel O'odham land and water. The army was growing increasingly concerned about keeping the peace in the Gila River Valley. The Akimel-Piipaash alliance was a formidable military force. The militarization of the Gila River tribes and the duplicitous intentions of the federal Indian policymakers led American officers to fear a possible collapse of the Akimel O'odham–American military pact: the Akimel-Piipaash alliance could rise up and attack the American civilians. The military commanders rightfully figured that the Akimel O'odham and Piipaash were on the verge of striking out against those who had encroached upon their water rights. The federal government outwardly supported the notion that Indians generally would eventually become yeoman farmers in the Jeffersonian ideal of American society. The Akimel O'odham were, in fact, one of the most "progressive" tribes in terms of the policy of Americanizing Native Americans. At the same time, Congress was passing bill after bill encouraging white settlement west of the Mississippi River. Arizona was especially prized because of its deposits of silver and copper. [36]

The consequences of this dichotomy in policy development were truly mind-boggling and ultimately detrimental to the Akimel O'odham and Piipaash way of life. The leaders of the Akimel-Piipaash alliance, as well as the federal officials, were acutely aware of the possible outcomes of opening the Gila River Valley to white settlers. More importantly to Ira Hayes' life story was the impoverishment of his people due to government policy and the duplicity of U.S. policymakers.

To those manipulating Indian policy at the time there were two straightforward solutions to the problem. Of course, the view from Washington and from the local Arizona territorial government was that the problem was the Akimel O'odham and not the American settlers. The first so-called solution was to remove the Akimel O'odham and the Piipaash from their homelands to the Indian Territory (present- day Oklahoma).

Tribal removal to Indian Territory was an established policy by the 1870s. In 1830, Andrew Jackson had signed the Indian Removal Act into law. The intention of the act was to eventually concentrate all the Native peoples into a relatively small area that became known as the Indian Territory. The idea underlying the policy was to restrict the movement of the tribes and to rid the individual states of indigenous tribes. Of course, its other purpose was to reduce considerably the territorial boundaries of the tribes, making white expansion supposedly less contentious. One author has called Indian removal the nineteenth century version of ethnic cleansing. By the 1870s tribes from all over the U.S. had been moved to the Indian Territory. [37]

The Indian Territory was established to contain Native peoples while handing over their traditional landholdings to the whites. The Akimel O'odham and Piipaash became candidates for removal. An 1868 flood ruined the Akimel O'odham crops the next year. Then in 1870 a drought brought on more crop failure. The Akimel O'odham and the Piipaash blamed the failure on the whites, who were siphoning off Gila River water. Tribal officials Antonio Azul and Kihua Chinkum warned the reservation agent John H. Stout that an uprising was imminent. That being so, the white people could be placed in great jeopardy, having two great military forces, the Akimel-Piipaash alliance and the Apache people, aligned against them. The Akimel O'odham were, by 1871, demanding that their reservation be expanded north of the Gila. At least one Akimel O'odham village moved across the river. The federal government opened talks with the Akimel O'odham and Piipaash leaders about removing the people to the Unassigned Lands in the Indian Territory.

Secretary of the Interior Columbus Delano was obsessed with the idea of concentrating every Indian, save for some nonthreatening remnant groups scattered in a few states and the supposed descendants of Pocahontas, in the Indian Territory. Several of his friends were involved in the "Indian Ring" scandals in the 1870s. Plainly put, the "Indian Ring" was a cabal of corporate suppliers of cloth, equipment, even foodstuffs to the reservations and Indian Office bureaucrats. They made profits and kickbacks by inflating prices for those goods. The main idea was that confining the Native nations within the boundaries of

Indian Territory would open lands in Arizona to white settlement and mining operations.

The first step was to invite some headmen from the Akimel O'odham to come to the Indian Territory and see the lands on which their people would live. Tribal elders were unwilling to negotiate at first. Consequently, it was not until 1873 that reservation agent John H. Stout convinced a delegation of five Akimel O'odham and Piipaash leaders to visit the Indian Territory. In the meantime, a number of Akimel O'odham and Piipaash moved to the Salt River, thereby forming the basis for the establishment of the Salt River Reservation by executive order in 1879. When the five headmen returned to Arizona from the inspection of the Indian Territory land, they held meetings in several villages. They discovered that most of the people feared removal, citing cold winters, the possibility of hostile tribes, the distance from their burial grounds and ancestral lands, and the risk of disease as the reasons underlying their opposition to relocation. In the end, the Akimel-Piipaash alliance refused to be removed and continued to argue for an expansion of the reservation or, at minimum, a recognition of their water rights. [38]

The water shortage continued, and the effort to find a solution for it that would satisfy American settlers and maintain good relations with the Akimel-Piipaash alliance actually hit a stone wall. During 1879, an executive order stopped the selling of acreage on the Salt River to whites and added the land that was not sold to the Salt River Reservation. In the same year, President Rutherford B. Hayes added more land to both the Salt and Gila River lands. The problem was not in the size of the Akimel-Piipaash alliance land base; it was the lack of water. [39]

Sure enough, drought came on like the desert dust devils that the dry winds whipped up. And disaster followed. Crops failed, and the Akimel O'odham and Piipaash were made, in Ira Hayes' words, into beggars. The once independent people of the Gila River became dependent on the white man's hand-outs. Starvation came with the failure of the crops. During the 1880s the influx of white settlers rapidly increased. With their coming, more land was put under cultivation, and water usage by whites rose appreciably. By 1892, Akimel O'odham water use had dropped by more than half of what it was in 1866. [40]

In the minds of many white policymakers and the reformers interested in "civilizing" Indians, the answer to the "Indian prob-lem" was allotment in severalty. That meant dividing reservations into individually owned plots of land, so that each Native fam-ily would be responsible for its own welfare. Allotment eventu-ally came in 1887 when President Grover Cleveland signed the General Allotment Act into law. It was soon discovered that allot-ment could not work on the Gila or Salt River reservations sim-ply because there was not enough water to irrigate individually held allotments, much less the large fields of cotton, wheat, corn, and beans the villages worked collectively. Besides, famine was spreading across the reservations.

Crops failed again and again over the course of the twenty years between 1880 and 1900. Akimel O'odham and Piipaash cat-tle died in droves, and hundreds of children on the reservation were reported to be malnourished. In some cases, tribal elders were found dead for lack of food and water. Deaths on the res-ervation, according to the agency doctor, were unusually high, likely due to dehydration. The physician also reported cases of scurvy. In 1896 the superintendent of the Phoenix Indian School said that the Akimel O'odham had nothing to eat but mescal (the roasted root of the agave plant, not the alcoholic drink) and mesquite beans, neither of which is very nourishing. [41]

News of starvation on the Akimel O'odham-Piipaash reservations broke in 1900. The *Los Angeles Times* carried a story that said the tribe was starving to death and the direct blame lay with the white settlers of the region. [42] The *Chicago Tribune* asserted that two-thirds of the reservation's cattle had died due to the drought and lack of fodder. [43] In seeking to place the blame on government officials, the *Pomona Progress* stated how Akimel O'odham suffering contrasted with the state of the Apaches, who were "sleek and well fed." It was a case, according to the *Progress,* of the "rewarding of enemies and killing of friends." [44] The paper evidently forgot that Geronimo and the Apaches who escaped the reservation had been rounded up, jailed in Florida, and confined to a reservation in the Indian Territory, far from their homelands in the mountains of Arizona.

If the Pomona newspaper did not appreciate the actual treatment of the Apache people, the article at least pointed out the historical betrayal of the Akimel-Piipaash alliance. This duplicity on the part of the U.S. government caused historical misery among the peoples of the Gila and Salt River reservations that has not been forgotten even four or five generations later. Collective historical trauma is the consequence of a catastrophic event or series of events that are suffered by a particular group of people. These experienced events begin to shape meaning within the victimized society and can become part of a group's identity. The group forms an ideological identity that can lead to insular behavior. [45]

As historical, or intergenerational, trauma applies to Native Americans, it is apparent that the mental anguish is cumulative. For Hayes' people, the Apache, Quechan, and Yuma wars began a friendship with the Americans, who, in turn, encroached upon their lands and stole their water rights. The famine that ensued added to the emotional distress. By the time Ira Hayes was born, the Akimel O'odham were impoverished and left without any kind of recourse politically. Arizona did not consider Native Americans to be citizens of the state with the right to vote until 1948. [46] Ultimately, the Akimel O'odham were completely dependent on the federal government.

Poverty and dependence took away the ability of Native people to undergo change on their own terms. The historical, intergenerational trauma bred various social and emotional and psychological problems, such as substance abuse, depression, unresolved grief, dysfunctional parenting, and chronic unemployment. [47] Even individual health problems arose through impoverishment. Diets changed radically for the Akimel O'odham, leading to diabetes and heart disease. In a matter of less than one hundred years Ira's people went from a healthy, independent, and prosperous society to a poverty-stricken and underprivileged community, still fighting for the civil and legal rights that once were theirs.

Ira Hayes lived this historical, collective, transgenerational trauma. He was a single generation removed from the terrible famine that beset the Akimel O'odham people. He deplored the fact that even after Akimel O'odham men and women had served the United States in both world wars, "the white race looks down on the Indian as if he were a little man." [48] And he was sure that no Native person was going to receive equal treatment by the Americans even after fighting a white man's war.

Chapter 3

The Education of Ira H. Hayes

As the nineteenth century waned, a group of non-Native men and women who thought of themselves as Christian reformers launched an effort to transform Native Americans into American citizens socially and culturally. The Akimel O'odham were leading candidates for this transformation. The white settlers of Arizona Territory differed greatly from the Christian reformers. The settlers could not have cared less whether the Akimel O'odham could be assimilated into American society and culture. In fact, ethnologist Frank Russell wrote that between 1850 and 1880, the Akimel O'odham were more or less living with "some of the vilest specimens of humanity that the white race has produced." [1]

Still, the Christian reformers forged ahead, praying that they could transform the Natives from "savagism" to "civilization" and rid them of the "reservation system." The means by which they proposed to make Native peoples "vanish" into mainstream society were numerous and complex. At the movement's roots was a series of laws and programs aimed at undermining each tribe's existence as a social, culture, and political entity. The movement established the boarding school system to teach Native children the three R's and to "fit in" with civilized society. The Christian reformers also pressed for the end of treaty obligations and the dissolution of the Indian Office. Lastly, they lobbied Congress for a bill that would break up the reservations into individually owned farms and impose a market economy on Native people. [2] These measures would eventually affect all Native peoples within the United States.

What the reformers hoped to create was a "New Indian": educated in the Western European model, Christian above all, dressing in "citizen's attire" (like white people), working alongside white Americans, taking on the civic responsibilities of U.S. citizenship, and independent of any kind of government handout or obligation. After the turn of the nineteenth century there arose a large number of these "New Indians." Easily the most famous of them was Charles A. Eastman. A Santee Dakota from Minnesota, as a child he witnessed the horrors of the Dakota War, which broke out when he was only four years old. It was thought that his father, Many Lightnings, had been killed in the fighting and so Eastman, then known as Ohiyesa (The Winner) and his brother were left in the care of their paternal grandparents. In actuality, Many Lightnings had been captured and imprisoned. Luckily, he escaped the mass execution by hanging of the Santee's leading warriors and chiefs. When Eastman was fifteen, his father returned. Many Lightnings had become Jacob Eastman and a Christian. His father immediately sent him off to the Reverend Alfred E. Riggs' Santee Indian School. The rigorous curriculum there readied Charles Eastman for entrance into Knox College. He went on to Dartmouth and finally to Boston Medical School. Eastman worked as a physician with the Office of Indian Affairs and, while on duty in South Dakota, tended the wounded of the Wounded Knee massacre in 1890. The Wounded Knee incident was the underlying reason that he soon left the Indian service. He began to write books and articles extolling his upbringing in the Santee way of life. He lived in Minneapolis and opened a private practice. Eastman's publications were highly regarded and brought him national recognition as a champion of conservation, Indian rights, and the preservation of Native knowledge of the environment. [3]

Equally prolific in writing about the beauty of Native American life and the injustice done to Native peoples was Gertrude Simmons Bonnin, or Zitkála Šá, of the Western Dakota or Yankton people. When she was eight, she was taken to Josiah White's Manual Labor Institute in Wabash, Indiana. She was torn between her own Yankton culture and the enforced assimilationist education. She rebelled against cutting her hair while at the same time enjoyed learning to read and playing the violin. Later, she would join the faculty at Carlisle Indian School in Carlisle, Pennsylvania, where she clashed with the director, Richard Henry Pratt, over his "Kill the Indian and save the man" assimilationist rhetoric. She would go on to write about her culture and she produced several political articles in both the *Atlantic Monthly* and *Harper's Monthly*. She also penned a libretto for the first Native American opera. She married Raymond Bonnin and moved with him to the Uintah-Ouray Reservation in Utah. They would later make their home in Washington, D.C., where they both would remain active in the Native justice movement. Like Eastman, she was a member of the Society of American Indians and, with her husband, helped found the National Council of American Indians in 1926. [4] They were survivors of the Indian schools and the white man's world, and both maintained their Native identity.

Although they did not receive the notoriety of either Eastman or Zitkála Šá, Ira Hayes' parents, Joseph E. or "Jobe" and

Nancy, were, in many ways, "New Indians" in terms of surviving the conditions on the reservation. Both were born in the new century, Joseph in 1901 and Nancy the next year. They were born during the famine, but they grew up attempting to farm the land. Water, though, was in the hands of the white men. Yet, despite the severe hardships they faced, they remained committed to the Presbyterian church and basic education and, at the same time, maintained their Akimel O'odham uniqueness and the group ethos of Himdag. Although there were no references as to how the Hayes family received their surname, it is likely that Ira's grandparents took the name as part of their conversion to Christianity. Ira's mother, Nancy, used Whitaker and Hamilton as surnames before she married Jobe. Ira's middle name was Hamilton, presumably after a maternal relative. Since at least the sixteenth century, renaming Native people who had converted to Christianity had been common practice in the churches. When allotment was carried out on the reservations, allottees were often given "Christian" names merely to keep land ownership records and the inheritance of property properly administered in the tradition of Western European land ownership.

Although it is not clear where Jobe and Nancy learned the "three Rs," it is likely that they went to a Presbyterian mission school located on the reservation. Charles H. Cook, called the "Apostle to the Pima" and who was said to be a master of the O'odham language, brought the Presbyterian mission to the Gila River community in 1871. Thereafter, he converted and baptized more than a thousand Akimel O'odham. He built fourteen churches and related schools. Cook firmly believed that religion went hand in hand with education. And so the Presbyterian church and its various elementary schools on the reservation and in Phoenix and Tucson were wedded. Reading the Bible and comprehending church doctrine were essential to conversion, especially in a John Calvin–and John Knox–based liturgy like Presbyterianism. [5] According to Anna Moore Shaw in her autobiography, *A Pima Past*, the transition from the traditional way to the new religion was not easy, but when Chief Antonio Azul was converted and the first group of people were baptized, "Christianity spread like wildfire." [6] To another Akimel O'odham man, George Webb, Christianity was acceptable primarily because "religion was natural to us." [7]

Nancy and Jobe were married in 1922, presumably in the church that Cook established in Sacaton. Ira Hamilton Hayes, their firstborn, arrived the next year. He received his elementary education at the local missionary schools. Within the span of seven years, they had five more children. The times were nevertheless difficult. Two of Ira's siblings, Harold and Arlene, died in childhood. [8] In 1932, the family moved from Sacaton to Bapchule. Two of Jobe and Nancy's children, Ira and Kenneth, the youngest, entered military service. Ira fought in World War II and Kenneth in the Korean War.

Until the age of seventeen, Ira stayed in Bapchule and worked as a farm laborer picking cotton and harvesting wheat, corn, and other essentials. His mother continued to encourage education among her children and sent Ira off to the Phoenix Indian School. The Phoenix boarding school for Native children was one of several government institutions that, at first, fit into the nineteenth-century reformers' scheme to "Americanize" or assimilate Native peoples. Richard Henry Pratt, the superintendent of the Carlisle Indian Industrial School in Pennsylvania, was a former army captain who had served as the commandant-warden of the Fort Marion, Florida, prison for Native Americans who had warred against the United States. Pratt took what he thought was the way to "rehabilitate" his Native prisoners and applied it to educating Native children. He became a darling of the Christian reformers and of their Lake Mohonk Conferences of Friends of the Indian, which began in 1883. [9]

He firmly believed, like most of the Friends of the Indian, that if Native children were removed from the reservations and given Western educations, they would become "civilized" people and be worthy of American citizenship. In essence, if the children were left devoid of their tribal cultures, they could be educated and be acceptable in the white world, hence the Carlisle motto, "Kill the Indian and save the man." Indian boarding schools soon sprang up all over the nation. The curricula were harsh and militaristic. Students wore uniforms, were marched to classes, were subjected to corporal punishment, were forced to keep everything spotlessly clean, and were not allowed to speak a word of their Native languages.

After the ultra-zealous Pratt was finally removed from the school in 1904, things began to change. Whites became interested in collecting Native artifacts, and the conservation movement had a renewed focus on the stereotype of Indians as "children of nature." Anthropologists decried the Christian reformers as "unscientific" and denounced the Office of Indian Affairs as a corrupt bureaucracy. The Indian boarding schools became more receptive to some aspects of Native cultures, especially arts and crafts. [10] But until the 1930s the schools were still reaching toward the goal of assimilating Native students into mainstream American society.

During the administration of Franklin D. Roosevelt, Indian policies changed significantly and abruptly. Day schools on the reservations were emphasized instead of taking Native children to far-off boarding schools. Even the boarding schools were taking students from relatively close-by reservations. At several schools, students continued to wear uniforms, and many of the graduates who would later enter the military service suggested that because of their boarding school experience basic training was not new at all. [11]

In fact, many of the Akimel O'odham students took the discipline they learned in boarding school to the trenches in France during the Great War. Phoenix Indian School was made into a recruiting station when the U.S. entered the war in 1917. At first, the superintendent of the school, John R. Brown, discouraged students from enlisting. But as war fever grew, Brown changed his position and supported those students who wanted to serve. [12] Eventually, Phoenix Indian School would have one of the highest rates of military service within the boarding school system. Richard Henry Pratt would have been proud of the system's martial traditions.

A large number of Akimel O'odham–Piipaash signed up for the war. One, Edward Nelson from Blackwater, entered the navy because "the Army had still to be organized." Nelson's training in Indian school helped him become a Blacksmith Second Class. On the other hand, he ended up playing in the band aboard the battleship USS *North Dakota*. [13]

Other Akimel O'odham were already serving in the Arizona National Guard and were first called up to protect the border while General John Pershing was chasing Pancho Villa in Mexico. The Native guardsmen were also activated during the First World War and served as the basis for Indian Company F of the 158th Infantry, 40th Division, that shipped out to France in August 1918. Company F was held in reserve for the rest of the war. [14]

The most famous of the Akimel O'odham doughboys during World War I was Mathew B. Juan. A member of the "Big Red One" infantry division, Juan was a graduate of the Riverside,

California, Indian School. He was killed in action by machine-gun fire during the battle of Cantigny. He was the first person from Arizona to die in combat during the war. He, along with Ira Hayes, is memorialized with a life-size statue at the Mathew B. Juan–Ira H. Hayes Memorial Park in Sacaton. Juan is buried at the Presbyterian church there. [15]

It was clear that a martial tradition had been active among the Akimel-Piipaash alliance since the late eighteenth century. The alliance warriors had been tested over and over again, and the American military elites wanted Native troops. The Scouting Service, in which the Akimel O'odham and Piipaash had served, was on its way out, simply because the "Indian Wars" were over. Although the last Apache scout was not retired until the 1940s, most Native members of the armed forces were in regular military units. During the First World War, in fact, nearly everyone who had anything at all to do with policymaking, from the Christian reformers to the scientists who studied Indians, insisted that Native Americans be integrated into white military units because of their "special" abilities. African American soldiers would be segregated into their own units; Native Americans would not.

By the early twentieth century, military elites, who at the time were all white, were afflicted with what I have called the "Indian Scout Syndrome." Al Carroll, in his very fine book *Medicine Bags and Dog Tags,* called the stereotype that caused the malady the "Super Scout Image." [16] The assimilationist reformers advocated Native American service in World War I, writing in the newsletter the *Indian's Friend* that "Indians in the regiments are being used for scouting and patrol duty because of the natural instinct which fits them for this kind of work." [17] The idea that Natives had inherent skills that gave them an intuitive understanding of stealth in warfare or the instinctive ability to read the terrain of a battlefield was inculcated in the American mind. In the 1890s the notion that Native Americans constituted a martial race was strong enough to inspire Secretary of War Redfield Proctor to authorize the formation of a few all-Indian infantry and cavalry units in the U.S. Army. To the secretary, military service would promote civilization among the Native troops and foster in them a sense of loyalty and patriotism toward the U.S. It would also give employment to Native men. Because the American officer corps objected to the program, the Indian companies were ultimately disbanded before the Spanish-American War. [18]

There is one source that indicates Jobe Hayes was a veteran of the Great War and could have influenced his son's decision to volunteer for service in World War II. An "Official Website of the U.S. Department of Veterans Affairs" called Vantage Point asserted that the senior Hayes was indeed a World War I veteran. [19] I could find no other reference regarding Jobe's service. Additionally, Joseph B. Hayes was only sixteen when the U.S. declared war on Germany—too young to enter military service in the first place.

Still, most of the factors that may have played a part in Ira Hayes' enlistment in the Marine Corps were extant. A strong martial tradition existed in Akimel O'odham culture as well as a long-standing record of alliance with and service in the U.S. armed forces from the Mexican-American War, through the American Civil War, the Scouting Service, and during World War I. Mathew B. Juan was a revered name in Sacaton, where Ira spent the first nine years of his life. The wars against the Apache, Quechan, Mohave, and Yavapai created an Akimel-Piipaash alliance that was highly militarized. Those wars were in living memory of several older men and women during the 1920s and

'30s. An underlying factor might well have been the notion that in aiding the white people in their wars they might alleviate the historical collective trauma that had been dealt to Ira's people in the form of stealing the tribe's water and land. At the time the Akimel O'odham ("O'odham" means people, so "Akimel O'odham people" is redundant) and every other Native nation within Arizona were denied the vote and every other basic civil right. Perhaps by demonstrating their loyalty to the U.S. they could gain the rights held by all other citizens of the U.S.—or, at minimum, demonstrate that they were not threatening. [20]

Little is known of Ira's early years. But there are two autobiographies of Akimel O'odham, Anna Moore Shaw and George Webb, that speak of life in the Gila River community in the period slightly before and during Hayes' childhood. As Hayes once told one of his comrades in arms, he would have liked living in the old days before the whites came to the Gila River Valley. If that was indeed the case, then Hayes must have grown up hearing the stories of his ancestors and his culture and how his people lived in harmony with the land and one another. He also grew up in the Presbyterian church that Charles H. Cook established in Sacaton. Such was the reputation of the church, or of Cook, that some Akimel O'odham would even walk two days to be at the services on Sundays. [21] The Presbyterian church, especially in its missionary activities, presumes that with grace or election comes a responsibility to serve the larger community by doing good works.

Ira Hayes attended the local school and the church. Many of his cousins and relatives lamented the dying out of the old ways but found solace in the new religion. As a girl, Anna Moore Shaw snuck off and joined in the festivals and dances at the local Catholic church, eschewing the severity of the Presbyterian injunctions against dancing and feasting. Her father, a strict member of Cook's church, admonished her for attending the festivals, and she dutifully returned to the narrow path of the church's strictures. [22] George Webb too told of his education and upbringing in the church schools.

Ira Hayes' childhood was probably not unlike Webb's, even though Webb was a generation older. The reservation was still impoverished, but children nevertheless played games, learned to read, and did their chores. And, of course, they went to church. Children took care of livestock, feeding chickens, horses, and cattle. Often, they cared for younger siblings and helped clean and cook for the household. They played soldier, mimicking the commands of military leaders and marching in columns like the white soldiers. When they attended the government Indian school they would be marched to class and to the school's mess halls for meals. When on vacation from the boarding schools, Akimel O'odham students often wore their school uniforms, which their younger relatives found smart and even inspiring. In short, many Akimel O'odham children were prepared by the martial aspects of the government schools. Webb also wrote about a traditional game the children played called "going to see the coyote." The game involved a boy lying down, pretending to be a sleeping coyote, while a line of children marched around him four times. After the fourth circuit the column leader poked the "coyote" with a stick. At that, the coyote jumped up and attempted to catch one of the fleeing children. When one was finally caught, he or she had to lie down, and the game resumed. Girls also played a game known as Toka. The game was something like field hockey but with very long sticks. [23]

Those who grew up with Hayes developed a mixed view about his character as a boy and as an adolescent. Generally, they suggested that he was a quiet, serious young man who rarely spoke unless spoken to. Hayes' quiet demeanor, in the words of one playmate, "was like his father." Another said, "Ira was a quiet guy... Such a quiet guy." Still another stated that Hayes was "very shy" and "preferred to stay in the background." Not only was he "shy" and "distant" but, according to one person, "Ira wasn't playful, he wasn't competitive." Hayes' cousin, Buddy Lewis, said, "Ira didn't go in for games." [24]

In contrast to these images, Hayes' brother Kenny said, "He didn't cause any trouble, but he liked to tease the girls." As a boy, Hayes was "telling stories on a rubber tire swing hanging from a tamarisk tree." [25] Teasing the girls and telling stories were hardly the characteristics of a self-effacing, silent, and unobtrusive boy. It was revealed in a 2000 article on Hayes' life in the *Arizona Republic* that he was the assistant editor of the 1939 *Autam Machick*, the Sacaton Indian school's yearbook. Later, as a student at the Phoenix Indian Boarding School, he played on the football and baseball teams. [26]

It seems as though Hayes was not really the introverted, inactive, and dour young man who has been portrayed. Hayes was a storyteller. His Marine buddies described him as a fun-loving, outgoing man who could, as a humorous trick, pry off a beer bottle cap with his teeth. He would also talk about his people and their struggle to regain their water rights. Hayes could be angry as well. He disliked being called "Chief" and would "glower" at whoever called him that. Hayes made a close friend in Teddy Draper, a Navajo Code Talker. [27] It was only after seeing the horrors of battle on Bougainville that Ira, as did every one of his friends, sought solitude while he relived the fighting.

When Hayes was seventeen, he went to the Phoenix Indian

Boarding School. At the time, the Phoenix Indian School served as a vocational school as well as a junior and senior high school. Military discipline was being edged out, and the students were no longer required to wear uniforms. The curriculum was standard for Indian schools at the time, and although most of them were conceding that there were some aspects of Native cultures that were worth keeping, the schools nevertheless emphasized that Native people would eventually have to find employment either on their reservations or in the larger society; hence, the emphasis on a so-called practical education for Native students. That is, speaking and reading English, learning basic arithmetic, and taking vocational or agricultural training or both. Gone was the "Kill the Indian and save the man" standard, but there was still an emphasis on holding a job in the outside world. The vocational side of the education was difficult enough; after all, the U.S. was in the Great Depression, and World War II was looming on the horizon. After the attack on Pearl Harbor, the students at the Phoenix Indian School heard the war news every morning. They sang the anthems of each of the services and were encouraged to participate in some way to the war effort. [28]

Hayes made no comment on why he left the Phoenix Indian School after two years. Perhaps it was because he thought that being in school was not aiding his home community in combating the poverty that was so rampant. On the other hand, he simply might have needed some source of income to help his family in Bapchule. Whatever the reason, in 1942 Hayes enrolled in the Civilian Conservation Corps–Indian Division. His two months in the CCC-ID probably led directly to his decision to serve in the Marine Corps. Poignantly, while in the CCC-ID, Ira worked as a laborer at one of the Japanese American internment camps.

Never once in any of his letters home did Ira equate the issei (Japanese-born) and nisei (first generation American-born) with whom he interacted in the camp with the Japanese he fought in the Pacific.

The CCC-ID was a result of the transformation in Indian policy that John Collier, as commissioner of Indian Affairs, attempted under the new Roosevelt administration. Collier's background was in social work and conservation. He was an advocate of cultural preservation in emigrant groups and was also a participant in Mabel Dodge's New York City salon, where political activists and artists gathered to discuss art, politics, economics, and culture. The attendees included the likes of D. H. Lawrence, the gifted author; John Reed, the reporter who documented the Communist revolution in Russia; Max Eastman, a political activist and writer; Isadora Duncan, the celebrated dancer; and Emma Goldman, the famous orator, feminist, and anarchist. [29]

Dodge moved to Taos, New Mexico, and married Antonio Luhan in the early 1920s. Collier visited her there and discovered for himself a "Red Atlantis." To Collier, the Pueblo peoples of Taos and other places were the height of gemeinschaft societies: cooperative, inclusive, culturally unique, and fully capable of governing themselves. He came away from Taos with a perception that Indians should enjoy the freedom of religion and cultural expression. Collier became committed to preserving Native cultures and recognizing the Native right to self-determination. [30]

Eventually, Collier was selected to head the Indian office within the Department of the Interior. He lobbied for and was rewarded with the Wheeler-Howard Act in 1934, also known as the Indian Reorganization Act. The new law essentially gave tribes back a few sovereign rights: an elected government, the jurisdiction over crimes and misdemeanors within their boundaries, the ability to determine citizenship, and the ability to levy taxes. The federal government also began several programs intended to help relieve the extreme poverty of Native communities. [31]

The year before Wheeler-Howard, the per capita Native income was $81 a year, hardly enough to keep a family of four alive. One idea to aid Native peoples that government officials were excited about was to enroll Native men in the Civilian Conservation Corps. Harold L. Ickes, the secretary of the interior, fought for a separate Native division of the CCC, and Roosevelt approved of the plan in April 1934. The idea was to enroll Native men over the age of eighteen and put them to work primarily on their own reservations. Officials envisioned a corps of Native enrollees working on forestation projects, soil erosion control, improving grazing land, and establishing fisheries. The men received $30 a month and, for married men, a commutation allowance of $12. [32]

Shortly after its organization, the CCC-ID began an education program. In Arizona, for example, Native enrollees worked on archaeological projects and had to learn the academic side of preserving historic sites. By 1939, the CCC-ID was conducting classes on topics as wide-ranging as firefighting, the maintenance of trucks, ranching techniques, carpentry, welding, and many more vocational subjects. The Phoenix office set up a mobile classroom to teach conservation techniques on the various reservations within its scope of responsibility. [33]

By 1940, the federal government was forced to cut back on the various CCC programs generally. The U.S. was stepping into a wartime economy, beefing up military service and moving the CCC-ID more toward vocational training specifically to mobilize Native manpower in the defense industry. Learning radio repair, welding, carpentry, auto mechanics, and the like practically guaranteed jobs in the factories that would soon produce tanks, trucks, ships, and sundry other items that would be used in making war. [34]

Ira Hayes quit the Phoenix Indian School to enroll in the CCC-ID in May of 1942. He would spend only two months in the program. He was in the CCC-ID during the period in which it underwent the change in emphasis from conservation work to vocational training. Indeed, during the time Hayes was in the program, it directed its educational agenda toward employment in the factories and shipyards of the industrial cities. Hayes trained in carpentry, which was useful on the reservation. But by then there was a war on, and apparently Ira Hayes was ready to join up. Hayes was drawn to the Marine Corps, and he had his mother and father give their permission for him to enlist. He left for recruit training after a community ceremonial farewell in August. [35]

One of the more perplexing questions that crops up is about the extraordinarily high Native American rate of enlistment in the armed forces during World War II. Almost immediately after Germany declared war on the U.S., Nazi broadcasters were reportedly asking this specific question. According to writer Richard Neuberger, Natives were enlisting in numbers that were disproportional to their total population compared to other Americans. This, according to Neuberger, left the Nazis with the rhetorical question of "How could the American Indians think of bearing arms for their exploiters?" [36] Natives were heavily recruited for the armed forces during the war because indigenous peoples of the Americas were indeed thought of as both a martial race and a politically reliable minority. [37] It was considered safe to arm them. Both the Germans and the Americans stereotyped Native Americans as scouts and warriors of the highest caliber. [38]

Other than being heavily recruited because of their supposed martial propensities, Native Americans, and especially tribes like the Akimel O'odham, have answered the call as military auxiliaries, allies, in the U.S. Army's own Indian Scouting Service, and as regular American servicemen. The reasons for this willingness to join and participate in a "white man's war" vary greatly but can be reduced to a few motivations or rationales. A number of Native people entered the service because it has become a family or perhaps a tribal tradition going back to military alliances based on treaties with the U.S. Another factor is poverty. In several rural Native societies there are very few rewards for young men, especially in the twentieth century, when warriorhood itself was devalued because there were no traditional enemies to fight. Finally, among a number of tribes a person gains status by returning to his or her homeland and taking part in time-honored ceremonies that either honor or purify the warrior of the taint of violence. Ceremonies among Native peoples always include many other members of the given society. The ceremonies are inclusive social-cultural gatherings designed to bring people together. The status gained from being the center of a tribal ceremony can also lead to political participation. The returning veteran is often seen as a person who has experienced both the Native and the white world and can somehow navigate both. A number of veterans have served on tribal councils and as tribal chairpersons. [39]

Becoming a Marine was, in those days, somewhat like a secular-sacred calling. The branch itself was seen in the public eye as an elite force made up of "tough guys" from the city streets and boys from hardscrabble farms in rural America who could toss hay bales ten feet in the air. It was also an armed force with a tradition and a culture all its own. In an article entitled

"Marine Corps Cultural Similarities to Native Americans," Anthony Hines lays out the case that Marine Corps culture meets the four-field approach to anthropology in defining a people. In a somewhat tongue-in-cheek style, he compares Marine culture with various aspects of Native tribal cultures. A cultural identity was the key. And that was acquired in Marine Corps boot camp. The new Marines spoke a brand of English all their own, performed rituals, learned Marine Corps lore, and lived and worked in bases forbidden to outsiders. [40]

When Hayes was sent to basic training in San Diego, California, boot camp was a seven-week ordeal of calisthenics, drill, hand-to-hand combat, and marksmanship training. In a recent award-winning article, Jessica Anderson-Colon analyzes Marine boot camp as the "gateway" to victory over the Japanese defense of Iwo Jima. In a report on the taking of the island, observers worried that several levels of training for the assault were unfortunately inadequate. Boot Camp was, according to Anderson-Colon, "the only steadfast principal training acquired by troops headed to Iwo Jima." [41] The importance of Marine boot camp during the war and to individuals like Ira Hayes was the inculcation of Marine Corps culture and a particular Marine Corps ethos.

Between 1939 and March of 1942, Marine Boot Camp had fluctuated back and forth from eight weeks' training to six to five, and on to seven when Hayes went to the Marine Corps Recruit Depot in San Diego, California. It was certainly a rough few weeks on the new recruits, but it has been demonstrated that this period of time was essential to their performance in the Pacific war. It would become all-important to Ira Hayes' survival for the next three years.

Chapter 4

From Boot Camp to Bougainville

Ira Hayes and the rest of the new recruits had been left standing on painted yellow footprints for what seemed like hours before they were ushered into the building where they could pack up their civilian clothes and mail them back to their mothers. The "boots," as they were called, were fed and went for medical examinations and shots. They would have their first military haircuts (shaved heads, really), take showers, and be given their first clothing issue. They were not issued the beautiful dress blues that their recruiters wore. In the 1940s they were given ill-fitting, olive drab herringbone-twill dungarees (later called "utilities") and the distinctive Marine Corps cap, known as a cover. The recruits received a pair of olive drab canvas and black rubber physical training high-top sneakers and a pair of brown, rough leather "boondockers." The boondockers' tops came up to about an inch or so above the anklebone; the boots were not unlike the ankle-high boots issued to army personnel as far back as the Civil War. Then they were issued their 782 gear—packs, canteens, cartridge belts, helmets—and weapons. [1] In 1942,

69

the Marines were still issued the 1903 Springfield bolt-action rifle with its 1905 model bayonet because of a shortage of M1 Garands. When the 1st Marine Division landed on Guadalcanal in August 1942, the Marines carried 1903 Springfields, 1917 Enfields, .30 caliber water-cooled Browning machine guns, .45 caliber 1911 semiautomatic pistols, and Thompson .45 caliber submachine guns.

Thoroughly fatigued, they had their pictures taken for identification cards and were given their dog tags. All the while, the drill instructors screamed in their faces and sometimes struck a recruit with a sawed-off broom or mop handle. The recruits ran everywhere: to get haircuts, to take showers, to draw their blankets, sheets, and pillows. For all Marines, then and now, that first day in boot camp was one of the most profoundly bewildering, exhausting, and frightening of their lives. It became more difficult once their platoon was fully manned.

When training days began, the harassment did not cease. It only increased as the recruits, disoriented as they were, made mistakes. Nothing was done correctly. Physical training stepped up both as punishment and as a way to get the recruits in condition for combat. The first few days of training were aimed at changing the recruits' identities from civilian to Marine. And learning one's new identity was perhaps the most difficult part of boot camp. But soon the recruits learned the camaraderie and esprit de corps that they would carry with them into combat and for the rest of their lives. [2]

To promote readiness in war, by mid-1942, the Marine Corps instituted a seven-week training program that emphasized physical conditioning, marksmanship, and military courtesy. The first two subjects were self-explanatory. Military courtesy primarily meant instilling in the recruit submission to higher ranks and the immediate obedience to orders. Even more important, perhaps, was the inculcation of the distinctive Marine Corps culture. [3] In repeating the history of the corps, boot camp instructors consigned a kind of secular sacredness to place, heroic sacrifice, unswerving loyalty, and pride in simply wearing the uniform. The recruits also learned teamwork through various exercises like the log drill, where several recruits lifted, raised, and carried a two-hundred-odd-pound log as a group. In some ways Indigenous recruits had a head start on their non-Native peers. Those who had been students in the militarized boarding schools understood military culture from the very beginning of their training.

But Marine Corps elites also knew the value of physical conditioning and weapons training. Close-order drill with rifles was essential and time-consuming, but it taught compliance with orders, quick physical reaction, and, most important, familiarity with the rifle the recruit carried. Field training probably took up most of the instruction time during the seven-week boot camp. It included instruction in first aid, tactics, cover and concealment, signals, and how to use a gas mask, which included being exposed to tear gas.

Ira wrote to his family that he was proud to be a Marine and happy that there were "a lot of Indian boys here." He made friends with Marvin Jones and other Native "boys," especially from Oklahoma. His drill instructor at one point introduced him to the idea that the Natives in the platoon should put on a "boxing show...to prove that Indians can fight better than most white men." As a result of several "bull sessions" Ira learned that "I never knew white boys cried so easy." "But not me," he wrote, emphatically declaring that he did not shed any tears during his training. Another observation he made to his family was that the white men in his platoon "don't seem to know anything at all about Indians." [4]

Time at the rifle range at Camp Elliott was easily the most important part of recruit training. There Hayes and his fellow recruits learned how to adjust the sites on their rifles for elevation and windage, to squeeze their triggers, and adjust their bodies to different firing positions: standing, kneeling, sitting, and prone. They also familiarized themselves with the .45 caliber pistol. To top it all off, Hayes had to shoot for qualification in one of three categories: expert, sharpshooter, and marksman. He qualified as a sharpshooter, missing the expert badge by just a few points. Hayes would be taught what sounded like a seemingly ancient skill: musketry. [5] The term was used to describe a concentration of small arms and automatic weapons on particular targets. It was another way of teaching teamwork in bringing the maximum amount of fire in a single direction. It produced what Marines would call in later years fire discipline. Despite the tough training and punishments, Hayes wrote home saying that he actually enjoyed certain aspects of his training and was proud of his accomplishments. [6] Finally, after seven weeks of training, the Marines graduated and were assigned general military occupations. This kind of advanced training, whether infantry or technical instruction such as intelligence gathering, motor transport, tank school, and artillery, at the time was called "replacement training." [7] Hayes was going to be an infantryman, but he also requested and was accepted to parachute school.

The Marine parachute battalions were a totally new idea, at least for the Marine Corps, which was originally a seagoing branch of the service. A number of military thinkers at the time considered the Marine Corps a superfluous branch of the armed forces. The Army provided ground forces and the Navy, with its growing number of great battleships, seemingly could sail across vast oceans and bombard enemy cities and control the sea-lanes. There was no Air Force, and when airplanes did come into military use, they were seen primarily as a scouting service for the Army.

The corps had been continually forced to justify itself since the turn of the twentieth century. The Marines appeared to be a holdover from an earlier age of wooden ships. Marines brought musket fire from the shrouds to enemy vessels and often served to board hostile ships. They also were detailed to perform "fire watch," a kind of nightly watch, fire being the greatest danger to a wooden ship at sea. It took an alcoholic Marine lieutenant colonel named Earl Hancock "Pete" Ellis to outline a war plan against Japan in 1921 that would ultimately give the corps a mission that would save it from extinction.

It was almost as if Ellis was gazing into a crystal ball when he foresaw an island-hopping campaign to build up forces and finally to invade the Japanese islands themselves all from the sea. His ideas were laid out in "Operational Plan 712-H, Advance Base Operations in Micronesia." In the plan he detailed a complete reformation of thought on amphibious warfare. The disastrous British and Australian Gallipoli campaign during World War I, for example, simply put combatants onto the beaches. From there, the British and Australian troops essentially set up a trench system in opposition to the dug-in Turkish army. To Ellis an amphibious assault was a tactical maneuver that transferred troops across the water and the beaches to capture a hostile force's inland command-and-control structure. He even described the types of assault boats and weaponry needed to perform an attack like the ones he anticipated in his operational analysis. Ellis conceived of the assaults swiftly taking place on narrow fronts and concentrating fire (musketry) on particular places on the enemy's frontline defenses. [8]

One of the obvious needs in Ellis' theory of amphibious warfare was instantaneous and secure communication between command and the spearhead of the assaulting vehicles and troops. An outcome of this particular need was the formation of the famous Navajo Code Talkers within the Marine Signal Corps. These brilliant men, all bilingual in Navajo and English, devised a code that could be altered at will and communicated back and forth in real time without being decoded by the Japanese. The code remained indecipherable for the remainder of the war. [9]

Ellis' ideas also led to innovation and an inclination among Marine planners to attempt to integrate new ideas and inventions into his amphibious warfare doctrine. The willingness to experiment led to the development of the select Marine Raider and Parachute units—the forerunners of the Marine Force Recon battalions. [10] Ira Hayes became part of these elite Marine forces.

Parachute training was as rigorous as boot camp with a projected 40 percent washout rate. The Marine parachutists were being trained to operate behind enemy lines, which meant "a limited ability to return to [their] parent organization." Thus, their mission objectives had to be "sufficiently important to warrant the sacrifice of the force." [11] Given the notion that the parachutists might on occasion or in certain circumstances be sacrificed, it must have taken a stout heart to volunteer for the service. Either that or the volunteer had thrown caution to the wind. The bond Ira felt with other Marines held all the way through the difficult training. "I don't think," he wrote to his family, "any of us would take $1000 to separate from the others." [12]

The Raiders and Parachutists had a parallel development.

Both, unfortunately, were on shoestring budgets from the beginning. The Raiders' mission was to use rubber boats to go ashore from submarines to seize terrain overlooking beachheads, create diversions, use guerilla warfare tactics, and gather intelligence. The parachutists' aircraft, when available, were to take the Marines into a target area flying low, then ascend quickly to a height so that they could jump behind enemy lines. After jumping, their mission was essentially the same as the Raiders'. At one point, the parachutists were to take rubber boat training and learn, like the Raiders, land navigation, demolitions, sabotage, and guerilla tactics. [13]

Volunteers had to be able to read and write. They had to be between nineteen and twenty-one years old, be unmarried, meet certain height requirements, and be physically fit. There was a high application rate because the trainees received a boost in pay. [14]

Parachute training, by the time Hayes volunteered, was taught in three stages. In the first phase, the Marines were conditioned and took part in what was called "ground" instruction. What ground training emphasized was scouting, patrolling, map reading, compass instruction, and familiarization with different weapons, like the collapsible Johnson M1 and M2 carbines, the Johnson light machine gun, the Johnson rifle, and the folding-stock Reiser Model 50 submachine gun, as well as sawed-off shotguns. All were light, portable weapons, presumably ideal for parachutists and close-quarter combat. [15]

In the second training stage, Ira and his mates became familiar with their jump equipment. They packed and unpacked parachutes and learned the rigging procedures so that if they packed a chute it would reliably open. Generally, the Marines bore two parachutes. The main parachute was harnessed to the

Marine's back and the secondary on his chest. Aboard an aircraft over a drop zone, the parachutists were ordered to stand and hook their main chute's rip cord to a static line running down the middle of the interior of the plane. Then, one by one, they would be ordered to stand in the door and jump. The static line would open the parachute. [16] During World War II, a parachutist had little control over the direction his parachute would take him in its descent, and sometimes wind gusts or drafts would pull the parachutist off course, away from the drop zone. Parachuting was a perilous profession at any rate, and the Marine might be descending into a hail of enemy fire as well.

Ira graduated from the Camp Gillespie jump school on November 30, 1942, and was promoted to private first class the next day. Following his parachute qualification, he was assigned to Company B, 3rd Parachute Battalion, Divisional Special Troops, 3rd Marine Division, at Camp Elliott, California. [17] As was usually the case, after boot camp and special training he probably got leave and went back to Arizona to visit family and friends before leaving for duty in the Pacific war. The entire 3rd Division, including the special troops, were being staged to go overseas early the next year. Staging for Marines was preparation for combat. For overseas duty they familiarized themselves with various weapons, underwent more physical training, and took part in "wet-net" exercises—clambering up and down cargo-like nets hung from the sides of ships into landing craft. They also went on forced marches, bivouacked, and underwent inoculations. There was no letup in training.

It seems that the parachute units were constantly being reorganized and redesignated. Actually, the Marines were kept in the same companies and simply placed under the umbrella of a larger military command structure. At the time the Marine

Corps was experiencing a huge influx of new recruits and was increasing its divisional strength. A Marine division was the operational basis of deployment. Until the late 1930s, the Marine Corps was a small force, limited to detachments aboard ships or on naval bases, or as an anti-insurgent force. During World War I, the Marine Corps grew to four brigades in France while under the control of the American Expeditionary Force and the Army's 2nd Infantry Division. In February 1941 the Corps activated the 1st and 2nd Marine Divisions, mainly made up of prewar regulars. The 3rd Division was formed in September 1942, the 1st and 2nd acting as "parents" by folding in 40 percent of the two divisions into the 3rd. By the end of the war, the Marine Corps would field six divisions. A Marine division was larger than an army division by nearly four thousand individuals, with double the number of crew-served machine guns. [18] The Marines learned early in the war that the Japanese launched all-out banzai charges that were repulsed only with increased firepower.

Ira joined the 3rd Parachute Battalion as part of the 3rd Marine Division, which was at the time being raised to its full complement of Marines and Navy personnel. At first, there were only two companies of parachutists. Those companies later became two battalions. In May 1943, Hayes' unit was redesignated Company K, 3rd Parachute Battalion of the 1st Marine Parachute Regiment. By that time, he was in Noumea, New Caledonia, in the South Pacific, undergoing more training and acclimating himself to the tropics. [19]

The 1st Parachute Battalion had undergone fire in the initial Marine offensive against Japan. In August 1942 the 1st Marine Division came ashore on Guadalcanal without opposition. The Japanese high command kept feeding troops into the maw of Guadalcanal and its numerous frightful engagements. The

Japanese navy also was able to cause the American naval forces to retreat and regroup, leaving the Marines alone to fight and catch the amazing number of illnesses, especially malaria, that the island spawned. [20]

The Marine parachutists took part in some of the bloodiest fighting in the Solomon Islands. The 1st Battalion landed on Gavutu on August 7. The next day, they participated in the battle for the small island of Tanambogo. Out of the fewer than four hundred Marines who landed on Gavutu, twenty-eight were killed and nearly fifty wounded. The 20 percent casualty rate was the highest for any unit involved in the initial fighting for Guadalcanal and the surrounding islands. For two days, September 13–14, Marines from the 1st Parachute Battalion joined with the Raiders to take a place known as Lunga Ridge on Guadalcanal. After the fight, the ridge was renamed Bloody Ridge and later named for the commander of the 1st Raider Battalion, Lieutenant Colonel Merritt A. "Red Mike" Edson, who was awarded a Medal of Honor for his actions and leadership. [21]

While the 1st Parachute Battalion was recuperating from the bloodbaths on Gavutu and Edson's Ridge and being reevaluated as to its total performance in the Guadalcanal operation, the 2nd and 3rd were being readied for battle to take the island of Bougainville. The campaign for the Solomon Islands was part of the larger Operation Cartwheel, intended to isolate the Japanese bastion at Rabaul on the island of New Britain. [22]

Hayes' battalion moved northward from New Caledonia to Guadalcanal to Vella Lavella in anticipation of taking part in the Bougainville assault. Repetitively doing the same drills strengthened the bonds between the members of the company. They moved together and had to cope together with settling into new environments. Additionally, they shared the same quarters, the same deprivations, the same rewards, and the same food. Hayes saw the bonds with his fellow Marines as he viewed his own community. The bonding and esprit de corps that were built in boot camp continued through the long hours of joint labor and aiding one another. It was truly a reciprocal relationship that developed between members of the same unit. If anything, it could be called a "tribal" society built without the use of kinship terminology, except perhaps for the word "brother." [23] The next step for the parachutists of the 2nd and 3rd Marine Parachute battalions was combat itself. Combat would forever seal the bonds of the Marines in Hayes' company.

The Bougainville campaign was an assault on and capture of an enemy-held island with significant strategic value. It was part of the plan to surround the Japanese base at Rabaul, pound it with aerial attacks, and let it and other Japanese garrisons "wither on the vine." [24] The Americans had the victory over the Japanese navy at Midway and finalized the Guadalcanal campaign. Those two successes set both the Japanese army and navy back on their heels and inspired the Americans, Australians, British, and other allies to continue the drives across the Pacific and northward through New Guinea.

The Japanese recognized that Bougainville was the key to defending Rabaul and the Japanese Empire. Rear Admiral Matsui Ijuin, of the Japanese Fleet, said prophetically, "Japan will topple if Bougainville falls." [25] The Japanese had built a total of six airstrips from which, if captured, the Allies could bomb the citadel of Rabaul. It was only 250 miles from the farthest Bougainville airfield. Those airfields could harbor the aircraft necessary to fight off American bombers and harass Allied troops all over the central Solomon Islands. Secondly, Japan's high command built up the island's garrison with the survivors of the defeat of Guadalcanal and also the bloodied veterans of several other campaigns. It was estimated at the time that the Japanese garrison on Bougainville numbered between forty-five thousand and sixty-five thousand troops. The garrison of highly trained and dedicated troops was to hold the island from invasion and protect the airfields. The Japanese were on the defensive by then, and Bougainville was a kind of "make-or-break" Japanese stronghold. [26] Of course, after Guadalcanal, everything in the Pacific was make-or-break for the Japanese Empire. Of all the Japanese higher command, the only person that seemingly recognized that fact was Admiral Isoroku Yamamoto, and he was killed when American P-38 fighters shot down his airplane in April 1943, just a few months before the Bougainville attack. Ironically, his plane crashed on Bougainville itself. [27]

The determination about how to take Bougainville was left to Vice Admiral William F. "Bull" Halsey. He got his nickname for his self-confidence and belligerent personality. He was not always correct in his judgment of particular situations. When the naval battle of the Philippines was raging, and MacArthur was landing troops at Leyte Gulf, Halsey steamed his battleship task force off in search of a diversionary Japanese carrier fleet, leaving a group of American escort carriers, destroyers, and destroyer escorts to fight off a flotilla of Japanese battleships and heavy cruisers. [28] Halsey's impetuousness was tempered somewhat when he and his staff planned the Bougainville campaign. The invasion was meticulously planned and carried out, but at the same time bold and aggressive. [29] Using the islands of the Solomon chain like stepping stones, Halsey needed to take Munda on New Georgia to secure another staging point. Nearby Guadalcanal and Vella Lavella were already in his hands.

The softening-up part actually began in August with Marine Corsair fighters from the Russell Islands attacking the southernmost airfields on Bougainville. Later, in October, the medium bombers began their runs over the island. The Munda airstrip began to launch sorties as well. During the night of October 27, General Alexander A. "Sunny Jim" Vandegrift, commander of I Marine Amphibious Corps, launched a diversionary attack on Choiseul Island using the 2nd Marine Parachute Battalion. On the same night, the New Zealand 8th Brigade was sent to the Treasury Islands to seize and hold a Japanese radar station. The New Zealand troops had light opposition at first but soon began to take casualties from snipers and intermittent Japanese attacks. By the time of the invasion of Bougainville, the 8th Brigade had wiped out the Japanese garrison on the small, rain-forested Treasury Islands. [30]

The 2nd Parachute Battalion's raid on Choiseul was a somewhat more difficult task, but it succeeded in its deceptive role. Under Lieutenant Colonel Victor H. "The Brute" Krulak the battalion embarked on four fast-attack transports (APDs). On the way to Choiseul, a Japanese airplane spotted the APDs and dropped a bomb, which missed the small convoy. The battalion landed at one o'clock in the morning (0100) at Voza on the northwest coast of the island.

Krulak and his force turned south and raided along the northwest coast. Attached to the parachute battalion was a platoon of machine guns, an experimental rocket unit, and four landing craft to give the force an added mobility in coastal waters. The parachutists were to act as if they were a much larger force and even set up a fake supply station on the beachhead. Krulak sent patrols to the southeast to look for potential patrol boat (PT) base sites. Another patrol was launched using landing craft northwest to the Warrior River near the tip of the island closest to Bougainville. [31]

On October 30, Krulak decided to attack the Japanese base at Sangigai. One company moved inland while another followed the coast toward the objective. The company that moved inland did so to flank Sangigai. A sortie of American bombers attacked the objective and sent the Japanese garrison into retreat. As they withdrew into the jungle, they met with the flanking Marine parachute company. A firefight ensued, during which the Japanese launched a banzai charge. The company's machine guns wreaked deadly damage on the Japanese force. [32]

Meanwhile, Krulak's other attacking company entered Sangigai without resistance. It destroyed what was left of the Japanese base, including enemy supplies and a barge. Most important, the company found a map that pinpointed the Japanese minefields laid out in defense of Bougainville. [33]

The executive officer under Krulak, Major Warner T. Bigger, took his patrol aboard landing barges to the Warrior River. The patrol was slightly less than fifty miles across the water due east of the Japanese airfield in Buin on the island of Bougainville. Bigger's patrol became involved in several firefights and was attempting to get back to Voza when it encountered a large Japanese force at its extraction point. The landing craft were late, but the Marines aboard them fired at the enemy unit engaged with Bigger's patrol. The increased firepower forced a Japanese partial withdrawal, and the patrol was able to board the boats. One boat was stuck on a reef, but a PT boat, commanded by the future president John F. Kennedy, extracted the Marines from the reef. Bigger joined Krulak, and on November 3 the 2nd

Parachute Battalion departed Choiseul. At that point, the 3rd Marine Division had already assaulted Bougainville. [34]

Although the island of Vella Lavella had been officially secured on October 7, the 3rd Parachute Battalion was participating in the mop-up and occupation of Vella Lavella island from October 14. Hayes' unit, Company K ("King" Company, in the phonetic alphabet of World War II) was patrolling the jungles, looking for Japanese holdouts and solidifying various bases of operation and occupation. It was onerous business for the parachutists, patrolling and standing guard in a rather inhospitable tropical volcanic island where earthquakes were common. [35]

On November 1, 1943, the 3rd Marine Division assaulted Bougainville. The 3rd and the 9th Marine Regiments, along with the 2nd Raider Battalion, swept into Saint Augusta Bay and took Cape Torokina on the division's left flank. The 3rd Raiders landed on Puruata, a small island off the cape. Aircraft from Munda bombed and strafed the beach. Captain Henry Applington II, who hit the beach on D-Day, later remarked about the strange feeling of eating steak and eggs in the officers' mess that morning aboard ship, and taking a "short boat ride," and later "rolling in a ditch trying to kill another human being with a knife." [36]

Once the Marines established a beachhead they began to move inland, attempting to fan out around the bay. The Japanese, meanwhile, were reinforcing their garrison on Bougainville. On November 6, four Japanese destroyers disembarked eight hundred Japanese soldiers in various types of landing craft to attack the left flank of the Marine perimeter. Although the attack surprised the American defenders, they reacted quickly and brought up more troops. The Marines enveloped the attack and beat it off. In large part the struggle for the island boiled down to narrow-front assaults on and infiltrations of the Japanese regrouping zones. Fortunately, American air attacks had rendered most of the Japanese air bases inoperable very early in the campaign. [37]

The campaign on Bougainville never came to a single decisive battle. There were some banzai attacks, to be sure, but they were carried out in the confined spaces of the swamps, jungles, and hillsides. Plus, the Marines always could rely on their collective firepower, utilizing machine guns, 60-millimeter mortars, and small 75-millimeter howitzers. The fighting was reduced to one battle after another, often hand-to-hand. The whole reinforced 3rd Division was engaged in the sweltering jungle, fighting not only the Japanese but also the mud, leeches, a thing called "jungle rot," mosquitoes, and fevers of unknown origin. [38] But the plan of taking the island was working as well as could be expected. The idea was to secure a base on Saint Augusta Bay, then expand a perimeter outward, securing interior lines of supply and maneuver. As the expansion of the perimeter widened, more troops were brought to the island.

And the buildup was relentless. The Japanese and the jungle seemingly contested every foot of the expanding perimeter. When the beachhead was established, General Vandegrift turned I Marine Amphibious Corps and the Bougainville operational command over to Major General Allen Turnage. The new commander was more than aware of the threat of a Japanese counterattack and correctly requested more troops. On November 5 the 21st Marine Regiment landed, and three days later the army's 148th Regimental Combat Team came ashore. Additionally, on the night of November 11–12 two more army regimental combat teams were sent into the growing perimeter. The combat teams were part of the 37th Army Division, the rest of which followed. [39]

Through the rest of November 1943, the American Marines, soldiers, combat engineers, and Seabees fought off Japanese attacks, patrolled the jungle, destroyed bunker complexes and pillboxes, and built roads and airfields. American airplanes bombed and strafed Japanese positions and blocked attempts at large-scale troop increases. What the assault troops were fighting for was the construction of airfields, PT boat bases, refueling farms, and medical facilities.

Actual construction began within days of the landings. A fighter airstrip on Cape Torokina was built. By November 24 a damaged dive-bomber made an emergency landing there, proving, more or less, that the airfield was operational. In early December the Marine VMF-216 and VMF-214 squadrons were based at Torokina. A bomber airfield was begun on November 26 by the Army's 36th Construction Battalion. By January 3, 1944, Army and Marine medium bombers were conducting sorties on Rabaul from Bougainville. Various construction units, despite Japanese sniper and artillery attacks, built barracks, mess halls, tank farms, a PT boat base complete with docks, and a large hospital. [40] The Americans declared Bougainville secure before the new year. The fighting continued well into 1944, and the Army infantry divisions were still clearing the jungle of intractable Japanese soldiers even into 1945 and until the end of the war.

Ira Hayes' 3rd Parachute Battalion was called upon to fill in the line on December 3. The days and nights he spent on Bougainville would test Hayes' physical and emotional limits more than anything up to that point in his life. Bougainville's environment affected the Marines physically and emotionally. The jungle was dark, enclosed, humid, mysterious, and depressing. Practically all life was hidden in some way or another, even one's own friends and fellow Marines. The dank atmosphere made it difficult even to breathe. Carrying heavy weapons, ammunition, and packs up steep hills through the forest taxed their strength. Ira's home environment might have been a hot desert in summer and chilly in winter, but it was also sunny, open, and familiar to him and his people. Ira moved with his unit through some of the most densely forested and fetid places in the world.

His company moved onto the line on Hill 1000, so called because the military topographical maps indicated that it was a "hill" that rose above sea level to one thousand feet. Of course, the maps the Marines had of Bougainville at the time were not all that accurate. In fact, the lack of precise cartography would cost Ira's Company K several casualties. [41]

The parachutists were placed on Hill 1000 as a result of a report that said that Japanese troops had occupied the high ground on the west side of the Torokina River. The commanding general of the 3rd Division ordered Ira's parachute battalion to occupy and defend three thousand yards of the front. The battalion's sector was difficult to defend because of the jungle and hilly terrain, but on December 6, an earthquake shook the entire island, causing a disturbance in the allocation of supplies and the tactical movement of troops. [42] Patrolling was necessary simply because of the length of the section of the perimeter that the 3rd had to cover.

Ira's Company K was sent out the day after the earthquake to patrol the ridgeline they faced and discovered a spur off Hill 1000 that was not on any of the American maps. Located on the spur was an abandoned Japanese defensive position. Hayes' squad went on patrol the next day to scout out the spur, which was later given the appellation "Hellsapoppin Ridge" after a famous 1938 Broadway comedy and a 1941 film, both starring the comedy team Olsen and Johnson. Hayes and two others were ordered to scout an area near a small hill. Hayes' detail covered about three-fourths of a mile and discovered a small creek. There was a large group of Japanese soldiers bathing and splashing around in the water. The three Marines watched for a while and decided that they could not take on the larger force. They backtracked to their company's position and were ordered to dig in for the night and maintain strict silence so as not to give away the patrol's position. [43]

In the darkness, the Japanese were at work cutting fire lanes through the dense jungle to set up ambushes. One Marine remarked that the Japanese were so close to the Marines' foxholes that he could have reached out and caught a soldier by the ankle. As soon as the sun rose, the K Company patrol broke from their holes and raced under fire back to their battalion command post on Hill 1000. [44]

The parachute battalion was put under operational control of the 9th Marines. Hellsapoppin Ridge was a thorn in the side of the Marines trying to tighten and secure the perimeter. The 3rd Parachute Battalion was ordered to assault the spur, but they were beaten back. Company K was to spearhead the attack but was forced to fall back on Hill 1000 once again. Taking the spur would shorten the American lines and secure the high ground. It turned out to be a natural fortress from which the Japanese could fire from a defilade position. Marine mortar rounds even bounced off the Japanese bunkers, which had been constructed from sturdy coconut palm logs. Try as they did, the men of Hayes' company were pushed back time and again. Late on the same day the Japanese launched a counterattack on Hill 1000 with mortars and attempts to infiltrate the Marine line. The horror of the situation was that in the retreat the Marines had left their dead on the trail and on the ridge. Finally, 105- and 75-millimeter howitzer fire was called in, and the Japanese attacks were halted—for the time being. [45]

That night and the next morning were possibly two of the most dreadful times in Hayes' already hard life. When the company dug in, its strength had deteriorated somewhat. Because the men had been fighting all day long, they were severely fatigued. It also had begun to rain. Their foxholes became mired in mud, and the rain came down in buckets. They had to stay in their holes or risk being shot down by Japanese sharpshooters who hid in the foliage and climbed up in the trees. Japanese soldiers attempted to infiltrate the parachutists' lines and used concealment and camouflage to their advantage. The Japanese yelled and threatened the Marines with calls of "Marine, you die tonight." [46] This threat would later become a cliché in war films.

Ira Hayes shared a muddy, sodden foxhole with a friend from jump school, William Faulkner (no relation to the famous author). Faulkner would later describe that night to historian Albert Hemingway in harrowing detail. Hayes was sitting in one corner of the hole, his legs drawn up, trying to keep the chill under control. His rifle was held straight up between his knees. [47] Hayes probably carried an M1 carbine. The carbine's bayonet was likely the M4, a relatively short-bladed weapon with a stacked-leather grip that resembled the Marine Corps Ka-Bar knife. A Japanese soldier had crawled through the mud right up to Hayes and Faulkner's fighting hole. The infiltrator sought to his use stealth and willingness to slip through the muck to surprise and kill whomever he came across.

When the soldier dropped into their hole, Faulkner was asleep. Hayes, awake and vigilant enough to defend himself, bayoneted the soldier. Faulkner awoke to the shrieks of the dying infiltrator. Faulkner assumed that the soldier had simply jumped into their hole and accidentally landed on Ira's bayonet. [48] Hayes himself never described the death of the Japanese soldier. But it could not have been pretty or quick. Blood would have been everywhere within the confined space of the foxhole. When the Japanese soldier died, Hayes and Faulkner naturally wanted to remove the body. And that presented another problem. They certainly did not want to expose themselves to enemy fire by crawling out of the fighting hole in order to haul the dead soldier out and away from their position. It's likely they pushed the body over the edge of the hole and left it there. Even more likely, they both spent the rest of the night on high alert, readying them-selves for another attack.

Sleepless and rain-soaked, they could not help but see the residue of spilled blood, especially in the muddy puddle of water at the bottom of their hole. Thankfully, the rain stopped, and Company K was ordered to retrieve the bodies of the seventeen Marines they had lost on the way back to their defensive posi-tions. The smell must have been terrible. In the humidity, the bodies of their comrades putrefied quickly. Hayes' platoon came under fire while carrying out the mission, and the platoon com-mander called in artillery on the enemy positions and drove the enemy away, except for the ever-present but hidden Japanese snipers. [49]

They continued on, and when the Marines of K Company finally made their way to the bodies of their dead comrades, they took in a horrific sight. If the sights and smells of the place were not bad enough, they had the awful duty of collecting and car-rying the bodies back to a rear area to be buried. In a fit of pure viciousness, the Japanese had driven stakes through the bodies of the dead, perhaps to terrify those Marines who would eventually come across the corpses. [50] The rain had contributed to the horror, distorting the dead men's facial features so as to make them seem almost inhuman. [51] The men of Company K probably carried stretchers with them, but if not, the bodies had to be placed on their ponchos. The survivors, after completing this harrowing duty, were ordered off Hill 1000 to rest, recuperate, and regroup.

When his company left Bougainville, Ira wrote home to tell his family that he was all right, thanks, he wrote, "to God." [52] He was not. The experience of Bougainville would live with him forever.

The act of killing another human being in combat is a rather delicate subject to tackle. One of the earliest studies of combat stress was 1949's *The American Soldier.* [53] The three-volume report seemed to emphasize that killing and seeing the dead caused stress. But the narrative did not get to the point of what happened emotionally to the men who actually killed enemy soldiers or how they brought themselves to kill. The persons who survive combat and have taken lives generally keep silent about killing to noncombatants for fear that their listeners will not understand. Those who might have killed from a long distance, such as artillerymen, do not have the same reaction as a person who killed an enemy in hand-to-hand combat. Distancing, in other words, perhaps made a difference. *The American Soldier* pointed out that Americans, and human beings, usually do not like to kill.

The idea of distancing and other notions about how humans can actually kill other human beings was the subject of Lieutenant Colonel Dave Grossman's 1995 book, *On Killing.* [54] Most scholars avoid studying what makes humans able to take the lives of other human beings. More often than not, they lapse into a "nature versus nurture" argument in the attempt to find out whether or not human beings are inherently prone to violence. Grossman leaves no doubt where he stands on this issue. Humans are not genetically violent. In fact, according to Grossman, humans kill other human beings only under particular circumstances, except for that 2 percent of the population who are psychopaths.

Grossman, unlike most scholars, made some very important points about the human ability or inability to take another human's life in *On Killing*. Grossman initiated his study after looking into S.L.A. Marshall's study of World War II combat veterans, entitled *Men Against Fire*. What Marshall found was that a large proportion of these combatants did not fire their weapons in combat. They did not leave the battlefield, nor did they surrender to the enemy. They simply decided that even attempting to kill an enemy soldier was too much to ask. One interesting point about Marshall's study is that veterans of the Pacific war were far more willing to kill than their contemporaries fighting in Europe. This might be the result of racial differences and racism but could also be the result of the fact that several units that fought in the Pacific war used more crew-served, automatic weapons, which made it easier to kill from a distance and without picking a specific target. [55]

Grossman took a deep dive into Marshall's revelations and did an analysis of what motivates the killing of other human beings. Grossman proceeded from the fact that probably only about 2 percent of human beings genuinely like to kill or at least have no compunction against killing. And no remorse. The vast majority of people recoil from taking lives, even nonhuman lives. Most cultures ritualize the slaughter of food and game animals.

Those who do not have qualms about killing are, simply put, psychopaths or sociopaths. Killing in combat is primarily the result of compulsion. As the authors of *The American Soldier* discovered, the primary reasons for soldiers to fight are not ideology or self-preservation as much as they are connected with ending the task at hand and group solidarity. Forming a tight-knit unit like a Marine Corps fire team and using crew-served weapons, so that the group tending the weapon is focused on its performance rather than taking lives, compels combatants to protect, rely upon, and follow their compatriots. [56]

Lately, Grossman has become a rather controversial figure because he has made a career of lecturing law enforcement officers on what he calls "killology." Basically, his ideas center on the notion that police officers must be trained or be prepared in some way to kill others without hesitation. These ideas have supported the notion that police officers are becoming thoroughly militarized and therefore have moved away from community-based, friendly, and neutral policing. Grossman's "killology" essentially supports the growing concern that law enforcement is on a war footing and that police officers have ceased being "peace officers." [57] His recent descent into lecturing on "killology" does not detract from his findings in *On Killing*. He remains the only person who has taken up the study of how soldiers go about dealing in death.

Whether the death of the Japanese soldier in Ira's foxhole was an accidental or an intentional killing, Ira took that soldier's life. A number of studies since the Vietnam War have indicated that post-traumatic stress disorder is the result of what happened to a combatant and what he or she did in combat. These studies emphatically state that personally killing an enemy leads to a "more severe functional impairment" than is seen in those who did not kill or were able to distance themselves when taking another human being's life. [58]

Ira Hayes' Bougainville experience was, perhaps, the impetus underlying his severe emotional crisis and why he wanted to stay with his more accepting unit. Among other Marines he was praised for being a good Marine, not as a heroic figure, but as a high-status member of the larger group. It was in that tribal-like acceptance and inclusion that Ira enjoyed and performed well. But Hayes' 3rd Marine Parachute Battalion did not last long after the Bougainville campaign. In February 1944, the Marine Corps disbanded both the Parachute and Raider units, and Ira was transferred to the 5th Marine Division then forming at Camp Pendleton, California. The whole division would sail to Iwo Jima within a year. The assault on Mount Suribachi would be his next combat assignment, and Joe Rosenthal's photograph of the Iwo Jima flag raising, although inspiring, well-intentioned, and framed perfectly, would change Ira's life forever.

Chapter 5

The Photograph and Its
Immediate Aftermath

"I wished that guy had never made the picture." [1]
Ira Hamilton Hayes

So intent were they on raising the flag that day that none of the men even noticed that Joe Rosenthal, a correspondent for the Associated Press, snapped their picture. Standing not even three feet away from Rosenthal was Sergeant Bill Genaust, who was later killed on the island, with his motion picture camera. Genaust started filming, and Rosenthal raised his camera and snapped his picture just as the men had the flag at about three-fourths of the way up. After the flag raising, all of the men on the summit of Suribachi posed for another photograph, now called the "Gung Ho" picture. It shows a smiling Ira Hayes at the far left.

The whole scenario smacked of victory: the flag raising, the shouting, the smiles, the pictures. When the rest of the world saw the picture, it *felt* like victory. It was a false sense of triumph, though. The battle for Iwo Jima was not over, much less the war against Nazi Germany and the Empire of Japan. And much less the return to civilian life many men and women had to face.

When Ira Hayes' Easy Company came off Suribachi it joined the rest of the battalion, which meant that he would spend nights in his foxhole and patrol the company's tactical area of responsibility within the 5th Division's position on the north side of the mountain. On February 26, Hayes' division pivoted northward to join the drive to take the rest of the island. Foremost on the commanders' minds was the capture of the two operational airfields, and the third under construction, in the center of the sulfurous and bleak landmass of Iwo Jima. Taking the airfields would be left to the 3rd and 4th Marine Divisions. The 4th would also drive up the east coast toward the Japanese main body. The 5th Division became the left tine of this offensive trident, moving up the west coast of Iwo. [2] Hayes' Company E of the 2nd Battalion of the 28th Marines was held back at first because of its heavy losses in taking Suribachi.

While the 26th and 27th Marines moved into an unnerving landscape of cliffs, ravines, gorges, rock fields, and tree stumps that hid camouflaged tanks, pillboxes, bunkers, and cave entrances, Hayes' 28th Marines held its position at the base of Suribachiyama. The 26th and 27th met not only obstacle after obstacle but also concentrated, overlapping fire from the bunkers, pillboxes, and ridgelines. On the last day of February, General Keller E. Rockey, commanding the 5th Division, ordered the 28th Marines to prepare to move north. That same day, Japanese artillery blew up the 5th Division's ammunition dump. The bulk of Kuribayashi's forces were concentrated in the northern and middle parts of the pork chop–shaped island. [3]

Another incident that alarmed those Native Marines who knew about it—and there were several Native Marines fighting on Iwo Jima at the time—was the seizure of a Navajo Code Talker by members of the 26th Marines who thought he was a Japanese soldier dressed in Marine Corps dungarees. [4] The problem of white Marines misidentifying Native Americans, especially the Navajo Code Talkers, plagued Native servicemen all through the Pacific war. On island after island, Code Talkers were detained and treated as if they were Japanese infiltrators until they were correctly identified by their own commanders. To combat this particular problem, the Code Talkers were assigned "body-guards" to protect them from being seized by American troops. The rumor quickly circulated that these bodyguards were actually there to kill the Code Talkers in case the Japanese were about to capture and torture them to crack the Navajo code. [5] The rumor was untrue.

Even though the 28th Marines faced the possibility of running low on ammunition because of the dump explosion, they nevertheless moved through the 27th Marines' position to attack Hill 362A. Hayes and his comrades made the assault with a unit from the 5th Tank Battalion. Hayes' Company E drew the unenviable center position of its attacking battalion. [6]

The entire northward thrust cost Company E heavily. The first day of the attack, March 1, the company assaulted across relatively flat but rocky ground toward the hill. They took fire from Nishi Ridge as well as the fortified Hill 362A. Naval gunfire began to hit predesignated targets, but unfortunately fell on the attacking battalions. Sergeant Mike Strank, Ira's squad leader, who was one of the six who raised the second flag on Suribachi, was killed by an exploding shell, possibly from one of the ships off the coast. At that point, Corporal Harlon Block took over Strank's squad. [7]

Later, Easy Company was crossing another relatively open

area north of Hill 362A when a Japanese mortar round killed Block. The company also lost Henry O. Hansen, another Marine who was present on Suribachi when the flag went up. [8] Hayes was especially close to both Block and Hansen. The three were Marine parachutists and members of the 1st Marine Parachute Regiment that fought on Bougainville. The parachute battalions were disbanded after Bougainville, and Hansen, Block, and Hayes together went to the 5th Marine Division. The three still maintained that special unit camaraderie and esprit de corps. [9]

The next day, March 3, the battalion was thrown against Nishi Ridge itself. Lieutenant Colonel Chandler W. Johnson, commander of the 2nd Battalion, 28th Marines, was killed while inspecting his front lines. [10] Even closer to home for Easy Company was the death the next day of Platoon Sergeant Ernest "Boots" Thomas Jr., who was to become a posthumous recipient of the Navy Cross for his actions while taking Suribachi. Thomas was also with the patrol that raised the flag on the strategically important dormant volcano. [11]

Combat is an ongoing disaster. It kills people over a period of days or even weeks. It destroys natural resources and human-built structures and equipment. The brutality is immeasurable. Most of all it takes the lives of those their fellow combatants depend upon. Strank and Hansen were sergeants, Block was a corporal who became a squad leader, and Thomas was a platoon sergeant. They were the noncommissioned officers who kept the fire teams, squads, and platoons—the basic elements of the Marine Corps—organized and focused.

Despite their crucial losses, Easy Company dragged itself to the next objective. The 1st and 2nd Battalions of the 28th took Nishi Ridge and then Nishi Village, or what was left of it, on the second and third of March. Taking Nishi Ridge brought Japanese fire from the overlooking Hill 362B. On March 4, the Japanese resistance was light until the 28th began to advance north near the coast. Once again, enemy fire stalled their progress. At that time, 3/28 took over 2/28's position and allowed the rest of the 28th Marines to reorganize. Within forty-eight hours orders came down to root out the enemy and seal off cave entrances. A war of attrition began, which meant that the battalion was to capture or kill the enemy when found and destroy their fortified positions and caves. The three division commanders knew that the Iwo Jima campaign was nearing its end. All three were closing in on the open terrain that lay before Kitano Point. That was where Kuribayashi was preparing his final stand. [12]

Mopping up and blowing caves, bunkers, and pillboxes was the mission on which Hayes' 28th Marines was focused. Every day the company had to be on alert and ready for just about anything. They were still moving north, but it was much slower going. After taking hills 362A and B, Nishi Ridge, and Nishi Village, Easy Company was subjected to sniper fire and intermittent shelling from Japanese artillery and mortar positions located in the hills and ridges of the island. They were entering the last enemy stronghold that would come to be known as Death Valley. By that time, the men of the 5th Division were all exhausted, dirty, soaked from sporadic rainfall, and nearly starving. The noise from constant explosions, whether from aircraft ordnance, artillery, or naval gunfire, created among the troops increasing tension and heightened startle responses that stuck with them even after their battles were over. The din of rifle and machine-gun fire also produced hearing loss and periods of tinnitus. The Japanese were not giving up the fight even though Admiral Chester Nimitz declared that organized Japanese resistance was at an end. [13]

A sniper killed Frank Sousley on March 21 while on patrol. Ira was only three or four feet from Franklin when the bullet struck him. When he was hit, he told those on his patrol that he was all right, but within a minute he was lifeless. [14] He and Ira had found the rusty pipe that they attached the second flag to, and both were among the six who raised it over the island. He was also the last of the six to die in the battle for Iwo Jima.

Ira Hayes' memory will be forever linked to the Rosenthal photograph. His personal courage was recognized by his company commander, Captain David Severance, who recommended him for the Bronze Star. The higher-ups downgraded the recommendation and Ira received a Letter of Commendation, later to be the Navy Commendation Medal with Combat "V" device. But one man, Rolla Perry, saw Hayes' valor at close hand. According to Perry:

> Near the end of the battle, I saw to my right a Marine from another company coming up the line. As he passed in front of me, I was astonished to notice that he had an unexploded shell lodged in his left arm. It was about eight inches long and three inches around. The man went on to pass in front of Hayes, and the Chief ran out to help him, put his left arm around his body, and with his right hand pulled the shell out and threw it as far as he could. It exploded when it hit the ground.

Without doubt, Ira saved the man's life. [15]

But the grinding horror of the Iwo Jima campaign was indeed coming to an end. Kuribayashi's defenses, strong as they were, had been crushed, and the general himself was surely dead. His body was never discovered. On the morning of March 26, the Japanese made a last-ditch assault on Airfield No. 2. The Army Air Force pilots and ground crews were hit first. The Japanese attack penetrated the army bivouac area but were stopped by the Marine 5th Division's Pioneer Battalion. They counted 196 Japanese dead. [16]

Taking Iwo Jima was slaughter on a grand scale. The U.S. Marine Corps, Navy, and Army dead numbered over 6,000; the Marines alone suffered 5,885 dead and 23,203 wounded. Forty-six Marines were missing in action, including Sergeant Bill Genaust, the motion picture cameraman who filmed the second flag raising on Suribachi. He had been sealed in a cave explosion and was presumed dead. His body was never recovered. The exact number of Japanese casualties remains unknown. Between twenty-one thousand and twenty-three thousand Japanese personnel and an unknown number of Korean slave laborers were on the island when the attack began. Out of that number only 219 prisoners were taken, primarily those who were wounded and unable to flee or fight. The Japanese were shot, were blown up, or committed suicide while trapped in their hidden caves in the hills and ridges. [17]

The 3rd, 4th, and 5th Divisions established their own cemeteries on the island. The 5th Division's chaplain, Navy Lieutenant Roland B. Gittelsohn, a rabbi from New York, led the final services for those buried in the cemetery. In his speech, Chaplain Gittelsohn paraphrased a few words from Abraham Lincoln's Gettysburg Address, saying, "from the suffering and sorrow of those who mourn this, will come…the birth of a new freedom for the sons of men everywhere." Ira and those who were left from Easy Company attended the dedication ceremony and were led around the graves by their company commander, Captain Severance. After visiting the graves of their comrades, they boarded a troop transport for home. [18]

Weeks before the battle was over, Iwo Jima was well known back home in the U.S. Rosenthal's picture of the flag raising appeared on the front page of America's newspaper of record, the *New York Times*, on February 25, less than a week after the event. The picture's speedy appearance in the newspapers from faraway Iwo Jima was due to the diligence, persistence, and good luck of Joe Rosenthal. Born in Washington, D.C., of Russian-Jewish immigrant parents, Rosenthal's interest in photography began in the late 1920s. In 1932, he joined the staff of the *San Francisco News*. After the attack on Pearl Harbor, he tried to join the army as a photojournalist but was rejected. In the same year, the Associated Press hired him to cover the war in the Pacific.

During the fight for Iwo Jima, Rosenthal shuttled back and forth in landing craft that were ferrying the wounded to transports. He was able to wire his photographs from a navy vessel to the naval base in Guam and thence to the U.S. His picture of the second flag raising on Suribachi was instantly recognized as perhaps the finest war photograph of all time. And its impact on society back in the States was profound. [19]

Secretary of the Treasury Henry Morgenthau created a method of raising money for the war without, it seemed, raising taxes. War bond drives were put, with the approval of President Franklin D. Roosevelt, in the hands of advertising tycoons, who turned them into wildly extravagant performances. They would center on celebrities congratulating and even adoring a group of servicemen or a single heroic figure. John Basilone, who was awarded the Medal of Honor for his actions as a Marine sergeant during the Guadalcanal campaign, was one of the first American servicemen to tour on one of these Morgenthau-inspired extravaganzas. [20]

As Basilone did, those who would later take part in one of

these tours found them tedious and somehow lacking in under-standing what the war was all about. The atmosphere of the ral-lies was a propaganda function, pure and simple. At the rallies movie stars' memorabilia, nylon stockings, and even underwear were auctioned off. And the rallies used, in combination, sym-bols of patriotism and of glamour. The servicemen heroes were kissed by sexy female pinup girls and Hollywood actresses. Basi-lone himself expressed the notion that he felt like a museum piece—an object, rather than a human being. [21] Basilone, a legend in the Marine Corps, requested that he return to the fleet Marine force and combat. He was assigned to the 27th Marines of the 5th Division. He was killed on the first day of the attack on Iwo Jima. [22]

Once the president saw Rosenthal's picture, he commanded that the picture itself was to be the focus of the Seventh War Bond Drive. The picture was unique and powerful in terms of its anonymity. Not a single face could be discerned, which might have been the source of its power as a symbol. It was as if the group, not the individual men, struggled to raise the flag. The viewer sees arms and helmets, feet, legs, some weapons, and, of course, the flag. In some drawings and paintings made from the picture, the flag is in full red, white, and blue colors while the Marines remain anonymous in greens and browns. James Jones, the best-selling author of *From Here to Eternity*, *The Thin Red Line*, and *Some Came Running*, addressed the anonymous nature of sol-diering in combat and especially dying in modern warfare. The soldier, he wrote:

> must work within the mass of anonymity...to accept
> dying unknown and unsung except in some mass acco-
> lade, with no one to know the particular how and when

except in some mass communiqué, to be buried in some foreign land...requires a kind of bravery and acceptance so unspeakable that nobody has ever given a particular name to it. [23]

The individual Marines did not matter so much as the team effort to raise the flag. The symbolism was instantly recognizable.

Despite the anonymous quality of the photo—except for the flag—the president demanded that the individual flag raisers who were captured in it be located and brought home to take part in the spectacle of the war bond tour. Rosenthal did not get the names of those who actually raised the flag. He snapped the picture in a hurry, and after the flag was raised, the men immediately dispersed to gather rocks to hold the pole in place. In short, no one in the U.S. at the time knew who raised Old Glory over Suribachi. The fighting on Iwo Jima was still raging, and for all that the president and Secretary Morgenthau knew, every one of the men could have been dead.

The job of identifying the men in the picture fell to the Marine Corps. Sergeant Keyes Beech, a Marine correspondent, found the only person who could possibly identify the flag raisers, the battalion runner, Rene Gagnon, who had carried the second flag up the mountain. Gagnon had a tough time remembering the men in the photograph and actually misidentified most of them. By the time the Fifth Division departed Iwo Jima, the Marines on board had heard about both the picture and the planned war bond tour. Gagnon was pressured again to divulge the names of the flag raisers. Ira Hayes, who did not want any part of the tour, confronted Gagnon aboard ship and told him not to disclose his name to anyone, most of all to those who would force him to leave Easy Company. Gagnon, in turn, revealed that three of the flag raisers were dead and named those as Henry Hansen, Mike Strank, and Franklin Sousley. He also named Navy corpsman Jack Bradley, who was in the hospital with shrapnel wounds. Bradley was a perfect pick for the symbolism of the tour. He had a Purple Heart and was recommended for and received a Navy Cross, the second-highest medal for valor the U.S. can confer on a member of the armed forces. Gagnon was true to his word and did not reveal Ira as one of the six. Without doubt, Gagnon knew that he himself was not a member of the six men in the photograph. But because he brought the second flag up Suribachi, he probably felt as if he deserved to gain some recognition for his action. Additionally, Gagnon, unlike Ira, simply wanted to get away from the hell of Iwo Jima. [24]

Likely there was some confusion about who was involved in the first and second flag raising. Bradley, who was in the first patrol up the mountain, certainly helped with the first planting of the flag. The second raising was problematic: memories may have been clouded as a result of being a part of the drive to the north of the island, and the picture itself was snapped so quickly that the men simply did not know they were being photographed. Gagnon was eager to get back home and gain some fame from being part of the planned tour. Bradley joined the tour, but Ira wanted to keep his anonymity.

The reasons underlying Ira's desire to remain unidentified as a flag raiser are somewhat complicated. James Bradley, in his *Flags of Our Fathers*, points out that Hayes was a dedicated Marine, and his unwillingness to take part in the war bond drive would be tantamount to disobeying a direct military order. On the other hand, if he kept his identity secret, even by threatening Gagnon, it would not technically be contravening an order given by a ranking NCO officer. Gagnon was a private first class, as Ira was. Bradley offered other reasons for Ira's wish to be excluded from the tour. In his words:

> The idea of going around the country being congratulated for his presence in a photograph, following a month of witnessing death and incessant killing, simply did not connect with his rural, tribal, almost nineteenth-century frame of reference. His memories of Iwo Jima had nothing to do with The Photograph. It certainly didn't jibe with what it meant to be a Marine. [25]

Although Bradley's evaluation of Ira's reasoning behind his wish to avoid going on the tour has merit, it is impossible to know what really motivated him to evade what would become the inevitable. For one thing, Ira knew perfectly well that Gagnon was not in the picture. Gagnon was a battalion runner who was in Easy Company at one time. He was not part of the companionship of the company's tight-knit, fraternal society. Ira probably did not want to spoil Gagnon's chances of going home. He was also aware that Gagnon had misidentified one man in the photo. Ira was probably reluctant to take part in a sham.

What is difficult to understand about Bradley's quotation is the reference to Ira's "rural, tribal, almost nineteenth-century" outlook. Few, if any, combat veterans, whether non-tribal, urban, or twentieth-century, tend to think of themselves as heroes compared to those who gave their lives in battle. Nearly every culture in the world recognizes the import of heroism. In all cultures, those who, in Abraham Lincoln's words, "gave the last full measure of devotion" are revered because of their self-sacrifice. In Native American societies the virtues of a hero are courage, honesty, generosity, and humility. Ira's Presbyterian teaching reinforced these merits and more or less syncretized them with those of Akimel O'odham traditional values of Himdag. Charles H. Cook, the Presbyterian minister and educator, preached in the O'odham language and, no doubt, knew about and compared O'odham values with those of Christianity to gain converts. One of Ira's many virtues, according to his relatives and friends, was his humility. To him, and to many combat veterans, the dead gave everything they had so that their comrades in arms could live. Ira was alive because of them. Whatever it may be called, whether survivor's guilt or humility, to Ira the real heroes were killed on Bougainville and Iwo Jima. He did not want to appropriate the importance of their sacrifice.

In addition to his Christian ideals, Ira's cultural heritage almost certainly played a part in his reluctance to go on the bond tour. Bradley's mention of Ira's tribal upbringing was correct but in a different way than generally perceived. Ira carried with him a long-standing Akimel O'odham avoidance of the dead. One of his specific burdens was the contamination of death, over and above survivor's guilt. Akimel O'odham warriors had to go through a long period of lustration before returning to their peaceful activities and their people. Being immediately forced to go on tour would not have allowed Ira to readjust to peace. In his mind, possibly, Ira had to relive and continually think about combat if he participated in the war bond rallies. A peaceful transition based on a calming and healing atmosphere in his homeland was what he needed.

Ira's attempt to avoid the tour ultimately failed. As soon as their troop transport docked at Eniwetok Island, Gagnon was whisked off to an airplane bound for the U.S. and eventually to Washington, D.C. Once in the capital, Gagnon was driven to Marine Corps headquarters, where a group of inquisitors grilled him for the name of the sixth man. He caved. Gagnon gave Ira Hayes' name to the interrogating officers. Jack Bradley was still recuperating from his wounds in Honolulu, and Ira was still aboard the transport headed for the port of Hilo. The Marine Corps and Henry Morgenthau had the names of all the figures in The Photograph: Mike Strank, Henry Hansen, Jack Bradley, Franklin Sousley, Rene Gagnon, and Ira Hamilton Hayes. Little did they know at the time that they had only three names of the men who actually raised the flag, and two of them were dead. [26]

Other than the three who were killed in action, Ira was the only one of the flag raisers who was correctly identified. It would take another seventy-five years to discover the rest. Ira knew, of course, but he objected only to Henry Hansen's participation. It was Harlon Block, Ira's fellow parachutist, and not Henry Hansen who was pictured securing the base of the flagpole. He was told to keep mum about the identification—just another reason why Ira was unhappy with the tour. [27] Two genuine flag raisers were still alive but unrecognized. Ira was stuck in a situation that he wanted to avoid in the first place. Honesty was an Akimel O'odham warrior's virtue. To Ira, the tour practiced deceit.

The controversy over who was, or was not, in The Photograph was rapidly silenced. But there were others that came up. The first was the result of the accusation that Rosenthal staged the whole shot. He spent years defending himself against that particular charge. What had happened, apparently, was that he did pose the "gung-ho" picture showing all the Marines on the mountain, plus Jack Bradley. When he was asked if he staged the picture, Rosenthal thought about the gung-ho shot and said that he did set it up. Upon receiving this bit of news, a *Time* and *Life* correspondent named Robert Sherrod gave the story to the radio show *Time Views the News.* [28]

The story, of course, bothered Rosenthal, and he generated a great pile of correspondence defending himself and his picture for the rest of his life. The picture, it should be said at once, captured a powerful, instantaneous moment that could never have been posed. And Bill Genaust's film of the flag raising proved that it was not staged. There was another problem, though. When the story came out that Rosenthal's picture was of the second flag raising, there were those who believed wholeheartedly that it lost its symbolic value. The first flag demonstrated that Suribachi's defenses had been crushed and fittingly symbolized the ultimate victory over Japan. The picture of the first flag raising was, unfortunately, not as stirring as Rosenthal's. Secondly, there was a problem over exactly who raised the first flag. At first, Raymond Jacobs, Louis Charlo, and James Michels were included in the official list of those who raised the flag. By 2016, these names were dropped from the list. Finally, the Marine Corps named First Lieutenant Harold Schrier, Ernest Thomas, Henry Hansen, Charles W. Lindberg, Jack Bradley, and Philip Ward as the first flag-raisers. [29] Neither flag raising was a demonstration of total victory. There were too many battles yet to be fought; too many lives to be lost.

Rosenthal's picture was much too powerful to dismiss. The photo of the second flag raising was far more dramatic and representative of what Morgenthau wanted to convey to the American public. Additionally, The Photograph was already being reproduced over and over again. To the organizers of the "Mighty Seventh" bond drive, Rosenthal's photo was a "lucky break" because it captured the American will to victory and stirred the public's sense of pride. It was as if the bright light of heaven had shone upon the American flag and on the six straining veterans that day. At least, that is how it looked on the poster. [30]

The 3.5 million posters made for the tour actually employed C. C. Beall's painting of Rosenthal's photograph. Rosenthal himself thought the painting was "a little overdrawn" but had to concede that it indeed made a powerful poster. [31] The poster was ubiquitous. According to the *Los Angeles Times*, "As everyone knows now it is difficult to look at a store window or poster space anywhere in the United States without seeing the picture... [the] moving spirit of the current Seventh War Loan Drive." [32]

Even before the events began, Ira dreaded the tour and especially its meaning. In many ways, Hayes was the most enigmatic of the three picked to go on the tour. He could appear to be angry and remorseful, modest and boisterous. He could also cry openly over the death of his comrades. Combat veterans often display a macabre sense of humor. Ira was no exception. There is a story about him taking handfuls of dirt and building a miniature graveyard while mimicking the playing of "Taps" while his friend Franklin Sousley was preparing to ascend Suribachi. Franklin was a "boot" in Marine Corps parlance. Iwo Jima was his first taste of combat. Sousley kicked the little mounds of dirt over and began his climb up the mountain. Ira, the old veteran at the age of twenty-two, followed shortly. [33]

Like a faithful Marine, Ira began the tour. President Roosevelt died of heart failure at a Georgia spa on April 12. Hayes, Bradley, and Gagnon met President Harry S. Truman and Henry Morgenthau in the White House nine days after Roosevelt's death. The actual start of the war bond drive was to begin on May 14 and last through the month of June. The planned starting date did not interfere with the thirty-day mourning period for the deceased president. Actually, the three Iwo Jima survivors participated in a flag raising in a Washington, D.C., ceremony on the ninth of May, which served as more or less a preliminary event for the drive. [34]

They came to New York the next day and were greeted with a parade, a stay at the Waldorf-Astoria, a Yankees game, and a tour of Times Square. Then it was off to Philadelphia, Boston, and back to New York. After the second New York appearance, they stopped in Rochester and boarded the train once again that took them to Chicago. [35]

The trio signed posters, waved to the crowds, and gave speeches to local groups. Actresses kissed them, and they shook hands with local, state, and national politicians. Ira walked off the stage when actress Ida Lupino started to kiss the three on their cheeks. She kissed Tech Sergeant Keyes Beech, their Marine Corps chaperone, instead. They also urged what one of them referred to as the "fat cats" to empty their pockets to buy the equipment that would bring an end to the war. Victory in Europe came on the day before Ira, Jack, and Rene raised their "sacred" flag in Washington, giving the tour an air of triumphant celebration. They were to move north and then west after leaving Chicago. After the Chicago rally, Jack, Rene, and Keyes Beech would be on their own. Ira was to travel west, but it would be back across the Pacific to Easy Company, 2nd Battalion, 28th Marines, to prepare for the invasion of Japan.

The tour events included parties, gifts of watches, and keys to cities. As part of the celebration, the events served alcohol, and the trio plus Keyes Beech took the libations as an inevitable feature of selling war bonds. Beech would later state that "Hayes was an amiable drunk." [36] While in Chicago, Ira hit the bottle a bit too hard. Police picked him up in Chicago's Loop area and brought him to his hotel. He was drunk but still ambulatory.

111

Beech, the Marine chaperone, plied Ira with black coffee and got him sober enough to appear at another flag raising held at Soldier Field. From the Windy City the four of them proceeded to Detroit, Indianapolis, and back to Chicago on May 24. On that day, Ira was given a plane ticket to California with instructions to catch a military flight to his unit. He had been fired from the tour by none other than the commandant of the Marine Corps Alexander Vandegrift, who was afraid that Ira—or, as Vandegrift put it, "your Indian"—would bring dishonor to the corps. [37] The "drunken Indian" trope was obviously behind the order.

It was clear that racial stereotyping spurred Ira's removal from the tour. In the late 1930s and the 1940s, the consumption of alcohol in itself simply did not rise to the degree of cultural condemnation that it had during the pre-Prohibition days in the U.S. Even some physicians were downplaying the potential health risks that had been known since the late nineteenth century and even earlier. A late Saturday night or early Sunday morning would likely have found dozens of uniformed young men in 1945 inebriated after a night of carousing. Drinking, at the time, went hand in hand with dancing in various clubs in the downtown area. So alcohol consumption was equated with recreation and entertainment. Most of the civilian population went along with servicemen seeking some form of entertainment because the boys in uniform were winning the war.

During the war, alcohol consumption among servicemen was relatively heavy in the rear areas and while on leave or liberty. The Department of Agriculture ordered that 15 percent of the production of beer be allotted to the military for consumption on certain bases during off-duty hours. Treatment for alcoholism did not exist at the time, and personnel who drank alcohol risked dishonorable discharges, which would affect their ability to get employment after the war. Most military doctors were sympathetic to the men who displayed symptoms of alcoholism and covered them with diagnoses of problems like gastritis. Military personnel themselves were reluctant to admit to any sort of alcohol use disorder. In short, alcoholism seemed to go along with enlistment in the military service. And covering up alcohol abuse in the military was systemic. [38]

Tolerating servicemen did not, it seems, extend to non-white servicemen or women. The police had very likely recognized Ira or simply saw a brown man in uniform who was out of place in Chicago's Loop. The police stopped Ira because he was an inebriated dark-skinned man. They either recognized him or he revealed who he was, and they brought him to the hotel and Tech Sergeant Beech.

Vandegrift's orders were obviously racial in their context. He used the terminology "the Indian" to describe Ira rather than his name, rank, or even "Marine." The underlying theme of his order was based on the "drunken Indian" stereotype. It is highly doubtful that Vandegrift would have issued his order for Ira to leave the tour if he had been white. Keyes Beech, for instance, was known as quite a tippler himself, and Jack and Rene were also known to drink. According to authors Karal A. Marling and John Wetenhall, "[B]ottles [were] shipped from stop to stop in the cases intended for the flag." Ira enjoyed drinking with Keyes Beech nightly. [39]

Vandegrift had bought into the drunken Indian trope; he was a white man of his times. Interestingly, the 1832 act that forbade the sale of alcohol to Native Americans was still on the books. And some bartenders and club managers held to it, depending on which states they were located in. In Phoenix, Arizona, near Ira's reservation, the law against selling drinks to Natives was enforced to a certain extent, depending on what the police might overlook. Of course, in Arizona Native Americans could not vote in elections either. Oklahoma, where a large Native population resided, was still "dry" during the war. Other states might enforce the law, or they might not.

The stereotype was a long-standing belief among whites. Drinking alcohol is a tradition among Europeans, yet they historically held a belief that too much liquor leads to degenerate behavior, licentiousness, and perversion. Natives, on the other hand, were "savages" in the first place, and drunkenness was simply proof of their savage nature. The English used similar tropes against the Irish, and Americans picked up this sentiment in the U.S. The image of the drunken Indian—and the drunken Irishman—reassured the whites that they were a superior race, but also that Natives could still threaten their civilization, political authority, and culture. The threat led to a policy of suppressing Native cultures and, essentially, stealing land, water, and minerals from indigenous peoples. A "drunken Indian"—"your Indian"—would, in Vandegrift's mind, ruin the tour. [40] The commandant wanted boisterous, proud, smiling young men to sell war bonds, preferably young white men. Bradley and Gagnon were young, good-looking white men. Gagnon was even known as the "poor man's Tyrone Power," after a movie star of the day. Ira was known as the "chief" or the "Indian," both racial appellations. [41]

Upon learning that he was to be shipped overseas again, Ira requested that he stop in Arizona to visit his parents and friends. He had been able to do so on several occasions, notably just before going to Vella Lavella and Bougainville. He also took leave to see his family before he shipped out to Iwo Jima. The special part of going home before he went to do his duty was the send-off his community gave him. Every time he came home, his family arranged for a special prayer meeting at their church. The entire community would come to pray for Ira's safe return, feast on Akimel O'odham foods, and say farewell to their warrior. It is not unreasonable to speculate that Ira's family believed whole-heartedly that their community's prayers played a role in his safe return from the terrible battles he fought. Because Ira emerged from these terrible battles remarkably unscathed physically, the white people would have considered him lucky. His people would have looked upon his safe homecoming as the result of the power stemming from their prayers and beliefs. To them, Ira's safe return was the result of a power greater than mere luck.

Vandegrift's action was lamentable. Ira was a deeply religious person, both in terms of his Presbyterian upbringing and his traditional understanding of the necessity of family and the strength of community. All Akimel O'odham people have a spiritual attachment to their land and its environment. Water, earth, the fauna, and the flora are sacred entities that give and preserve life. Returning home, especially before going into battle, brought Ira a renewal of his Native identity and sense of purpose. At the time, his 5th Division was preparing for the invasion of Japan, and he knew full well of the dangers of the operation— if the Japanese defended their homeland as they did Iwo Jima the coming battle was sure to be the worst fight of the war, even worse than invading Hitler's Fortress Europe. To refuse Ira a visit to his family was cruelty on top of cruelty and an unforgivable act of racism.

A reporter for the *Boston Globe* got wind of Ira's departure and wrote that Ira was "much more at home with a BAR or a tommy-gun." [42] Another reporter wrote that Ira preferred "action to steak feasts" and that "his hunting was terminated too soon." [43]

Tucson, Arizona, was to be an important stop on the tour. Ira was to have seen his family and, as he had done before, reassure his people that he was proud to be an Akimel O'odham warrior. Unfortunately, it was not to be.

The news media was complacent with the Marine Corps' story of why Ira wanted to return to combat and developed it into a tale of Ira's self-sacrifice. Even before the bond tour began, Ira was reported to be itching to get back into action. On April 29, 1945, the *Arizona Republic* stated that Hayes "went through the hell of Iwo Jima...and came back unscathed." Yet, according to the report, "He still wants to go back and help until the fighting is over." [44] When he returned to the States, his home community of Bapchule held a celebration at his church because "his people are anxious to show him they appreciate what he has done...They are honoring a hero." [45]

On May 16, the *Boston Globe* reported that Ira actually wanted to stay with Easy Company because of "the memory of his many buddies killed and wounded on Iwo Jima and with plenty of war against the enemy Japs still ahead of us." [46] Back in Arizona, the papers reported that Ira "requested that he be sent back to combat to help speed the end of the war." [47]

The virulent hatred of the Japanese in the U.S. seeped into the articles about Hayes' supposed desire to get back into the fight. In Hawaii, the Honolulu newspapers reported the surprise the officers of the 5th Division felt when Ira reported for duty and printed that Hayes was a stubborn man more than willing to turn his back on the easy life of the bond tour because he just "couldn't take hero worship." [48] Killing the enemy was Ira's only concern, according to the *Tucson Citizen,* and "evidently the Indian hero...prefers the dangers of battle to the mass adulation of American crowds." The article concluded, "Good luck and happy hunting, Marine Private Hayes." [49]

On June 2, the *Tucson Citizen* reported that the scheduled war bond drive would feature Gagnon and Bradley, but not the Arizona hero Ira Hayes. The headline on the first page read, "Prefers Duty on War Front." The article explained further that Ira had left the tour a week before because he had already done two overseas tours and "didn't want to leave his outfit in the first place." A few days later the Mighty Seventh reached Tucson without Hayes. There was disappointment in Ira's absence but, as the paper explained, he "returned to combat by his own request." [50]

At the end of June, perhaps to gloss over the fact that Ira had been ordered off the tour, the Marine Corps presented a plaque commemorating the flag raising to the Hayes family. The corps sent Native American sergeant Roland Justin, who had served in both the Iwo Jima and Okinawa campaigns, to Bapchule with the plaque. The family insisted on a prayer ceremony at the local Vah-Ki Presbyterian church. Akimel O'odham leaders and elders spoke and offered prayers at the ceremony for all the Akimel O'odham men overseas. The Vah-Ki choir sang hymns in both English and O'odham. The *Tucson Citizen* covered the ceremony and explained that Ira had requested to leave the Seventh War Bond Drive for duty in the Pacific. [51]

There is some degree of controversy over whether or not Hayes really wanted to leave the tour. The newspapers of the period were being fed the story that Ira was itching to get back into the fight. He wrote to his family while in San Francisco, waiting for passage to Pearl Harbor. Ira told them not to be afraid for him and that General Rockey, commander of the 5th Division, wanted him back because "there's some show out there," and his experience was necessary to train the new men in his company. He reassured his family that he would rejoin Gagnon, Bradley, and Beech when it was over. He may have been downplaying the seriousness of the "show" for his mother. [52] Later, in June while in Hawaii, he wrote, "The bond tour was really lots of fun for a while. We found out it would not be so easy after a week on the road. We done the same old stuff. It got so boring and tiresome." [53] Tiresome it surely was for Hayes. During the tour, it seemed that there was always one person in the crowd who yelled out, "How many Japs [has] the chief killed?" [54] For combat veterans this question is one of the most irritating and ignorant. Few, if any, want to be reminded of the bloodshed, let alone being directly involved in taking another person's life. At most, Ira had an enigmatic love/ hate feeling about being on the tour.

The tour finally wound its way to Arizona, where a rally was held in Tucson. Taking Ira's place was his mother, Nancy. The Mighty Seventh honored her for bringing her son up in a patriotic household, despite its being on a desperately poor reservation. In explaining his absence from the rally, the *Arizona Republic* stated that Ira "was back in the Pacific—where he wanted to be— fighting the Japs." [55]

It was plausible that, given the propaganda, anyone who killed or was ready to kill Japanese people in numbers was a hero. And he was about to be sent into the conquest of the Japanese home islands. That battle, had it happened, could have been the costliest invasion in history in both lives and treasure. The Japanese had fought to nearly the last man on numerous small and seemingly insignificant islands. It was expected that the entire Japanese population would oppose an Allied invasion of the homeland to the same or a greater extent.

After Hayes returned to the 5th Division in Hawaii, the *Tucson Citizen* published an article that read, "The Pima Indian hero...has served two tours of duty and didn't want to leave his outfit in the first place." Moreover, he was "unhappy in his hero role" but that although "he realized the importance of selling war bonds ...he wasn't cut out for that kind of job, being able to do more good 'out there.'" [56]

Hayes rejoined Easy Company in Hilo, Hawaii, on May 28. He knew that few of his friends would be there, but he nevertheless followed orders and began the rigorous training for the "show out there." The "show" was the planned invasion of Kyushu, the southernmost of Japan's four main islands. The first phase of the operation was called "Olympic" and named the 5th Marine Division as one of the units spearheading the assault.

Olympic was to take place in October 1945. As planned, the 5th Marine Division would be part of the V Amphibious Corps that would land in Kagoshima Bay along with the 40th Infantry Division of the U.S. Army on the west side of the island. Several other army divisions would assault the island's eastern flank. Once inland, the entire 6th Army, including Hayes' 5th Division, would establish a line across the island protecting its entire southern half. Shipping would come into Kagoshima Bay. Bases and airfields would be built as soon as the divisional areas of responsibility were established.

The Japanese were busy building up defenses, knowing full well that an invasion of their homeland would take place that year. On Kyushu, the Japanese army based at least fourteen infantry divisions and two armored brigades. In addition, they reinforced their air defenses. During the Leyte Gulf, Iwo Jima, and Okinawa campaigns the Japanese air forces used kamikaze tactics and no doubt would use them again while defending the home islands. B-29 incendiary bombing in major cities was taking a toll, and the Japanese civilian population was incensed. Civilians were being taught to wield bamboo spears to fight off the invading Americans. Like the battle for Iwo Jima, the Japanese would operate on interior lines and on what is known in military parlance as "owned ground," meaning that, as the sacred homeland, the populace would be willing to protect it at all costs. [57]

No one, except for the select scientists, the high military command, and the president's closest advisors, knew that the atomic bomb was about to be used in the war. By July 1945 two bombs, "Fat Man" and "Little Boy," were ready for deployment. The idea of dropping the bomb was frightening. The scientists worried that since the bomb itself was based on a chain reaction of atomic particles, it was not unreasonable to think that the chain reaction might extend outward and set the atmosphere on fire. The test firing of a bomb in New Mexico proved otherwise, and the decision was made to drop Little Boy on Hiroshima and Fat Man on Nagasaki. Ultimately, President Truman had made the decision based on the projected high American casualty rate that an invasion would result in. He had no compunction about giving the order to drop the bombs and never regretted taking the chance on the bomb's ability to coax the Japanese to surrender. Fortunately, perhaps, Japan's emperor Hirohito, hearing about the devastation the bomb caused, ordered the final surrender. Emperor Hirohito announced the surrender on August 15, six days after Fat Man leveled Nagasaki. Ira's 5th Division was given a reprieve from going into combat once again. [58]

While still in training for the "show," as he called it, Ira was promoted to corporal. The promotion, which came in June, would have automatically raised him from rifleman to fire team leader, or even to squad leader, depending on the position needed at the time. The 5th Division stayed in Hawaii until after the Japanese surrender. Hayes and Easy Company once more boarded a ship headed out in the Pacific, this time to occupy a defeated Japan. The 5th Division arrived at the port of Sasebo on September 22. Sasebo lies immediately north of the nuclear ruin of Nagasaki on Kyushu, the same island that the 5th Division was to assault if Japan had to be invaded. Upon their landing, Ira's 2nd Battalion of the 28th Marines joined the Marine shore party and began unloading cargo. After that first arduous job, the Marines began the task of demilitarizing the Empire of Japan. The 5th Division was in Kyushu for more than a month, taking part in repatriating Japanese soldiers and supervising the surrender of armaments. Ira, as a veteran whose tour of duty was over, shipped out on October 25. On October 30, the 2nd Marine Division relieved the 5th. It was transferred back to the U.S. 2nd Battalion, and the 28th Marine Regiment was deactivated in January 1946. [59]

Ira Hayes was only twenty-two when he ended what was probably the most haunting and significant period in his life. One aspect of being a combat veteran is known as age acceleration. He or she has experienced the deaths of friends and peers on a level not normally faced until much later in life. There is substantial evidence in recent years that stress can lead to aging in people. Age acceleration is a psychological and biological condition. In testing the DNA methylation of combat veterans, it was found that that those with symptoms of post-traumatic stress disorder had "significantly lower...age profiles than those without PTSD." [60] In short, this chemical reaction to stress accelerates biological aging, which can cause despair leading to depression. Accelerated aging in the emotional sense can be cause for an assumption of despair and doom, leading to depression.

Of course, the discovery of DNA came after Ira's death, and so it will never be known if he actually had a lower age profile than noncombatants. It is known that Native Americans in general had lower life expectancies than whites, especially in Ira's lifetime. On the other hand, it can be stated unequivocally that Ira suffered from PTSD and that witnessing death was without doubt a cause of that trauma. It would be reasonable to assume, then, that he had a lower epigenic age profile than those persons who had never been in combat. In many tribal societies, including that of the Akimel O'odham, age is equated with wisdom. A person simply has a number of life experiences from which he or she can draw upon to impart knowledge. Age acceleration, especially as a result of participation in war, is a life experience that gives a person an understanding of something that few others have faced. Years ago, a Ho-Chunk elder put it this way: "We honor our veterans not only because they are brave, but by seeing death on the battlefield, they truly know the greatness of life." [61]

Most humans do not like being around death or the dead and certainly abhor taking lives. This assertion holds true with Ira Hayes' people. Traditionally, they saw death as an unnatural occurrence that had to do with the spirit world, illness, enemy attack, or possibly murder. Death occurred as a result of evil intent. The spirit of the dead person was sent on to the other world with prayers and a request for a speedy and safe journey. [62] The spirit of an enemy could bring illness and insanity, and so had to be addressed with rituals of lustration. [63]

If an Akimel O'odham warrior killed an enemy in battle,

he (and sometimes she) left the battle immediately and began the rite of purification (lustration). If the warrior did not go through this ritual, he could be pursued by the spirit of the deceased enemy. Observers of Akimel O'odham warriors in the nineteenth century noted frequently that they were particularly observant of this religious ceremony. The warrior fasted, prayed, sang songs honoring fallen enemies and their own warriors, and drank only river water. They bathed and observed certain prohibitions against touching their faces, hair, and certain other parts of their bodies. The sixteen-day isolation period was essentially a period of healing for both the body and soul of the warrior. It was the way to attend to the dead and remove the taint of death from one's own spirit. Additionally, the Akimel O'odham warrior's lustration prevented the dead enemy's spirit from causing spiritual harm to the enemy slayer. [64]

It is not known if Ira took part in any kind of healing ceremony other than for church services and his own community's welcome home. Hayes' people had only come to Presbyterianism around sixty years before Ira's birth. Traditional beliefs and institutions die hard. Those new ideas and practices are filtered through a given people's sense of peoplehood. Peoplehood is a consciousness of a distinct identity based on a group's understanding of its own history, a ceremonial cycle that corresponds with the changes in their home environment as articulated in their historical narrative in their unique language. These four elements of peoplehood, language, history, ceremonial cycle, and place give the group its own set of values and customs. These elements also outline relations, both domestic and with other peoples. Ira's people were able to syncretize much of their tribal ethos with that of the Presbyterian missionaries.

Ira had to deal with death without the traditional ritual of healing. The modern battlefield did not allow time to attend to the dead properly, nor did it allow the space for the isolation of the "enemy slayer" so that he could internalize all that has to do with killing and death. The purification ceremonies could not take place on Bougainville or Iwo Jima, and so, in the end, the dead haunted the living.

In a way, the photo haunted Ira Hayes. Once he returned home a civilian, he was still a hero in the minds of many Americans. He had called the Rosenthal photograph into question. That presented a problem, because Congress had commissioned the sculptor Felix de Weldon to create a statue out of the famous photograph. In addition, the Postal Service had issued a green three-cent stamp with the Rosenthal picture. Ira, along with Bradley and Gagnon, posed for de Weldon's sculpture. [65] Ira continued to insist that the Marine guiding the flagpole into position was his friend and fellow parachutist Harlon Block instead of Henry Hansen as Gagnon had indicated. As it turned out, Gagnon had half the names in the picture wrong, except for Ira's, Mike Strank's, and Franklin Sousley's. It was not until 2019 that the names of the men who were really in the picture were finally revealed. Ironically, when he was arbitrarily kicked off the Mighty Seventh War Loan tour, Ira was the only one of the actual six flag raisers who had been sent back to the U.S.

The fact that neither Gagnon nor Bradley was in Rosenthal's picture was unknown or covered up at the time. Ira probably knew who was really involved in the flag raising, and he was adamant that Harlon Block had been part of it. He did not expose Gagnon and Bradley because Gagnon was about to be married and Bradley was already severely wounded. If anything, Ira acted nobly and humbly in shielding Bradley and Gagnon. He kept quiet about being sent back into the maelstrom of war. Although he certainly missed stopping in Arizona to see his family, he was probably happy with being transferred back to his old unit. He would be away from the crowds, the parties, the disrespectful questions, the liquor, and the forced enthusiasm he had to display on the tour.

During World War II, imagery played a very important part in the war effort. For example, rationing some consumer items, like gasoline, was intended to get the folks at home to feel as if they were contributing to winning the war against the Nazis and the Japanese Empire. In fact, the U.S. was producing more gasoline than any other county and, moreover, its production was in the United States and not really in danger of being destroyed by Axis mass bombing raids.

The image of heroism was all-important during the war. Americans have long cherished those who have performed valiantly under stress. But Americans have often democratized and romanticized heroism to the point that merely surviving catastrophe is heroic. [66] That is, perhaps, what bothers combat veterans about being called heroes. One's own survival and the survival of those in one's unit might be difficult, but survival is often a matter of inches or of certain circumstances, like a sniper picking out a person to target standing two feet away from another, who might have been just as easy to shoot. Ira and his own family undoubtedly believed that his survival was the result of their prayers. Other combat veterans might think of their survival as simply a matter of luck.

The fact that a Native American was given heroic status solidified the American crusade against fascism and Nazism and showed that U.S. forces were truly democratic. If an Indian could join the crusade, then the cause itself must be even more righteous. [67] Ira, as well as Gagnon and Bradley, began to come under the scrutiny of the press. They equally became icons in American popular culture. Gagnon and Bradley returned to "ordinary" life in white America, although Gagnon's life was hardly prosperous. The media painted Ira's return as a particularly harsh homecoming to an adobe hut and a barren desert reservation. Because of his distinct background, he became more closely scrutinized and stereotyped.

The democratized American Indian hero was seen in newsreels and in newspaper photographs and in popular magazine articles. Although Ira's face did not appear on the covers of *Life*, *Look*, *Time*, and the *Saturday Evening Post*, he was part of a feature story in the 1945 winter issue of *True Comics*, which carried the subtitle "TRUTH is stranger and a thousand times more thrilling than FICTION." [68]

The story was titled "Who Were the Men Who Raised the Flag at IWO JIMA" (no question mark) and depicted Ira climbing up Suribachi on his stomach with a walkie-talkie in hand while a fiery shell blast is detonated behind him. The story itself introduced each of the presumed six men who raised the flag: Ira, Gagnon, Bradley, Mike Strank, Franklin Sousley, and Henry Hansen. In the comic book, the flag raisers were an all-American team. They also represented the great American melting pot. The story described each man's ancestral heritage and the stereotypical features that gave them the abilities and the will to win the war.

During the war, comic books were a form of propaganda. [69] A large number of servicemen read them, partially because they were easy to carry around and also because Captain America and other superheroes were fighting the battles they were fighting. They were also fun to read. *Parents* magazine was the publisher of *True Comics*, and its purpose was to educate rather than thrill or chill young readers. Wartime issues were blatantly propagandist and featured stories of heroic figures, both animal and human. All the stories had a basis in reality but were also hyperbolic to the point of absurdity.

Like film, fiction, and the newspapers, *True Comics* utilized stereotypes to tell stories without going into full-scale character development, and to connect with readers who had had these images and labels already implanted in their thinking. Strank's parents were simple immigrant farmers from eastern Europe; Gagnon descended from French coeur de bois; Henry Hansen's ancestors were Vikings; Bradley was of English extraction; Franklin Sousley was a Kentucky mountaineer; and Ira was an Indian scout. In short, these six, although misidentified in part, epitomized the melting pot—ignoring, as was usual in that period, African Americans.

The stereotype associated with Ira Hayes was the most brazen. He was, even in comic books, the American Indian warrior of the white man's imagination. In the story, Ira acted as a scout and called back to his squad, "I've spotted them, come on up." To which an anonymous Marine bringing up the rear stated, "That Indian can see around corners." Down the page, an Indian in stereotypical red headband with a tomahawk tucked in his belt, lying on his stomach, is peering over a rock at several figures. "Ira Hayes' ancestors had formerly ruled the deserts of southwestern America," the comic book said. He would live with this label the rest of his life. [70]

Ira upon graduating from the
U.S. Marine Corps jump school.
The image was immediately
reprinted in the Bureau of Indian
Affairs publication *Indians at Work*.

Kerr Eby's masterful and powerful drawing of a Marine patrol in 1943. The
artist captured the essence of patrolling the Bougainville jungle.

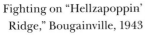

Fighting on "Hellzapoppin'
Ridge," Bougainville, 1943

Three members of the 1st Marine Parachute Unit are on patrol on Bougainville.

Joe Rosenthal's iconic photograph shows the second flag raising on Iwo Jima.

Gung ho fighters photographed by Joe Rosenthal

After the flag raising
on Mount Suribachi

L to R: Jack Bradley; Secretary of
the Treasury Henry Morganthau, Jr.;
President Harry Truman;
Rene Gagnon; and Ira Hayes at
the start of the Mighty 7th War
Loan tour

Opening the Mighty
7th tour: raising the
flag over the Capitol

Ira pointing to himself
in the famous Rosenthal
photograph

Stereotyping Ira:
the Indian scout
image in the comics

Ira Hayes (at left) and
Sgt. Henry Reed (at
right) visit Los Angeles
mayor Fletcher Bowron
with members of the
L.A. Native community
about the Isabel Crocker
eviction case.

Ira visits the American Freedom
Train in Phoenix, Arizona.

Rene Gagnon, Ira Hayes,
and Jack Bradley reunite in
Los Angeles to make *Sands
of Iwo Jima*.

Sgt. John Stryker (portrayed by John Wayne) hands the American flag to Rene,
Jack, and Ira to raise it atop Mount Suribachi in *Sands of Iwo Jima*.

John Wayne's war face is on the *Sands of Iwo Jima* poster, with the Rosenthal picture in the background.

The children called him "Chief." Ira at the piano with Betty and Dean Martin's children: Gail, Deanna, Craig, and Claudia.

L to R: Jack Bradley; Goldie Price, mother of Franklin Sousley; Vice President Richard M. Nixon; Belle Block, mother of Harlon Block; Rene Gagnon; and Ira Hayes at the Iwo Jima statue dedication

Ira Hayes lies in state under Arizona's capitol dome.

At Ira's funeral at Arlington National Cemetery, his family sat in the front row.

Rene Gagnon comforts Nancy Hayes at Ira's grave in Arlington.

Actors Tony Curtis and Vivian Nathan visit Jobe and Nancy Hayes (both at left) during the filming of *The Outsider.*

Ira Hayes, portrayed by Tony Curtis, visits the grave of his mentor and friend James Sorensen in *The Outsider.*

The poster from *The Outsider* had a very different look than the *Sands of Iwo Jima.*

Chapter 6

Heroism and Hollywood

Heroism seems to be a relatively easy thing to understand and define. It is performing some act to save lives or taking some kind of stand against evil at great peril to one's own life. A Muskogee-Creek-Seminole surname, Harjo, is an old term meaning something like "courageous, without fear, spirited." United States poet laureate Joy Harjo entitled her American Book Award–winning memoir *Crazy Brave*, boiling down her surname to its basic nomenclature and definition. [1] "Crazy Brave"—Harjo—means that a person is, or can be, brave to the point of self-sacrifice. The notion also has a spiritual side to it. A vision or a dream or a fetish or a drink or some substance can give a person the internal spiritual power to face an unknown or known threat that has the potential to take that person's life. Take the story of David and Goliath. Was David a hero because he relied upon the technology of the slingshot, or was he "crazy brave" because the deity gave him that spiritual power? How did the Israelite army see him? Did his peers think him insane or possessed of the power of God? Or both? Heroism is a much more complex idea, and defining it is difficult. The ancient Greeks thought of heroism as an individual demonstration of military prowess. And the western tradition has been passed from generation to generation to this day.

Ira Hayes had been defined by American society as a hero. He did not, however, think of himself as such. In fact, few actual combat veterans think of themselves in that way. Hayes was on leave after the Bougainville campaign, and his parents hosted a traditional feast and prayer service at the Vah-Ki church in Bapchule. He was asked to say a few words to close out the farewell ceremonies. He put into words how he felt about his survival of that bloody fight in the Bougainville jungle. He owed his life to God and his comrades in arms. In his own mind, he came through the fighting not because of his prowess as a professional Marine but as part of a brotherhood that looked out for one another. He was also beholden to his community and family for their appeals to an unseen deity that, in turn, protected him in battle. To Ira, his safe return had nothing to do with luck or his own particular skills. His dead comrades and the deity had protected him from the enemy. [2]

After the Rosenthal picture was plastered on walls all over the U.S., Hayes became a hero even eclipsing Bradley and Gagnon to a certain extent. Bradley and Gagnon were heroes, to be sure, but they were also ordinary in a single aspect: they were white and, therefore, like most of the people who turned out at the war bond rallies. Ira was "your Indian" in General Vandegrift's terminology, and that made a difference in the way the American mentality could be manipulated into thinking of Ira as some kind of primitive being who had emerged from the stark desert wilderness to fight alongside the white man against Nazism, fascism, and malevolent imperialism. At one time, "the Indian" was the ruthless enemy of American manifest destiny, but now he had become a friend anxious to prove himself worthy of American acceptance. Ira exemplified the supposed transition from savage to super scout to American hero.

The media played up the notion that Ira, after being pulled from the bond tour, was eager to get back in the fight rather than "getting fat on steaks twice a day while his buddies are still carrying on." [3] Few people could figure out why a young man would throw himself back into combat and leave what was perceived as basking in the admiration of the nation. No one in their right mind would leave the good food, the cheers of the multitudes, the company of movie stars, and the excitement of traveling across the country for the grimy and bloody horrors of combat on faraway islands. Ira was exchanging luxury for the possibility of a gruesome death. Given his veteran status he was sure to be a participant in the future invasion of the Japanese homeland. He must have been "crazy brave." The newspapers, in fact, were in on the deception and printed story after story based on his presumed martial proclivities. The public did not know, nor could they have conceived of, the fact that Ira had actually been kicked off the tour—sent back into abnormality of warfare—because of a racial stereotype.

Of course, white Americans were still using terms like "Redskin," "Injun," and "Blanketass" to describe Native Americans. So it must not have disturbed very many of them to include nomenclature such as "Jap" or "Nip" to dehumanize the Japanese. This dehumanization and politics of racism led to the incarceration of the Japanese Americans during the war. In fact, two Japanese "relocation" camps—called "Butte" and "Canal"—were located on Ira's own reservation against the protestations of the Akimel O'odham tribal government. In making a rather cynical presidential decision, Harry S. Truman appointed Dillon S. Meyer, the head of the War Relocation Authority, to be the commissioner of Indian Affairs in 1950. Truman obviously equated imprisoning Japanese Americans with handling Native American affairs.

The dehumanization of the enemy is a basic form of propaganda in wartime. It is a method of distancing soldiers from the enemy in order to kill and even commit atrocities. In 1864, when Colonel John Milton Chivington, who was also a Methodist preacher, led his cavalry unit to massacre the Cheyenne and Arapaho camp at Sand Creek, Colorado, he stated unequivocally, "Damn any man who sympathizes with Indians...nits make lice." [4] Dehumanization was and is a short step from slaughtering other human beings, and America was more than ready to slaughter the Japanese.

Through it all, Ira Hayes insisted that he was no hero. At the same time, he did not reveal that he had been told to remain silent about who was and was not in Rosenthal's photograph. He also kept quiet about his being foully booted off the bond tour. He received his corporal's stripes and a letter of commendation for his service. The letter more or less turned into the newly authorized Navy and Marine Corps Commendation Medal. The *Casa Grande Dispatch* announced that "honors had been piled up for the Sacaton Indian Reservation boy, Pfc. Ira Hayes." [5] The use of "boy" is a sure indicator of the continued view that minority males were not on the same level of intelligence or valued social status as white "men."

Given the honors and the camaraderie he enjoyed in the Marine Corps, it was a wonder Ira did not reenlist, or "ship over" in Marine Corps parlance, and make a career of the service. Of course, "shipping over" would have prevented him from speaking out regarding placing his friend Harlon Block's name among the Iwo Jima flag raisers and from telling the world that he had

132

been unceremoniously removed from the rest of the war bond tour. Five years later, he likely would have become a squad leader or even a platoon sergeant fighting another war in Korea.

After the war, military funding was cut back, and the 5th Division, in fact, was disbanded. It was not reactivated until the Vietnam War. Perhaps Ira did not want to continue to serve in an unfamiliar unit. He might have simply thought that his family needed him back home. When he did return, he immediately set to work on his father's small farm and began farm labor picking cotton and taking care of other crops on the reservation. Once again, he had returned to a poverty-stricken land and bigoted Arizona state government. Indians there were not considered citizens.

War veterans, when they leave military service, have to adjust to civilian life. They have to adjust socially, culturally, economically, and politically. Combat, although horrific in many ways, is also exhilarating. It heightens a person's reactions and stimulates an acute sense of awareness of the person's surroundings. This is probably the result of the body's adrenaline system. Some combatants have experienced a "high" in firefights.

Farm labor is difficult and unexciting. In the Gila River Indian community at the time, agriculture was not very profitable. In fact, because of the continued water shortage, life was almost at a subsistence level. Cotton farming was more remunerative, but it was seasonal and costly in terms of water usage. Cotton crops put a heavy cost on the soil as well and required a great deal of expensive fertilizer.

Ira's notoriety impeded his labor. Tourists were constantly asking for him and getting him to sign his autograph. He moved out of his parents' house and bought a small house that was once part of the Japanese internment camp on the reservation. The imprisoned Japanese Americans had all been released by the end of November 1945, and the house that Ira purchased was likely one of the new units that were built on or near the former encampments. It seems that he was constantly looking for something else to do that would somehow live up to his status as one of the people who won the greatest war in history and yet remove him from media and tourist scrutiny. [6]

He had always been somewhat politically minded. At the start of the bond tour, the National Congress of American Indians held their second organizational conference in Chicago precisely at the time the tour and Ira came to town. He spoke at an NCAI luncheon held in his honor and was appointed commander of the NCAI's organization of Native American veterans. His brief thank-you speech was primarily about reforming Indian policy, ending racism, and demanding equal rights as American citizens. He talked about Native American service in the war effort with an emphasis on his duty as a Marine. "Nothing," he said, "in the world mattered but to put the flag up." [7] There had been a consistent call for reform in Indian policy, and since the tribes had contributed soldiers, sailors, Marines, land, and treasure to the war effort, the demand for American Indian civil rights increased. Formed in 1944, the NCAI was leading the charge for equal rights for Native peoples. [8] Ira's name was invoked on many occasions as representative of a Native American warrior who fought in one of the grimmest battles of the war yet was denied the right to vote in his home state. [9]

Native American warriors and veterans have always been held in high regard among their own people. In fact, they are often given valued status because, as recounted in hundreds of stories of sacrifice and bravery, they hold virtues that nearly all tribal societies seem to hold dear. When a Lakota warrior counted coup or told how he had touched an enemy in battle, he was expected to be completely honest. When a Cherokee took a captive in battle, he was expected to be generous and hand that prisoner over to the women of one of the seven clans to replace, in body and spirit, a deceased loved one. When a Kiowa went to war, he was expected to be brave. And when an Akimel O'odham took an enemy's life, he was expected to humbly leave the battlefield and go through a sixteen-day period of lustration. All of these virtues were regarded as supremely important to a person's status in tribal life. [10]

Ira possessed the spirit of these qualities, causing him to attempt to right a wrong and let everyone know that Harlon Block had been one of the Iwo Jima flag raisers. He made that announcement in 1946 and forced the Marine Corps to investigate who the individuals really were who had raised the flag atop Suribachi. Ira took it upon himself to walk and hitchhike to Texas to tell Harlon's family the reality of the situation. It was a brave, humble, honest, and generous act. As soon as she heard about Ira's trek to tell everyone about her son, Harlon's mother immediately began to enlist supporters in the effort to get Harlon recognized in the most important photograph of the war. The Texas newspapers took up the cause. In December 1946 a number of Texas newspapers heralded that Harlon Block, a Texas native, was one of the six in Rosenthal's picture. Rosenthal himself was quoted in the *Corpus Christi Times* saying, "There is no reason for me to doubt Ira Hayes' statement... [A]s a civilian now, [he] is in a position to speak more freely than he could as a private first class." [11]

Within a few months, Ira became involved in a controversial court ruling against a Native woman by the name of Isabel Crocker in California. On February 6, 1947, Judge Ruben S.

Schmidt ruled that, because they were members of the Indian "race," Isabel Crocker, a Seneca, and her three daughters were to vacate their house in West Hollywood, a suburb of Los Angeles. The housing development in which Crocker and her husband, Harry, had bought the property was a "restricted" neighborhood. The deed actually read that no one other than members of the "white or Caucasian race" could own a home there. Homeowners in the area, Harold M. and Franklyn Pearce, W. Eugene and Jean Saxton, and William A. and Colleen R. Douglas, brought the suit alleging that the Crockers had violated the restrictions of their contract. [12] Judge Schmidt, who later said that "I don't make the law, I interpret it," ruled that Isabel's husband, Harry, who was of French-Canadian descent, could stay, but his wife and children could not. [13] Immediately after the Schmidt decision, reporting on the Crocker case filled column after column of the local Los Angeles newspapers.

The Crocker case has distinct historical significance for at least three reasons. First, it concerned a relatively new phenomenon in Native American and white relations. Until the late 1940s, Natives had been viewed as a rural population generally confined on large but poverty-stricken reservations. By the late 1940s, though, a Native migration was taking place. Native Americans were not only joining the military in large numbers but also taking jobs in war-related industries. Isabel Crocker owned and operated a Hollywood gift shop, and her husband was a motion picture cameraman. They were gainfully employed and were part of a growing Los Angeles postwar middle class. The policy of assimilating Native Americans into mainstream American societies that had been in effect since the late 1800s had worked, at least in the case of Isabel Crocker.

The Crockers were victims of a well-established racist practice of residential segregation. In many areas across the U.S., neighborhoods were restricted to Caucasians, to the exclusion of all else. Native peoples rallied to the Crockers' aid. Significantly, the Crocker case raised the ire of Native American veterans, who were becoming increasingly political in outlook. Many of them felt betrayed and marginalized. Most importantly, perhaps, a number of them saw in activism and advocacy a method of conveying their sense of being deceived into fighting for an America that overlooked the poverty and bigotry that they encountered almost daily. Following the war, numerous veterans ran for tribal office and participated in protests demanding equal rights. The Native populace of the Los Angeles area, especially those veterans who had made their homes in California, was spurred into action.

Under the headline "Indians Fight Eviction of Mother and Girls," the *Los Angeles Times* reported that a meeting had been held to organize a protest against Judge Schmidt's ruling. Native veterans were taking a leading role in organizing the event. Tom Humphreys, a Hopi veteran of the Army Air Force, explained, "We want to find out where we stand...A lot of us are veterans and we're beginning to wonder what we fought for." [14] Humphreys made the point that his freedom to protest injustice was exactly why he fought in the war.

The initial meeting of Native Americans protesting the Crocker decision was held in Patriotic Hall in Los Angeles on February 19. Patriotic Hall was opened in 1926 to honor the veterans of the Indian Wars, the Spanish-American War, and World War I, as well as the veterans of the Grand Army of the Republic who fought in the Civil War. The location of the meeting was intended to stir the soul of the attendees and emphasize the contribution that Native Americans had made to the war effort. In addition to Tom Humphreys, a noted artist named Ralph Roan Horse gave a speech and promised to continue the fight until the kind of prejudice that led to the eviction of Isabel and her daughters from their home was wiped out. The local representative of the National Congress of American Indians, Leta Meyers, was also in attendance. [15] In a remarkable twist of fate or circumstance, Judge Schmidt died of a massive heart attack just five days after the meeting. His law clerk said that Schmidt had "been disturbed for the past two weeks about public reaction to the case." [16]

Under a headline that read, "Indians Open Fight for Racial Equality," the Los Angeles chapter of the National Congress of American Indians' representative told the audience that the legal services of the ACLU had been accepted. Will Rogers Jr., the son of the famous Cherokee humorist, actor, and writer, joined the cause. He would add that the Crocker case pointed out that this type of racism was a blight on American democracy. [17]

The next assembly received the Hollywood treatment. Native heroes and Native celebrities put on a rousing show for the one thousand protesters who met at Hollywood High School. Will Rogers Jr. had been a member of the House of Representatives but resigned to accept a commission in the army during World War II. He was wounded and won a Bronze Star for gallantry in action in France. He was a founding member of Los Angeles' American Indian Citizens League and its first president. [18] He was also an actor, later playing the role of his father in the film *The Story of Will Rogers* (1952). He personally appealed to Ira to come to Los Angeles to aid in the protest Rogers and others were organizing. Ira was ready to come to California and add his voice to the protest. Rogers no doubt thought that Ira's status as an American hero would lend credibility and notoriety to the protest. Ira was, after all, the most famous Native veteran in the U.S., except for Rogers himself.

Three other well-known Native actors of the time played roles in the Hollywood High rally. Monte Blue, who claimed Cherokee and Osage ancestry, starred in several films as a leading man from the 1920s. Chief Yowlachie, whose real name was Daniel Simmons, a Puyallup who was born on the Yakama Reservation, made more than one hundred films, one of which was the John Wayne film *Red River* (1948), in which he played Two Jaw Quo. Simmons had been, interestingly, trained in opera, and sang the national anthem opening the meeting. Also present was Chief Thundercloud, who claimed to have Muskogee-Creek ancestry and who played Tonto in the Lone Ranger films and radio show. Thundercloud escorted Ira and Henry Reed, a Kickapoo survivor of the Bataan Death March, to the meeting. [19] The hydra of racism that the rally was against consistently raised several of its ugly heads. The day after the mass meeting, the *San Pedro News-Pilot* reported that the rally was held to protest what Native Americans "regard as the discrimination of the redskin race." [20] The appellation "redskin race" simply reinforced the fact of racist thought.

Rogers started the rally with a speech promising both a legal fight on behalf of Isabel and her daughters and federal and state legislation against the kinds of restrictions that had affected the Crockers. The speakers were from various friendly offices, including the Los Angeles city school superintendent, a U.S. attorney from the county, a lower-level official from the Bureau of Indian Affairs, and Monsignor Thomas J. O'Dwyer, president of the Citizens Housing Council. Monte Blue delivered an impassioned speech and introduced the dramatic tableau of the Flag Raising on Iwo Jima, with Ira Hayes acting out his part in the event. The Native hero of Iwo Jima took a central position at the rally as a symbol of the Native American war effort. Ira's remarks to the audience covered both the Crocker case and Native veterans. He offered a subtle threat about the potential Native political influence, saying, "The court hasn't served the woman eviction papers yet because they're afraid of what we might do." He echoed Tom Humphrey's earlier observations about the apparent government duplicity in praising Native valor on one hand and denying Native Americans the same rights as white Americans. Something had to be done because "Indian veterans are having a rough time." [21] One of the maestros of country-swing music, Spade Cooley, a Cherokee originally from Oklahoma, and his orchestra provided the music. Terry's Rough Riders of American Legion Post 516 formed the color guard. All in all, the rally was a spectacular Hollywood performance more than a political protest. [22]

Aline Mosby, the Hollywood correspondent for the United Press, wrote a cutting review of the night's festivities. The list of American Indian Citizens' League members, including the likes of Hollywood stars Ann Sheridan, Johnny Mack Brown, Richard Dix, and Linda Darnell, according to Mosby, "reads like an opening night at Ciro's." She went on to write, "The actors and actresses whose ancestors used to live in teepees got scared that they'd be right back there, too. What if Linda Darnell and Ann Sheridan got tossed out of their houses?" She finished her column, which had a wide distribution, with a comment on the AICL itself: "First they're going to rescue the evicted woman, if she needs it, and then they'll see to it that Indian veterans get a better deal from the G.I. bill of rights." [23]

But the rally had a political outcome, despite being framed as a Hollywood spectacle. Under the headline "Indian Heroes

Visit City Hall," the *Los Angeles Times* reported that Ira and Henry Reed met Mayor Fletcher Bowron. [24] Bowron, a vociferous supporter of Japanese internment and the unconditional surrender of the Japanese Empire, was more than willing to have Ira and Reed in his office for a photograph together. The two Native men were symbolic of the beginning and the end of the war. Reed was a prisoner of war at the very start of the conflict, and Ira planted the flag that symbolized the American victory. The opportunity to have his picture taken with them must have thrilled Bowron. They were, nevertheless, able to present the case that very many Indians could be evicted from their homes if the ruling in the Crocker case were allowed to stand. They also were in city hall to emphasize that they, like so many other Native people, had served honorably in the military during the war. They had put their lives on the line for America, and now that they had returned from the war, they were nevertheless discriminated against. In Ira's words, they were being treated like "little men."

But after the Hollywood High rally, the Crocker controversy abruptly came to a halt. The newspapers out of Los Angeles County simply stopped writing anything related to Isabel Crocker and her family. But there was already a case heading for the Supreme Court that would make the property restrictions illegal. An African American man, J. D. Shelley, his wife, and six children moved into a house in St. Louis in 1945. They were unaware of the restriction covenant attached to their deed. Neighbors Mr. and Mrs. Louis Kraemer brought suit to have the Shelleys removed from the house, citing the housing restriction. Circuit Court judge William K. Koerner ruled in favor of the Shelleys, but the Missouri Supreme Court overturned Koerner's findings. The case eventually reached the Supreme Court, where the justices ruled that these kinds of restrictions violated

Article 14 of the Constitution. The Shelleys won and stayed in their home. [25] The Crocker case in California was no longer an issue.

Ira had returned home immediately after the rally in Hollywood. He found employment with a construction company operating out of Sacaton, his birthplace. In May, misfortune struck. He was involved in a car accident and hospitalized for a wrenched shoulder, some bruises, and some severe lacerations. His injuries made it difficult to work construction, and he sat idle for at least a month. Typically for the time, the press hinted that the cause of his accident was drunk driving. But he was not driving the vehicle at the time of the crash.

Even though the property restriction fight was over, Hollywood was still interested in Ira Hayes. The famous gossip columnist Louella Parsons wrote in early February 1948 that Ferenc Fodor, a wealthy inventor and businessman, was signing Ira on as the leading man for his film *Children of the Sun*. She misidentified Ira as an "Oklahoma Indian." Nonetheless, according to Parsons, the film was to be about "the problems of American Indians." [26] Parsons observed that Ira was in the "unforgettable" Rosenthal picture. She seemed to imply that Ira's heroic status led to him being picked for the lead role in Fodor's film. Parsons' column ran in hundreds of newspapers, and her association of Ira as being part of the picture and the possibility of him becoming a leading man in a movie about Indian "problems" enhanced his heroic image in American popular culture. Nothing came of the proposed film; at that time, Ira was back on the reservation, laboring in the cotton fields.

Meanwhile, in February 1948, the so-called Freedom Train wound its way to Phoenix. The Freedom Train had been organized primarily by corporate magnates to sell the country on

American free-market capitalism. In short, the tour was intended to sustain the ideology of freedom and patriotism that had reached its height during the war. The National Archives provided several key documents that were displayed aboard the rolling exhibition, including the Constitution, the Declaration of Independence, a copy of the Emancipation Proclamation, and the German and Japanese articles of surrender. The public turned out, and Ira Hayes was welcomed aboard the train by a fellow Marine veteran of the Iwo Jima campaign. The flag he helped raise on Iwo Jima was on display as well, and Ira was photographed standing before it with a smile on his face. [27]

Hollywood was not done with Ira Hayes, either. War films were being produced at an astonishing rate. An interesting aspect of these films was their messaging. Unlike the numerous war films that followed World War I, these movies reflected a militant nationalism. At best, the movies following the First World War promoted an ambiguous meaning of the cost of war. *The Big Parade* (1925), for example, viewed the war as a glorious adventure but also revealed its terrible cost. The woman whom the protagonist leaves behind as he marches off to the front is literally left crying in the dust of a truck convoy. Later, the convoy is a fleet of ambulances carrying the wounded, including the protagonist, who lost a leg, back to the ruined village from which he left his lover behind. [28] Five years later, Lewis Milestone's *All Quiet on the Western Front* was released. It was, perhaps, the quintessential anti-war film. Every character, is seems, is killed in one way or another, and throughout the film there is a sense of hopelessness and the nightmare of the trenches. [29] Moreover, American-made World War I films portrayed the war as a purely Caucasian affair.

World War II produced films that were pure propaganda. They depicted soldiers as weary fighters of wars that had to be fought. In American film, World War II was the good war. Conditions were harsh, the fighting was terrible, but the war itself was a necessary battle against evil. The heroes were all-American boys fighting against the autocratic and racist regimes ruling Germany, Italy, and Japan. The soldiers were battle-scarred and exhausted, but they fought on knowing that American values would prevail. American World War II films truly democratized heroism for the whole war effort. The All-American platoon was born, depicting a military in which Poles, Italians, Jews, Irishmen, New England Yankees, Southerners, and the lower, middle, and upper classes all fought on one side. Black Americans were excluded, but once in a while a brown person, whether Mexican, Puerto Rican, or Native American, would sneak into the All-American platoon to demonstrate that the melting pot was actually simmering. [30]

In the same year that *The Big Parade* was released, Hollywood produced a film that brought World War I to Indian Country. Directed by George Seitz, *The Vanishing American* was intended to be an indictment of the bureaucratic system and missionary zeal that led to the poverty of the reservations. In hindsight, though, *The Vanishing American* is a war film that seems to be ignored as such because of its Native American content.

The film begins with a prologue based on Thomas Hobbes' idea of primitive societies using warfare to replace one another through time. Native invaders from the north defeat and displace Puebloan peoples at first; then come the Spanish conquistadors, then the Americans. Through it all one warrior stands out. Nophaie fought against the Pueblo peoples and, in several incarnations through time, fought the Spanish and then Kit Carson. Finally, Nophaie's people are herded onto a reservation under the rule of a slimy bureaucrat who not only steals from the tribe but stalks and harasses the local white schoolmarm. Nophaie, in his modern embodiment, is in love with her and keeps up a running feud with the bureaucrat. He calls her "White Desert Rose."

When the U.S. enters World War I, an army captain is sent to the reservation to obtain horses from the Indians. The schoolmarm manages to win Nophaie to the American cause and, in turn, he convinces his people to sell their horses and also to join the army and take up the fight in the trenches. The Native soldiers acquit themselves quite well in battle, and Nophaie saves the life of the captain who was sent to buy the reservation horses in the first place. The battle scenes are well done and printed on red film stock, an innovative idea for the period and one that is striking compared to other 1920s war films.

After the war, Nophaie's comrades in arms return to the reservation, which is even more poverty-stricken than when they went to war. The Native veterans discover that the bureaucrats have been robbing them and raise the battle cry once again. This time, the Indian agent's friend and subordinate, armed with an illegally obtained machine gun, fires on the Native uprising. Nophaie, acting out of his love for the schoolmarm, tries to stop the slaughter but is killed. The schoolmarm reaches into the shirt pocket of the dying Native veteran and pulls out a Bible that she had earlier given him. She discovers that the bullet that killed Nophaie has passed completely though the Bible. Seitz's film is filled with this kind of irony. Although Nophaie's people, and his line of warriors, have fought and died at the hands of the white men, they stood with the U.S. against the Germans. They returned from the trenches only to discover, as Ira did, that the America they helped to defend did nothing to help the people out of poverty. The second irony in the film had to do with a bullet-pierced Bible and Nophaie's death. The trope that a Bible in a soldier's pocket stopped a death-dealing bullet goes back at least to the Civil War. But in Nophaie's case, the Bible did not prevent his death. The Bible that White Desert Rose presented him with was shot through. War films with Native characters have followed paradoxical twists and turns in their messaging since Seitz's *The Vanishing American*. Even the movies that feature Hayes as a character retain these dramatic themes. [31]

And then along came John—John Wayne, that is. Wayne's persona in film is that of a tough, no-nonsense, self-righteous fighter for the American way. He is the epitome of the rugged individualist of the American mythos. Modern Native Americans often ridicule this figure, because in many of Wayne's movies he is the exemplar of the western bigot who kills Indians with regularity. In one film, *The Searchers*, Wayne's character actually threatens to kill his own niece (played by Natalie Wood) because she cohabited with a Comanche Indian. [32]

Marines in Vietnam also had a bit of fun at Wayne's expense. They called the C ration can opener the "John Wayne" opener and joked that the "John Wayne" crackers in C rations could be used as deadly weapons when thrown at the enemy. These jokes are aimed precisely at Wayne's character in the film *The Sands of Iwo Jima*, Sergeant John Stryker. In the movie, the Stryker character fought at Guadalcanal, Tarawa, and Iwo Jima, among the most heralded Marine invasions during the war. The notion that Stryker was at all three battles is difficult to fathom, because he had to have been reassigned three times to three different divisions. Marine divisions were created during the war by folding veterans from one division into another along with new recruits. But Stryker moved from the 1st to the 2nd to the 5th Division within a span of two years with his same squad intact. That would have been next to impossible. But then it was a movie, and an audience, even a skeptical Marine audience, is supposed to suspend its disbelief once in the theater. Additionally, most Americans knew that Wayne was "4-F" and did not serve in the military during the war. The suspension of disbelief was necessary to attending a John Wayne film.

The battle-hardened Sergeant Stryker trains and leads his men through the horrors of both Tarawa and Iwo Jima. His squad hates him at first because of his harsh demeanor and cruel physical training. But they begin to understand the rigor of his training methods because Stryker has taught them to be physically and mentally prepared for combat. The movie made good use of actual combat film. Stryker's squad lands on Iwo Jima and begins the assault on Suribachi. While climbing the mountain, Stryker is wounded. He hands the flag over to, of all people, the real Rene Gagnon, Jack Bradley, and Ira Hayes. Stryker then dies, and the three go to the summit and raise the flag. The filming required only two days of their time and around a half an hour of acting. Bradley wrote to a friend, telling him that if he sees the picture, he'll be "sadly disappointed." He wrote further that "Hayes says they have the picture so fucked up he isn't even going to see the movie." [33]

Although it was a small part, the three heroes' appearance in the film was exploited to the fullest extent. Republic studio executives had guessed that recruiting the three would boost ticket sales. Ira, Bradley, and Gagnon were indeed the subjects of several newspaper articles. According to James Bradley in *Flags of Our Fathers*, the papers created the feeling that the picture was really about the three heroes and their experiences in the battle.

Once again, though, it was really about The Photograph and not the heroes who raised the flag on Mount Suribachi. Although John Wayne's warlike countenance was on the posters

advertising the film, Rosenthal's picture was always there, sometimes in the foreground, sometimes hovering over Wayne's shoulder. For Wayne's part, *The Sands of Iwo Jima* bolstered his status as
a Hollywood star. He was even considered for a Best Actor Academy Award. Ira went home to work in the fields. Given his roles
as frontiersman, athlete, soldier, seaman, and lawman, Wayne,
for the period, was the very personification of masculinity. He
was a tough, rugged individualist who was domineering, used
violence to achieve some greater goal, and won the hearts of
many women on the silver screen. He was a highly valued actor
who always portrayed the archetypical masculine role in American culture. The movie hero displayed a stoic acceptance of pain
and heartbreak. [34] In Hollywood, Ira was pressured into playing the role of heroic American warrior. Even though he was a
real hero of the battles in which he fought, he was not particularly
suited for or comfortable with the role he played in Hollywood.
Ira's upbringing in Akimel O'odham society gave him a contrasting view of heroism and masculinity. Movie heroism, to him, was
very different than the real thing. Reality in war was basic survival and dependence on others. It was not rugged individualism
and domination.

In the first half of the twentieth century, Akimel O'odham
women were the property owners and, from an early age, were
viewed as having the divine power of procreation. Their valued
status was inherent. Men had to acquire powers and earn valued
status. Boys were taught to work from a young age. As boys, they
collected firewood, tended the livestock, and helped with planting and harvesting. All of these chores were geared toward the
strengths of the young men involved. Both girls and boys were
instructed to recognize and respect older people and practice
group solidarity, especially when it concerned work. Tending

livestock, or gathering wood, or helping with the harvest were generally done in cooperative groups. [35] The idea of mutual aid was instilled in Ira from a very young age as part of Himdag.

By the time Ira was born, training with the shield and war club had been mostly discarded. Boys were still expected to help out in cooperative labor and respect their elders. Those who learned ceremonies and songs and traditional stories were valued as keepers of Himdag, the good way. Akimel O'odham elders held great value in society. Once the warrior tradition had been deferred or put away, younger men earned status by way of hard work, participating in ceremonies, learning from elders, and exhibiting virtuous behavior. Akimel O'odham children were also taught not to brag and, according to tribal elder Urban Giff, that it was improper for "a person to seek recognition." [36] Ira's supposed stoicism was no more than the Akimel O'odham male virtue of humility. Seeking individual preeminence while performing a group task like chopping wood or going to war was not part of the O'odham ethos of Himdag.

Although Ira had no desire to exploit his celebrity in white society, he was not happy with his lot in life following the war. White supremacy ruled in Arizona, and Ira hated the way his people were treated. He also hated that he had been branded a hero when all the real heroes were either dead or severely wounded and handicapped. The poverty of the reservation rankled him. It has often been reported that Ira escaped Iwo Jima unscathed. That was not true. Although he probably would not have admitted it, he too had been wounded and handicapped. His wounded soul had left him alive but fragile. He deserved at least a Purple Heart as much as anyone who shed blood in battle. There are no medals for that particular kind of suffering.

Chapter 7

"Call Him Drunken Ira Hayes" [1]

It was not called PTSD back then. They really did not know what to call it. Consequently, they named it "the thousand-yard stare," or "shell shock," or "battle fatigue," or "combat neurosis." No one really knew what it was, but the people who dealt with those who suffered from it realized that it was bad. There are in existence motion pictures of shell-shocked British veterans of the First World War shaking uncontrollably with eyes wide and staring, yet seeing only images of the horror they went through.

Post-traumatic stress disorder was actually noticed during the Civil War. One major problem with the diagnosis was that it was thought to be a relatively quick reaction to the stress of combat. Some veterans had long-term psychosis, but it was thought that combat fatigue could be cured with rest and a return to a more normal atmosphere of stability and quiet. It has been found, however, that PTSD can be the result of recent combat trauma or crop up again and again throughout a person's entire life, hence the use of "post-" in its name. [2]

Another problem is that PTSD is an extraordinarily complex emotional condition or, actually, a series of conditions and adjustment difficulties. And even that does not cover the entire spectrum of the disorder. Generally, the focus is on the stressor, which is considered beyond normal or usual human occurrence, be it a natural catastrophe like an earthquake, a rape, a disaster such as a plane crash, or combat. Combat can be viewed then as an extraordinary experience that is not quite supernatural but far from customary human pursuits. Warfare would then have to be considered an abnormal human event that puts the combatant in a situation that could mean death or serious injury. [3] However, as psychologist and scholar Wilbur J. Scott argues, PTSD was largely contrived as a disease because of political considerations that relied heavily on Peter G. Bourne's conclusions in his book *Men, Stress, and Vietnam.* But Scott did not deny that battle fatigue existed. He pointed out that "the flow of soldiers out of the Army on psychiatric grounds during World War II at one point exceeded the numbers of new recruits." Scott also posed the hypothetical query that PTSD might be a normal, rather than an aberrant, reaction to combat. It was certainly usual. [4]

Ira Hayes' stressors were multiplied several times over. He had participated in a brutal war. And even before he went into the Marine Corps, he experienced the poverty of the reservation that had, in actuality, been imposed upon his people. The Akimel O'odham people as a whole were still undergoing a very difficult transition from a peaceful and sophisticated agricultural society to a society burdened with extreme poverty. Ira's people were also setting aside some of their traditional culture in order to persevere as a distinct people in a changing world. Ira himself persevered through it all. But he survived with a great deal of emotional pain.

Because the terminology was not even invented until the late 1970s, Ira's complexities of emotional trauma must be considered with a degree of retrospection. It can be concluded that combat is perhaps the most traumatic of events beyond the normal because it generates numerous stressors over a sustained period of time. Ira Hayes took part in two major battles during the war. The Bougainville campaign took place in a jungle setting filled with unseen enemy troops, where disease was rampant and living conditions were horrible. On Iwo Jima the climate and terrain were different, but the defenses of the island were markedly more deadly than those on Bougainville. In both, Ira had survived hand-to-hand combat, sudden and mostly unexpected bombardments and small-arms attacks, and nerve-wracking patrols within the enemy's beaten zone. Moreover, he was physically present to see his friends die of bullet wounds or explosions. He saw enemy and friendly dead on several occasions and likely helped retrieve and remove bodies from the combat zone. His combat experiences were a myriad of horrors, none of which were easily forgotten and put aside. The intensity of the trauma put Ira in a continued state of bereavement and psychological pain. His stressors were not only cumulative, but they also extended for days and even weeks. A diagnosis of PTSD can easily be made in the case of Ira Hayes, even in hindsight.

In 1979, psychologist Charles R. Figley edited a volume of monographs entitled *Stress Disorders among Vietnam Veterans: Theory, Research and Treatment*. The book was more or less a preview of the American Psychological Association's *Diagnostic and Statistical Manual of Mental Disorders*, 3rd Edition (DSM-III). Although the volume concerned Vietnam veterans specifically, it was a succinct evaluation of what would be called PTSD for the time. DSM-III itself would become quite controversial. On the other hand, the Figley book does offer a number of clues as to the level of Ira Hayes' trauma. The book is certainly not definitive but, used as a research tool, it provides quite a few answers to important questions that arose during Ira's lifetime. The extensive research done on PTSD in Vietnam veterans can provide insight into Ira's own social and emotional difficulties. Very little new research contradicts in any way the findings in Figley's collection of essays. The revised edition of the third volume of DSM-III simply listed the five criteria for diagnosing PTSD. [5]

The most recent diagnostic manual (DSM-V) expanded the criteria for the PTSD diagnosis. A victim had to be exposed to death, serious injury, sexual violence, or the threat of death. In addition, a person had to witness trauma or be indirectly exposed to it via professional duties including first responders, police, and medical personnel. Gone was the criterion of sustained combat, recognizing it only under the criterion of exposure to serious injury or death. It seems that combat, in which a person's exposure to threats is prolonged over a longer period of time as opposed to seeing or being in a car wreck, has been dropped to a lower position on the PTSD scale. It appears that time of exposure is no longer a consideration in the diagnosis. Otherwise, DSM-V lists the same symptoms of PTSD as DSM-III did. [6]

Generally, the early research done on World War II combat veterans led to the conclusion that combat neurosis was a temporary nervous condition linked to the fear of death. When the veteran was removed from the environment of warfare, so the argument went, the condition would simply go away. Today, what little there is in terms of research on PTSD in World War II combat veterans employs the theoretical constructs developed to examine Vietnam veterans, primarily because of DSM-III and DSM-III-R. In consequence, World War II veterans are compared to those from the Vietnam war, and these comparisons can be used to examine the complexity and intensity of Ira's personal emotional circumstances. It might be added that World War II veterans generally had low expectations for jobs upon their return to the U.S. The Great Depression and its consequences were still on their minds. It was only later that their emotional problems were even noticed. [7]

Recent research has found that there was no significant difference between the emotional responses of World War II veterans and those of veterans who fought in Vietnam, except that among World War II veterans the onset of PTSD symptoms came toward middle age. One study found World War II veteran neuropsychiatric symptom rates were higher among those who served in the Pacific theater. It was thought that the conditions in the Pacific were much different from those in Europe, and that location might have been a factor in combat neurosis. Battle conditions were different. In the Pacific, military personnel had to deal with heat, lack of recreation, monotony, isolation, and disease. [8] Vietnam was more of the same.

Psychotherapist Ron Langer has done extensive research on PTSD in World War II veterans. Although he looks at DSM-III, as do other scholars, he focuses on the 2000 PTSD criteria for diagnosis. The first is referenced as *intrusive recollection*. This aspect of PTSD is simply a flashback of a distressing event that interferes with usual thoughts and activities. The flashbacks can be recurring and triggered by sights, smells, and sounds. Another aspect is *avoidance/numbing*. This is the avoidance of people, places, activities, feelings, or conversations that might prompt a traumatic memory. A third facet of PTSD is *hyper-arousal*. Hyper-arousal might include irritability, bursts of rage, heightened startle responses, sleeplessness, and difficulty concentrating. Langer essentially argued that PTSD was probably as prevalent in World War II veterans as it was in Vietnam veterans. It also sparked a kind of spiritual discord in what was otherwise a period in American history that emphasized organized religious dogma. Traumatic memories, wrote Langer, are more "vivid and immutable" than other kinds of memories. They are visceral, profound, and related to feelings rather than rational thought. "Wounded souls" is an appropriate diagnosis for a very large percentage of World War II combatants. [9]

In his actions, words, and personality, Ira Hayes displayed nearly every symptom of PTSD. Although Ira joked and generally had fun with his comrades in the Marine Corps, he was quite reticent when it came to talking about his experiences with his close relatives. This is common among combat veterans; the inability to speak about their experiences is often assigned to the veteran's sense of guilt or isolation or even of estrangement from others.

Survivor's guilt is a distinct emotional reaction to combat and can be called a syndrome in and of itself. Basically, survivor guilt, or survivor syndrome, is defined as the guilt, grief, and shame felt by a person who has endured a disaster or life-threatening event. The survivor typically believes that his or her survival is a matter of luck because others died in the incident or experience. Another reaction is that the survivor often feels that he or she could have done more to save the lives of others. This reaction adds to the prevailing aspects of post-traumatic stress: nightmares, flashbacks, feelings of rage because of the unfairness of simple luck, depression, isolation, and fear of speaking to others who might not understand the survivor's feelings about his or her "luck." Being lucky, in the minds of most noncombatants, is good. Survival in itself is considered fortunate. "Luck," in the minds of combat veterans, might be providential, but it is also cause for grief in the aftermath of battle. The difference in the views of what is "luck" and the idea of staying alive when others did not is part of the complexity, not only of the human mind, but also of survivor guilt. [10] An indication of Ira's own struggle with survivor syndrome is that he continually insisted that the real heroes of Iwo Jima were his dead comrades. The fact that he survived the fighting was because of the prayers of his people, the sacrifice of his comrades, or simple good fortune.

Another aspect of veterans' reticence in speaking about combat experiences has to do with the feeling that a listener might not want to hear, understand, or believe. And some combat veterans simply do not want to relate their experiences and feelings to someone who knows nothing about combat in the first place. At the same time, veterans get together and tell one another war stories without feeling judged or misunderstood. William Broyles Jr. wrote a brilliant essay for the magazine *Esquire* years ago that got to the heart of this. In the essay, published in an anthology about the Vietnam War, Broyles repeats a story told by Michael Herr in his book *Dispatches*. "Patrol went up the mountain. One man came back. He died before he could tell us what happened." Broyles called this three-sentence story a "combat haiku." This kind of war story goes back perhaps as long as people have gone to war. According to Broyles, "Its purpose is not to enlighten but to exclude…I was there. You were not." [11]

Ira could talk to fellow veterans, but he could not force himself to speak of the fear, anger, hatred, and exhilaration of combat to his mother. She would not have understood. Ira Hayes needed that sixteen-day lustration following a battle that his ancestors had practiced. The ritual aimed at the revitalization of the spirit, a cleansing of the stigma of death. If ever there was a time to revive a ceremonial purging of wartime trauma in the Akimel O'odham way, it was during World War II. Many

Americans are somewhat reluctant to believe in ceremonial healing and write off rituals like the Akimel O'odham postwar lustration as superstitious behavior. On the other hand, it has been demonstrated that ritual has its place in aiding the human spirit to heal from psychological trauma.

But the attacks on traditional Native ceremonies and the Christianization of Native peoples had been in effect at least since the early 1800s. It could likely extend further back in time if Father Kino and other Catholic missionaries had their way during the eighteenth century. But my study of more than one hundred Native American Vietnam veterans found a correlation between a decline in the severity of PTSD symptoms and the participation in tribal healing, cleansing, and honoring ceremonies. [12] Stan Steiner, in his book *The New Indians,* wrote about the healing that World War II veterans received in their own traditional ceremonies that brought them home from the death and destruction of the battlefields. He also wrote that the "rites of purification were inadequate. The young warrior...was a veteran of life, as well as of death, in the world beyond his reservation." [13]

Ira had fought in a war like no other, and it appears that he only had the faith of his family and friends to fall back on. Unfortunately, the Presbyterian church did not have the kinds of rituals of lustration that had sustained Akimel O'odham warriors in times past. Presbyterian doctrine is based on John Calvin's interpretation of the sovereignty of the deity. Part of the doctrine is predestination, which entails confession and submission to God and not necessarily to a prelate or a congregation. Baptism comes early in life. Ira may very well have reached a "state of grace" as the Calvinist tenets teach, but there is no specific ritual that cleanses a warrior of wartime trauma—only prayer.

One of the aspects of combat that veterans reluctantly talk about is death. Combat veterans are often asked if they killed anybody. It was a question that was continually put to Ira, Gagnon, and Bradley while on the Mighty Seventh Tour. Many veterans reply that they simply did not know if they killed anyone in a firefight. Most will admit that they tried to kill because of either peer pressure, hatred, the dehumanization of the enemy, or because they were on a crew-served weapon team. Historically the fear of death in battle was thought to cause combat neurosis. This notion was on full display in the film *Patton*, when George C. Scott, as the general, slaps an obviously shell-shocked soldier and calls him a coward.

But it is not the personal fear of death that explains all of the PTSD symptoms. The novelist James Jones wrote in his history of World War II that combat veterans go through what he called the "evolution of a soldier." Part of that evolution is simply acknowledging that one could be killed at any time during one's period of time in a combat zone. It is an acceptance of death and knowledge that it is better to die quickly than have it linger. [14] Additionally, it was better to fight sooner than later. Waiting only prolonged the misery.

Viewing the dead is altogether a different question. One can be inured to seeing corpses, but one never forgets the sight, especially if the body is maimed in some way. A person never forgets the sight of a good friend's corpse. The development of Ira's relationship with his fellow Marines is important in this respect. He was present when Franklin Sousley, Harlon Block, Mike Strank, Henry Hansen, and "Boots" Thomas were killed. Strank was his squad leader, Thomas his platoon sergeant, and Sousley was a young Marine who became close to Ira in a kind of veteran-to-novice relationship. Block and Hansen were Ira's fellow parachutists who shared previous combat experiences and a camaraderie that developed as members of an elite cadre like the "chutes." Seeing their deaths at close hand and likely handling their bodies reinforced the notion that Ira himself might be killed at any second, and, importantly, seeing the wounds they received, their blank eyes and faces, and feeling the limpness of their bodies either sickened him or left him with a sight of horror than would never leave him. Hayes was also part of a culture that, although certainly changed as a result of the introduction of Christianity, abhorred death. When a person died and was interred, the body was reverently treated, and the spirit was asked not to return from the land of the dead. It was also a custom to destroy the dwelling in which a death had occurred, thus removing the contamination that death had brought into the home. [15]

Ira experienced every stressor that physicians, psychiatrists, and sociologists have found linked to PTSD. He witnessed death and destruction, experienced life and death in a combat zone, had his own life threatened on numerous occasions, saw his close friends die, was constantly asked to relive the events of his life, and had killed other humans with his own hands. Just in terms of his combat experience, even ignoring the stresses of reservation life in the 1920s and 1930s and at the Phoenix Indian School, his job at one of the "relocation centers," and of his celebrity status, he was predisposed to PTSD.

The disorder surfaced in several ways. He was feeling isolated or alienated because of his unwillingness or inability to speak to an understanding listener. He very likely had nightmares and intrusive thoughts about his experiences. He probably suffered flashbacks that could have been set off by certain sounds, smells, and sights. His sense of betrayal, which he expressed on several occasions, led to an inward, unexpressed feeling of rage. While all of these symptoms and responses are conjectured, all of them are based on psychological observation of other veterans who have had the same kinds of experiences as Ira Hayes.

Ira attempted to adjust to civilian life. In order to stay with his family in the Gila River community, a presumed basis of support and cultural acceptance, he had to accept work in the economy of place. Low pay and grueling agricultural labor was essentially a step back from his status in the Marine Corps. Ira was, after all, a combat veteran and a noncommissioned officer. After his service, he was characterized as the poor Indian the government and the postwar conservative bureaucrats were attempting to uplift. The hypocrisy of turning him into a hero but not letting him vote in elections was staggeringly irrational. Ira felt that absurdity deeply. He once said, "I think of those things all the time." [16]

In post–World War II America, racism was the norm. Lynching black people, although declining in number per year, nevertheless plagued the U.S. "Whites Only" signs were practically everywhere, especially in the South. Education and the dispensation of justice were very different for African Americans. A series of attacks on Latinos and African Americans who wore "zoot suits" occurred in 1943, and the bigotry persisted well into the 1950s. During the late 1940s an effort to pass an anti-lynching law in Congress was stopped by a filibuster in the Senate. The argument against the bill was that the states all had laws against murder, and because lynching was murder the perpetrators would be tried in their own communities by their peers. Such murder trials resulted in not-guilty verdicts. The lynching of a fourteen-year-old boy named Emmett Till in 1955 sparked within the Civil Rights movement a renewed sense of outrage and a willingness to launch a new series of protests that extended into the 1960s and 1970s.

Prejudice against Native Americans largely rested on white images and stereotypes. Hayes and his family fell into that fallacy about Indians being wards of the government and on the dole. The reservation life, in the American imagination, was one of doing nothing and waiting on handouts because Indians could not sustain themselves. The myth was that Indians could not or would not accept Western civilization because they lived in the past. Veterans, according to this line of thought, were willing to fight for the U.S. beside white Americans. Surely, with the Nazis, Japanese, and Fascists beaten and the Communists on the rise, Indians would want to become full American citizens. They just had to be lifted up from the degradation of reservation life. Indian veterans would lead in the evolutionary process of becoming fully assimilated into Western civilization. [17] American hubris at the time seemingly had no bounds. All it would take was the correct policy.

It was assumed that Native Americans would overlook the historical, intergenerational trauma of genocidal policies and of being robbed of land and resources. In the minds of policy-makers, there was no such thing as cultural genocide. Cultural change, even if it was carried out on Native terms, was viewed as an inevitable process of modernization. Ira suffered from PTSD as a result of war and historic government policies toward his people. And PTSD, whatever the form or the number of stressors, nearly always leads to social problems. Sufferers tend to have high divorce, incarceration, and unemployment rates. They also commit suicide in relatively high numbers relative to society as a whole. Another problem is a tendency toward substance abuse. [18]

Alcoholism has been cited as Ira's downfall over and over again. But Ira's drinking has to be placed in context. Alcohol has a relatively long history in Akimel O'odham traditional society. Ritual drinking of alcohol and the use of other substances to produce some kind of conscience-altering experience was present in North America before the Europeans. According to authors Don Coyhis and William White, cultures indigenous to the Americas produced "highly refined healing practices." While Europeans had only 10 or so medicinal plants, Native Americans were employing more than 150. Indigenous peoples of America used tobacco to send prayers into the firmament, or it could be used as an analgesic for minor wounds. Alcohol was not widespread but nevertheless used by quite a few Native peoples in what is now the southwestern United States, Mexico, and possibly the southeastern U.S. Intoxicating beverages were distilled in Mexico by the Mexica or Aztecs and spread through northern Mexico and into Arizona. In fact, more than forty types of alcoholic beverages were produced in that geographical area alone. The Aztecs strictly limited alcohol use and punished those who were drunk and disorderly. They even limited quantities of alcohol for imbibing. Alcohol, in Aztec tradition and law, was not for "secular use." [19]

The Akimel O'odham, Ira's people, discouraged intoxication except in an annual ceremony. At that time, the number of people allowed by the chiefs and elders to drink the wine was limited to about one-third of a village population. The rest of the villagers were there to take care of those who were intoxicated. Again, alcohol was not consumed for recreational purposes. It was limited to a ritual for fertility of the earth. The Tohono O'odham and the Akimel O'odham made a wine out of the saguaro cactus. It had a low alcohol content and was used, primarily by men, in ritual. Specifically, it was consumed on New Year's Day in the summer during a ceremony that called upon the spirits to bring rain. The ceremonial drinking was linked to fertility and was a "complex agricultural ritual with the use of intoxicant beverages." [20]

For Native peoples like the Akimel O'odham, alcohol, as well as tobacco and peyote, had healing and spiritual power. Their use in sacred rituals was common and necessary. Often the powers associated with these substances could be good or ill, depending on the ritual in which they were used. In short, Native Americans knew about the dangers of each of these substances and avoided, as much as possible, abusing them. Since they came from the earth, they were sacred and required a balanced and constrained approach to their consumption. Coyhis and White list eight points about how Native American peoples avoided alcohol's "untoward effects":

- Rejecting alcohol as a culturally sanctioned intoxicant
- Reducing exposure of children and (in some tribes) women to alcohol
- Defining intoxication as a sacred state and discouraging the informal, secular use of alcohol
- Defining the right to get intoxicated as a prerogative only of the mature or the elderly
- Limiting the quantities of alcohol that could be consumed
- Limiting the frequency of intoxication (to religious or other ceremonial events)
- Defining alcohol consumption as a component of a ceremony
- Ritually structuring the consumption of alcohol in ways that minimized risks [21]

Reverend Charles Cook, although revered, did much to mitigate the power of traditional rituals and put an end to the consumption of even saguaro wine, except secretly. In each village where a Presbyterian church was established, deacons were appointed to act as a kind of ecclesiastical police force, admonishing congregants to practice temperance and obey the commandments. He established what has been called a "clerical state." [22] On the other hand, Frank Russell declared, "For a period of about thirty years, or from 1859 to 1880, the Pimas were visited by some of the vilest specimens of humanity that the white race has ever produced." Moreover, "the tribe was without a teacher, missionary, or, to judge from their own story and the records of the Government, a competent agent." [23]

Russell marked the 1870s as a period of noticeable change in Akimel O'odham society. It was about the same period that Cook, and the Presbyterian church, began to establish predominance over the tribe's secular life. Even after many Akimel O'odham accepted Christianity, the consumption of alcohol, in this period the white man's whiskey, changed for good. Russell quoted Hubert Howe Bancroft, a prolific author and prominent American historian and ethnologist, writing:

Swindling traders had established themselves near the villages to buy the Indians' grain at their own prices, and even manipulate Government goods, the illegal traffic receiving no check, but rather apparently protection from the Territorial authorities. Whiskey was bought from Adamsville or from itinerant Mexicans; the agents were incompetent, or at least had no influence, the military refused support or became involved in profitless controversies. [24]

Bancroft could not help but pass some of the blame on "itinerant Mexicans" even when the border towns (those on the borders of the reservations) were actually providing the intoxicants at relatively cheap prices. A turnaround in Akimel O'odham fortunes it was not.

Despite Cook's and the village chiefs' best efforts, alcohol consumption on the reservation increased. The "clerical state" was unable to quash the liquor trade. The border towns, the swindlers, and the "vilest specimens" continued to make distilled spirits available to Native Americans despite their being against the law. The liquor the whites sold was a much higher-proof beverage than the saguaro wine the Akimel O'odham men ingested ritually. Alcoholism on the reservation became a "major problem" after 1878, "resulting in many deaths." [25]

Outsiders in the late nineteenth century saw the drinking on the Gila River reservation as confirming previously held ideas that Indians were genetically prone to alcohol abuse and that they were too childlike to moderate their intake of liquor. These racial stereotypes translated into policy. To non-Indian policymakers, Native Americans would and should be "wards" of the government and as such should not have the same rights and privileges as white Americans. These inaccurate and racist ideas led to the disenfranchisement of Native peoples in Arizona and several other policies that subordinated Native Americans. [26]

Unfortunately, Russell's assessment of the conditions on the Gila River Reservation was correct. Bootleggers from the border towns literally plagued the Gila River people as they did nearly every other reservation in the U.S. And like nearly every other reservation, Gila River instituted prohibition whether by the federal agent or by the "clerical state." Tribal elders cautioned against the use of alcohol, coming out against even the traditional ritual alcoholic beverages. Liquor from the border towns had contributed to the anomie of Akimel O'odham society.

In the early 1950s, psychologists and physicians, as well as clerics and politicians, were trying to define alcoholism as either a disease or an individual moral failing, or as some kind of genetic circumstance largely tied to the idea of race. It had only been twenty years since national prohibition had ended. The whole ideology behind the experiment of prohibition assumed that certain immigrant "races" were genetically prone to alcoholism.

Scholars Roxanne Dunbar-Ortiz and Dina Gilio-Whitaker argue that the trope of the drunken Indian is one of the most damaging and intractable images of Native Americans in history. The drunken Indian is assumed to be morally flawed and without the ability to control his primitive compulsions. It makes him, in the American mind, prone to rape, pillaging, and murder. In short, drunken Indians are a danger to society. Dunbar-Ortiz and Gilio-Whitaker conclude that there is no evidence that Native Americans are genetically predisposed to become addicted to intoxicating drink. The drunken Indian is nothing but a myth used to confirm Native inferiority and the destruction of tribal cultures. [27] In the words of Coyhis and White, "To colonize or exterminate a people, you must first define them as a weed." [28]

Ira Hayes' battle with alcohol has to be seen in the context of the times in which he lived, his stint in the Marine Corps, his notoriety, his various jobs, and his culture. Regrettably, there was no idea, theory, or hypothesis about what ailed him that might have helped in his adjustment back to civilian life. He certainly tried to deal with his emotional, social, and economic problems, but there was nothing in place to help him cope with the anxiety, depression, feelings of rage, flashbacks, and nightmares that typify combat trauma.

Substance abuse has been a chronic problem for veterans. In Vietnam, both alcohol and some kinds of consciousness-altering drugs were almost unavoidable. American troops could obtain marijuana easily and cheaply. In Vietnamese cities, substantially more effective, and deadly, drugs like heroin and morphine were available. In the field, surettes of injectable morphine could be found in every first aid kit for the treatment of the wounded. The substances were there and, for a number of servicemen, highly addictive. Benzedrine, an amphetamine, kept soldiers awake and alert in World War II, Korea, and Vietnam. [29]

In particular, World War II veterans seemed to have been prone to alcoholism. But there is a difference between alcoholism per se and a prevalent form of alcohol abuse among military personnel known simply as binge drinking. [30] The consumption of alcoholic beverages is socially acceptable, even in the military service when off duty. Military bases have officers' and enlisted men's clubs that sell liquor. Not only that, but towns that border military bases have strings of nightclubs and bars, the numbers of which rival large cities. Overseas American bases are surrounded by establishments that cater to the military's seemingly endless need to imbibe alcohol. Even some on-base post exchanges (PXs) sell bottles of liquor at very low prices compared with stores in off-base towns.

Military service, in any period of time, is more often than not simultaneously demanding and mind-numbing. In World War II, drills were constant, whether marching in formation, running to battle stations on board a ship, recovering aircraft, weapons familiarization, or moving and setting up artillery pieces. Equally incessant were labor parties. Soldiers and Marines dug trenches, foxholes, and berms. They filled sandbags, strung barbed wire, constructed obstacles, and laid mines. Military personnel were also expected to do their own laundry, stand inspections, clean weapons, and do general janitorial work. Drudgery was a soldier's lot when not in direct combat; combat was of a different sort of drudgery. When troops were given liberty or furloughs, they used the time to celebrate. Recreational drinking was the norm in World War II. [31]

Becoming a chronic alcoholic is a somewhat different matter. The alcoholic cannot control drinking and, through time and continued drinking, develops a tolerance to alcohol. The alcoholic can consume intoxicants at a higher rate without being poisoned—unless, of course, he or she goes on an extreme spell of imbibing. Alcoholism might very well be put on the highest rung of the addiction ladder.

Binge drinking is a high-level sort of alcohol addiction that can lead to death. Normally, binge drinkers can function at their workplaces. But it is a far darker side of recreational drinking. Military men and blue-collar workers are seemingly prone to bingeing. Servicemen dare not show up for duty in a state of inebriation or they will be subject to the code of military justice. [32]

Ira started out, like many military men, as a binge drinker. It all added up. He had not graduated to a daily drink or two that would have built up his alcohol tolerance. He did not become a confirmed alcoholic who needed the liquor as if it were life itself. He articulated the need to stop drinking several times and went into rehabilitation on at least two occasions. He joined an Alcoholics Anonymous program. The rehabilitation at a sanitorium did not work, but that could have been the result of inadequate knowledge or a lack of treatments that could be applied to

Ira's personal alcohol problem and PTSD. At the time, treatment for alcohol-related problems simply did not consider the historic Native American experience with liquor and the cultural and societal wreckage it caused. Over time, the bingeing became more and more frequent, and he soon developed a tolerance to alcohol. In his day, the treatment for alcoholism and rehabilitation was rudimentary, even though by the early 1950s, many health professionals did commit to calling alcoholism a disease rather than a moral weakness.

The origin of Ira's drinking lies in his PTSD. But in that period, combat neurosis was recognized as a temporary problem unless the victim had a previous mental disorder. All that one needed to cure the problems of the malady was rest and relaxation. Commonly, rest and relaxation meant drinking as well. For Ira Hayes, the therapies for both PTSD and alcoholism were in their infancy. Rest was the answer for combat neurosis and temperance was the answer for alcoholism. Nor was it understood that one, PTSD, led to another, binge drinking and alcohol abuse. Ira's service was likely the major factor leading to his bouts of drinking. The Marine Corps did not officially condone alcohol consumption, but NCOs and officers often simply overlooked it because it was more or less accepted as typical behavior of lower-class recruits from the urban slums or the poverty-stricken rural areas of the U.S. or because their troops needed it to relax or prepare themselves for combat. Ira's service begot PTSD, which in turn begot binge drinking.

Ira had layer upon layer of traumatic experience. Drinking was more or less a way of relieving combat trauma. So many emotional and physical conditions arise in combat: excitement, fear, disgust, hatred, muffled hearing, terrible smells, pumping adrenaline, innumerable cuts, scrapes, illnesses, soreness, bruises, and fatigue. On and on. Monotony and routine come in between fights. Getting drunk is a way to rid oneself of the boredom of not being in combat. Getting drunk with friends is a way to relive the camaraderie. Alcohol might also be imbibed to create a false sense of courage. Many people are taught that alcoholism is a disease or an addiction. But most alcoholics don't think in those terms. Alcohol becomes a friend—the only friend. For Native peoples it was a mysterious power, used ceremonially. When some tribes got it from the whites, they thought of it as a power that took away fear. So it can be seen as a neutral power with good and bad characteristics. Some medicine people say that it should be respected but not abused, honored instead of affronted. Use it to clean wounds but do not drink it unless it is used as a sacrament in a traditional religious rite.

Ira loathed his drinking problem. When he was undergoing Marine Corps training, he wrote several times to his family that, unlike his fellow recruits, he had not taken a drink while on liberty. In boot camp he went to church every Sunday and, during one such meeting, listened to a sermon the chaplain titled "Alcohol versus Christianity." The sermon "made me cry to think of the times when like a fool kid, I've taken drinks." He swore in the same letter that he would try to avoid alcohol because he did not want to "bring shame on myself or on my family or on my church." He steadfastly believed in his church and that God will "be on my side" in combating his urge to drink. [33] Unfortunately, Ira's bouts with alcohol shamed him beyond his sense of religious guilt.

Traditionally the Akimel O'odham people used saguaro wine as a sacrament. It was used much like members of the Native American Church use peyote in ceremonies to heal and to communicate with the spirit world. In the early days of its

171

existence the Native American church was seen as an instrument to combat alcohol abuse in Native communities. But Ira had gone beyond using alcohol in a traditional sense. His bingeing was indeed more on the order of many blue-collar workers who used alcohol in the U.S. It might not have been good for him, but it was a matter of fact.

By 1953, Ira was weary of the reservation. Whether it was because of the soul-devastating poverty of the reservation, the repetitiveness of the work he was doing, or the restlessness of simply being a young man wanting the seemingly greater opportunities of the city, Ira wanted to strike out on his own. The federal government had, by then, developed a program for Native Americans that was aimed precisely at getting them jobs in an urban environment. Outwardly, the program was invented to "modernize" Native life and, at the same time, rid the federal government of its historical, legal, and moral responsibilities to Native peoples as outlined in treaties, court decisions, and legislation. It was called, simply, "relocation."

Chapter 8

Ira Hayes and the Failure of Relocation

Ira certainly realized that his bouts with alcohol had their origins in his attempts to deal with the traumatic effects of warfare, but, like the more than twenty-five thousand Native Americans who served during World War II, he probably did not fathom that his stint in the Marine Corps would also provide the finishing touch justifying a change in America's policy toward Native peoples. Generally, it became known as "Termination and Relocation," but it was much more multifaceted than those two words indicated. It was also much more insidious than most Natives could have perceived at the time. Ira's sense of betrayal was heightened because his service seemed not to have altered Akimel O'odham lives for the better. Ultimately, the policies of relocation and termination failed him as well.

Native Americans entered the military in unprecedented numbers, and they also invested heavily in the war effort. Tribes bought war bonds, and hundreds of Native people left the reservations to work in war-related industries. With tribal permission, and sometimes without, Native lands were used as bases and bombing practice areas. Japanese Americans were herded into internment camps located on Native American lands as a result of widespread racial and political antagonism toward them. John Collier, the commissioner of Indian affairs under President Roosevelt, commented, "The war has brought about the greatest exodus of Indians from the reservations that has ever taken place." [1]

For all of their sacrifices and hard work, Native Americans generally were still subjected to a systemic brand of racism. Banks would not loan the former GIs money for housing. Reservations, in that regard, were subject to redlining. Numerous Native Americans were subjected to "whites only" rules in several states, as in the case of Isabel Crocker in Los Angeles. In some states, Natives were not allowed to vote because they were "wards" of the federal government.

But most importantly, politicians, corporate elites, and conservatives began issuing complaints that the Roosevelt policies were socialistic and only a stone's throw away from communism. The Cold War was on and, significantly, government policies toward Native Americans were carefully scrutinized for any hint of Marxist thought. Rugged individualism and capitalism, not collectivism, were the watchwords of the day. President Truman favored civil rights and equal opportunity for all. Truman even desegregated the military. He also appointed William Brophy to head the Office of Indian Affairs. Brophy was especially interested in securing basic civil rights for Native veterans. In 1947, Arizona, one of the last holdouts on Native voting rights, gave in and enfranchised Native Americans. The new inclusive ideas were based on the notion that each person in the U.S. was acting in his or her own self-interest and that social programs and welfare of any type did not promote American ideals. Anything else simply smacked of communism. The Red Scare and Cold War affected everyone and everything, including Native American reservations and Native peoples. The ideas underlying American individualism and capitalism were liberal in some ways but steadfastly opposed to any program that promised social and economic justice for those who had been bypassed by the American dream.

The American sense of Western cultural and economic superiority muddled the liberalism of integrating Native peoples. Donald Fixico's brilliant and detailed book *Termination and Relocation* offers the most compelling evidence that the idea of assimilating Native peoples into the body politic was not so much a notion of liberal inclusion as it was a rather opaque form of cultural oppression. Fixico quoted one government official as saying that everyone, Natives included, recognized:

> the futility of attempting to maintain an isolated system of primitive community life. The outside world did offer to the participating Indians exciting, desirable and worthwhile possibilities of individual achievement.

Fixico underscored the fact that, at the time, "Dark skinned people were considered second class citizens." [2]

Building a policy that skirted all of the promises made to Native peoples was not very difficult. First, policymakers had to underhandedly settle and essentially remove all the demands for rights particular to Native tribes and tribal members and the promises made in treaties. The idea was to end direct federal-tribal relationships, cut the budget of the Bureau of Indian Affairs so that it would eventually cease to exist, and resettle as many Natives as possible to urban areas for industrial employment. By 1945, the plans to get the federal government out of the "Indian business" once and for all were working their way through the political process. And, according to Congressman George Schwabe, the Bureau of Indian Affairs should be done away with because "it encourages paternalism and socialistic and communistic thinking." [3]

In American politics, interest groups are important in that they often define, for legislative purposes, what kinds of policies are in the public good. Accordingly, the interest group is the first, and often the only, party in making policy that benefits from it. The problem in making "Indian policy" is that Native Americans have historically been removed from the policymaking process. So it was in the post–World War II era that as interest groups that should have influenced or benefited from government policies, the tribes were totally ignored.

The case made for relocation and termination was relatively straightforward. It was based squarely on this notion that because Native Americans joined in the war effort, they were demonstrating their desire to join mainstream society. Native veterans were never asked why they joined the service during the war. It was simply assumed that they, the men and women who worked in war-related industries, and the tribes that donated money and land to the war effort, did so because they were working to assimilate themselves and become part of the American economic system.

But Native American participation in the war effort was far more complicated than non-Native lawmakers chose to recognize. In fact, the lawmakers and bureaucrats actually fabricated the notion that all Indians were striving to leave their reservations behind and become "true" Americans. Individual Native peoples did indeed, like Ira, show up at the recruitment stations ready to fight. In several cases, young men from the Indian schools were encouraged to join and serve as a group. There were in World War II all-Native units like the Navajo Code Talkers in the Marine Corps and the Army's Comanche equivalents in the European theater. There were also Lakota and Hopi Code Talkers. These gifted bilingual servicemen were utilized within larger units to transmit orders and information in real time. Their contributions in both the Pacific and the European theaters of operations have not been fully documented, but on both the tactical and strategic levels they helped deceive the enemy so that American forces could concentrate and maneuver and direct fire on the enemy. Company C, 180th Infantry Regiment, 45th Division, was made up of men from the Chilocco Indian Boarding School. The regiment had two Native Medal of Honor recipients, Earnie Childers (Creek) and Jack Montgomery (Cherokee), who fought in Italy. Phoenix Indian School students and alumni made up Company F, 158th Infantry of the 40th Division of the Arizona National Guard. They would later fight in the Pacific theater as the 158th Regimental Combat Team, also known as the "Bushmasters." But for the most part Natives joined the branches of service individually or with a friend. [4]

Some Native American leaders advocated the formation of all-Indian units for training purposes, with the idea that their so-called primitive brothers needed a great degree of preparation before being thrown into all-white units. Not only that, but there was opposition to conscription on the basis of tribal sovereignty. In Arizona, a Tohono O'odham elder, Pia Machita of the town of Hickiwan, led a protest against the draft based on the belief that his people were not American citizens but an independent group that had not agreed to be subject to United States jurisdiction. Machita was imprisoned for a time for his and his Tohono O'odham followers' resistance. The Seminoles of Florida also resisted the draft on the same basis. [5]

Contrary to the American propaganda of the time, there was not a full consensus among Native Americans in favor of participating in the war effort. Numerous Hopis, for example, became conscientious objectors based on their religious beliefs against warfare. It all boiled down to individual decisions and the tribal governments' view of the war "from their own personal perspective," according to one leading historian of the Native American war effort, Jeré Franco. [6] The tribes wanted to remain sovereign entities with special relations with the American nation-state. In short, tribal officials knew full well that the federal government was waiting for an excuse to terminate its treaty and trust responsibilities and thus put tribal sovereignty on the chopping block as well. Tribal citizens were certainly willing to fight, but not at the cost of their tribal identities. That was true of most Natives in military service and certainly true of Ira Hayes.

The insidious nature of the plan was apparent soon after the war's end. The first step in terminating the federal-tribal relationship was the formation of the Indian Claims Commission in 1946. It was the government's attempt to settle all the Indian claims once and for all. If all claims were settled, then the tribes would gain independence from the Bureau of Indian Affairs, and the government could end its trust responsibility to the Native peoples. Or so it was professed. By 1979, when the commission was disbanded, it had paid out $800 million in claims. Afterward, there were still hundreds of claims unsettled and sent to various courts of claims. Most of them languished for years. [7]

The Indian Claims Commission did not settle all the claims, nor did it get the federal government out of the "Indian business," the point of which was terminating federal treaty responsibilities, bureaucracy, and, of course, money spent on Native health and welfare. The attempts to carry out these policies were protested at every turn by a large number of Native veterans of the war, even though the programs were supposedly intended to fulfill the dreams of Native veterans to fit into mainstream society.

The second scaffold of the termination policy was erected bit by bit. Or, to put it more bluntly, bill by bill, the first of which came in 1948. In June, Congress passed a bill that placed the Sac and Fox Reservation under the jurisdiction of the state of Iowa. [8] It meant that Iowa state and local law enforcement could go onto the reservation to serve warrants and basically enforce statutes enacted by officials outside the reservation. It was like blasting out a great hole in Sac and Fox sovereignty. At the time, government officials considered tribal sovereignty limited and subject to alteration by the federal government. As sovereigns the tribes had the power to determine their own membership, decided who could and who could not reside or do business on tribal lands, tax individuals and businesses located on the tribal estate, and maintain jurisdiction over civil and lesser criminal offenses. Native activists could clearly see that even these sovereign powers were under attack.

The bills came one on top of the other. Less than a month after Congress allowed Iowa to extend its jurisdiction over the Sac and Fox people, Congress enacted a blatant attempt to rid itself of its responsibilities to the tribes. [9] The bill simply ended all federal obligations to New York members of the Haudeno-saunee peoples, supposedly to emancipate Natives from federal wardship status. On the bill's heels, Senator Hugh A. Butler of Nebraska proposed that all trust restrictions on Osage land be removed. Under Butler's proposal, Osages would no longer have to submit to government interference if they, as individuals, wanted to sell their property. Again, the bill was introduced under the rhetorical framework of "emancipating" American Indians. [10]

One by one, tribes were being "emancipated" while losing federal protection and sovereignty. The final blows came in two acts. First, H.R. 108 allowed the government to determine which tribes were ready to have their special rights terminated. The second measure, Public Law 280, allowed individual states to assume jurisdiction over reservations within state boundaries. Combined, these two acts led to the cancellation of the federal responsibilities to the tribes. The tribes then began to be picked off individually. [11]

The groundwork laid, the Menominee of Wisconsin and the Klamath of Oregon were terminated. Then came the Rancheria tribes of California and Agua Caliente band near Palm Springs, California. More tribes were added to the list of potential groups to be terminated. By 1968, 109 tribes had been "emancipated." That meant that more than two million acres of land were removed from the protection of the federal government and handed over to the states. [12]

Throughout the period that termination was being put into place, Ira was called upon time and again to play the hero's role that he disliked so intensely. The press seemed to hound him as soon as he set foot off the reservation. In the almost ten years between Iwo Jima and his death, the newspapers covered nearly all of his movements and filled column after column with the news of both his ups and his downs, especially his downs. He was a transformed figure that went from American hero to the degraded and disgraced "drunken Indian" trope. It seemed that the journalists covering him played on this stereotype, whether it was to suggest that Indians were incapable of dealing with a changing industrialized America or that Indians were weak, dependent, and incapable of controlling their impulses. In the minds of the policymakers of the period, there were only two ways of solving the "Indian problem." Native peoples and their governments were capable of handling their own affairs if their nations were dealing with the federal government on a level playing field. That meant a government-to-government relationship, nation to nation, and keeping treaty obligations that Native peoples had already negotiated. The alternative was a "sink-or-swim" individualistic policy of terminating tribal governments and shipping tribal citizens off to the cities to work in America's industries. The first method would be too costly. Essentially, America would have to pay for the land, water, health care, education, and economic development the federal government had promised in hundreds of treaties, conventions, agreements, and covenants. The second was already in place at the time Ira and other Native World War II veterans were still dealing with the trauma of war.

In February of 1948, Ira made the national news again. Seemingly out of the blue, Hollywood columnist Louella Parsons announced that Ira had been "paged to play the lead" in a film titled *Children of the Sun*. [13] Another film was in the making as well. The *Baltimore Sun* carried a story under the headline "Three Men from Suribachi: Road Back Rough for Two" that revealed that the broadcasting company CBS was making a documentary about the three survivors of the flag raising, telling the story of their lives after Iwo Jima. While Bradley was portrayed as being relatively stable in terms of his profession and family life, Gagnon had had a disappointing time after the war. Rene's job prospects were not hopeful, and the employment that he did find was insecure. He dwelled on the fact that while a number of businessmen had made promises of employment to him, none had actually come through. Ira was described as "lolling around his desert home and going into Phoenix whenever he gets the chance." While the reporter was acidic toward Ira in his depiction of the "hero" lounging in the sun, he nevertheless wrote that Ira "doesn't like the way the Indians are being treated. In the Marines he was treated as an equal. In fact, he was a favorite of his buddies because he was rough and tough." The reporter offered the opinion that "Chief Hayes is no longer completely satisfied with life on the reservation. He wants to come East. But how and when he will do it, he doesn't know." [14]

Then, in 1949, there came another call from Hollywood. On July 28, the *Tucson Citizen* announced in an attention-getting caption that "Ira Hayes Leaves His Farm to Raise Iwo Flag in Movie." The Hollywood correspondent, Bob Thomas, wrote that the three surviving flag raisers, Ira, Rene Gagnon, and Jack Bradley, would be reunited for the first time since the Mighty Seventh bond drive and that the flag to be used in the film was the same one they raised on Mount Suribachi. It was on special loan from the Marine Corps. [15]

Thomas was one of the first to portray Ira in a negative light, mocking Hayes' appearance and demeanor, in writing about the "chubby, laconic Indian." Thomas hinted that Ira was certainly out of his element in Hollywood, although the author did not say the same about Gagnon or Bradley. To Thomas, Ira was a brown-skinned yokel raising corn, wheat, and vegetables and working construction. When Thomas asked if Ira was married, he replied, "No thanks, I get along better without 'em." [16]

Another reporter would, in February 1950, continue in the same vein. Ira, according to an article in the *Knoxville News Sentinel*, showed up in Hollywood wearing dungarees and a plaid shirt. The writer reported that the filmmakers were forced to buy him a proper suit of clothes, presumably so as not to embarrass him around the Hollywood elite. The Knoxville paper went on to describe Bradley and Gagnon as being somewhat dispirited because the film's script was not fully truthful about the Iwo Jima campaign. Ira, on the other hand, was described as "happy-go-lucky." When asked about marriage, Ira was reported to have answered, "Why should I ask for trouble?" The reporter then reached into the "drunken Indian" trope for the next question. Would Ira like to have a drink? "Don't mind if I do" was the reported response. [17]

Before he set off to play his cameo role in *The Sands of Iwo Jima*, Ira was in demand to make personal appearances. The papers advertised his appearances. He had been, since his release from the Marine Corps, appearing at local events, like the opening of the Thunderbird American Legion Post in Phoenix, a Flag Day Parade, and meeting the Freedom Train at its stop in Phoenix. [18]

The number of requests for Ira's personal appearance shot up after *The Sands of Iwo Jima* was released and then re-released. Soon, he made a personal appearance at the New Mesa Theater in Mesa, Arizona, on the occasion of the opening of the second release of *The Sands of Iwo Jima*, when the Mesa Veterans of Foreign Wars and American Legion posts of Mesa honored him for his service in the war. He was also asked to reenact the flag raising, along with Bradley and Gagnon, on Pike's Peak in Colorado. Neither Bradley nor Ira accepted the invitation. Ira was also later invited to be the honored guest at the twentieth annual American Indian Exposition in Anadarko, Oklahoma. [19]

The three flag raisers got together again in Washington to view the plaster version of the de Weldon statue for the Marine Corps War Memorial. Bradley, Gagnon, and Ira were pictured touring the de Weldon facilities and posing with the gigantic statue. Their ultimate purpose was a follow-up bond sale. This time it was intended to pitch federal savings bonds instead of war bonds. All three urged their fellow veterans to invest their G.I. insurance dividends in the new federal savings program. [20] The three would not see each other again until the de Weldon statue was finished and dedicated.

Despite the fact that Ira and so many other Native Americans served honorably in the war, things had not really changed for them. The Southwest has a very long history of overrepresenting indigenous people in the total number of arrests, and predominantly for "alcohol-related offenses." Poverty had not disappeared, and the long-standing Arizonan hatred of Indians still caused problems. After he returned from his moviemaking sojourn in Hollywood, the number of his arrests for public drunkenness went up. In Arizona, Native and Mexican American arrests on those charges far outstripped those of white citizens. [21] Ira's arrests were publicized. Known celebrity veterans who were alcoholics, like Lee Marvin, who also had symptoms of PTSD, never came close to the number of arrests that Ira experienced. Unfortunately, dark-skinned people like African Americans, Mexican Americans, Puerto Ricans, and Native Americans were hauled into jail for minor offenses in disproportionate numbers compared to the Euro-American population.

By 1952, Ira was openly eager to leave Arizona's bigotry behind. He had always said that Indians were treated like "little" people in Arizona and that the only option was to move east. But Ira did not at the time have the means to do so. His family and people were in Arizona, and leaving them behind was seemingly a rejection of his own sense of identity. He belonged with his people. If nothing else, he was Akimel O'odham to his very core.

Just as the policy of termination was initiated to "emancipate" the tribes from the guardianship of the Bureau of Indian Affairs, relocation was getting underway to "free" Native Americans of the poverty of reservation life. By that time, 1950, Dillon S. Meyer had been appointed commissioner of Indian Affairs. A career bureaucrat, Meyer had served for several years in the Department of Agriculture in various positions. Meyer headed the infamous War Relocation Authority. He notoriously took charge of imprisoning thousands of Japanese Americans in relocation camps, many of which had been situated on Native American lands. He was a natural cheerleader for termination and relocation. In fact, he argued that the two programs were not only for the public good in that they would ultimately lower the cost of government but that they would also promote the independence of Native Americans across the country. He requested that Congress allocate several million dollars to implement the policies. Although he never received the monies he asked for, he nevertheless established an office to oversee the relocation and vocational training needed to ship those who volunteered off to cities like Dallas, Los Angeles, and Chicago. [22]

Ira, convinced that Arizona offered him and other Native Americans nothing of value, volunteered to relocate to Chicago and train as a tool grinder. Because of his notoriety and hero's status, Ira got off the train in Chicago on May 18, 1953, to face a line of newspapermen and photographers. Soon nearly everything that Ira did was fodder for the papers.

The American Indian Club of Chicago welcomed Ira to the city. Two young women in traditional dress, Betty Maney and Ione Junesse, along with tribal elder Eli Powless, welcomed Ira as he exited the train at La Salle Street Station. The *Chicago Tribune* ran the picture of the four the next day. [23] Ira's arrival in Chicago also caught the attention of syndicated columnist Henry McLemore. McLemore's column was printed in a number of newspapers across the country within a week of Ira stepping off the train.

McLemore's column began with the premise that Ira was in Chicago looking for a job. From there, the correspondent wrote an entire editorial asking why Ira should have to look for employment in the first place. As McLemore put it, "I felt ashamed of myself and millions of my countrymen." The columnist wrote further that Hayes was "a worth-while, solid citizen who shouldn't be shunted around on some sort of Federal relocation and placement program." Ira had fought a dreaded enemy and struggled to raise the Stars and Stripes on Suribachi. The picture Ira was in rekindled in McLemore "the spark of national pride." That Ira was not being taken in and taken care of was, as McLemore put it, a "heck of a note, isn't it?" [24]

Ira took a job with International Harvester, learning the trade of tool grinder. His responsibilities included maintaining tools and smoothing and sharpening operating parts of machines. He did his work well and was fast becoming a reliable, skilled worker. Ira settled into a schedule of work and staying in his home on Huron Street on Chicago's near north side.

Relaxation and entertainment to many Chicagoans was hobnobbing and dancing in the local taverns. Ira avoided the bars at first, hoping to get used to the workaday routine. Practically anything was better than picking cotton for three dollars for every one hundred pounds that came from the fields. He still had to field requests for appearances and photographs. And they were numerous. Even the International Harvester telephone switchboard was packed with calls for Ira. The company took advantage of the fact that a Marine hero was working at the plant. His picture was printed in the company's publication. Eventually he would join his co-workers in weekend barhopping.

Ira apparently kept to himself and continued to work through the next few months. He had been fighting against his use of alcohol, but he started going to the bars after work. He was easily recognized. Bar patrons bought him drinks and toasted his bravery. Ira's supervisors at work got wind of his drinking and forced him to quit his job at International Harvester. He joined a railroad crew outside the city. Bradley and Powers relate a poignant story about the tribal chairman of the Gila River Reservation, Jay R. Morago Jr., running into Ira in O'Hare Airport. Ira had recently taken a job as a janitor there. Morago recognized Ira and asked him to come home. Ira told the tribal chairman that "we've had this conversation." At that, Ira simply continued to clean the men's room and ignore Morago. [25]

On October 14, 1953, Ira was picked up by Chicago police wandering the Loop without money or shoes. His fight against alcohol was a losing cause. The authorities threw him in jail on a drunk-and-disorderly charge. He had, according to the *Arizona Daily Star*, fallen in with strangers and went on a "tour of taverns [that] left him in the condition in which police found him." [26] The strangers had evidently robbed him after plying Ira with alcohol. In the jargon of the period, Ira had been "rolled," a reference to stealing a person's money roll after getting the person drunk or drugged. It is the equivalent of being mugged without the threat of violence. He lost his job. The city of Chicago had already seen Ira lose the bond tour in 1945. Now the city seemed to have it in for him in 1953.

His saving grace was the *Chicago Sun-Times*. The newspaper not only picked up Ira's story but paid his fine and began a campaign to aid in the comeback of the heroic Indian Marine of Rosenthal's photograph. Ira was placed in what was called a sanitarium, presumably to "dry out" and become a recovering alcoholic. The term "sanitarium" also implied serious mental illness, plus hygiene and healing. The sanitarium personnel utilized the drug Disulfiram or Antabuse on Ira. The drug, usually taken orally, causes vomiting if alcohol is in the patient's system. In short, it uses sickness to cure sickness, acting as a purge and a shock treatment to psychologically create a violent repulsion to the liquor. Ira wrote to his family about his time at the Hopecrest Sanitarium. In five days, he had "10 treatments, 16 shots" and was "pretty sick." [27] He vomited constantly. Abstinent but not necessarily cured of the root cause of his drinking—PTSD—he was ready to move on from Chicago. [28]

Ira was a binge drinker on the verge of becoming a clinically diagnosed alcoholic. He had not raised his tolerance of alcohol to the point that he needed to consume it on a daily basis. Given the knowledge of addiction in that period, Ira was considered an alcoholic. Ira could go without it for a period of time and then the need arose to ease his mind over his feelings of rage, guilt, or melancholy. He also had, as most workers do, the need for entertainment and relaxation. In Ira's case, alcohol must have been seen as having a power to heal even if it only temporarily put aside these powerful emotional states. For even a brief period of time Ira could overlook the horrors he had encountered in war, his feelings of betrayal by the federal government, and the bigotry he faced in Arizona. Drunkenness is certainly not a cure for all of these emotions, but it did offer a fleeting respite. As it happened, the use of Disulfiram cured Ira of nothing.

Ira's status as an American hero offered him a degree of help, but only insofar as help was seen from a certain perspective.

It is apparent in American society, then as now, that the cure-all for war trauma is a job and an enthusiastic pat on the back. And immediately after World War II, jobs for veterans were not available in great numbers, but there was plenty of praise for them. As has been pointed out, healing is much more complex than just being applauded for having spent time being shot at or seeing one's friends die. But, at minimum, the *Chicago Sun-Times* attempted to cure what was thought of as the sickness of alcoholism.

Aid also came from California. Elizabeth Martin, the former wife of Dean Martin, the singer and comedy partner of Jerry Lewis, offered to hire Ira as a chauffeur. Betty Martin, as she was known, was rumored to have a drinking problem of her own. She had probably read about Ira's troubles in Chicago and decided to help. Her 1949 decree of divorce left her with a substantial alimony of nearly $4,000 a month and a mansion in Beverly Hills. Her motives were not clear, but it might have had something to do with the breakdown of her marriage and the rumors of her own alcohol abuse. Her former husband, a known imbiber, adopted the persona of a carefree, always tipsy comic and singer for his television show in the 1960s and early 1970s. A drunken white man was apparently a source of amusement.

When Ira heard of Betty Martin's offer of a job in Hollywood, he readily accepted. He had some money left over from the *Sun-Times* funds. He bought some new clothes, packed his seabag, and booked a flight to California. Once in Beverly Hills, he obtained his chauffeur's license and moved into the Martin mansion. He had room and board and a $300 a month salary. He specifically became the chauffeur and bodyguard of the four Martin children. They called him "Chief" and were pictured in the newspaper with him playing the piano and singing. One of the Martin daughters had her arms around Ira's neck. He was smiling and apparently happy with his new position. [29]

Ira read to the children, played with them, and drove them to and from school and to parties. He had long talks with Betty Martin and accepted some interviews with reporters. One extremely meaningful day for him was his appearance on Ken Murray's variety television show. While doing the show he met ventriloquist Edgar Bergen and, most importantly, Joe Rosenthal, the man who took The Photograph. Ira was to write to his family that it had been a "very important day in my life" because he had finally met Rosenthal. Although at one time Ira had said that he wished the picture had never been taken, he declared that Rosenthal himself was a "very wonderful person" and that he would "never forget him." [30] Rosenthal, after all, was a veteran of Iwo Jima and therefore a person who understood the price of warfare. Rosenthal, like Ira, was one of the few people who "had been there."

On Halloween night 1953, Ira unfortunately went into a local bar to have a drink. Early the next morning he was stopped by police a few blocks from the Martin home. A brown man in the middle of a posh neighborhood in Hollywood was unacceptable. After being bailed out of jail, he fled and started frequenting the bars of Los Angeles. Elizabeth Martin searched for him and finally a taxi picked him up and deposited Ira at Martin's front door. He did not want the children to see him in that state. Once again, he was checked into a sanitarium to take the cure. Elizabeth and the children wanted him to continue working for them. Martin herself was a tremendously tolerant and forgiving person for whom Ira had a great amount of respect. "I will do anything I can to help him," she said.

Within a week, a friend asked Ira to attend a football game. He went and disappeared. Elizabeth Martin went looking for him once again and found him at the friend's house, recovering from a bout with alcohol. He ran when she tried to talk him into coming home. Finally, the police arrested him and sent for Betty. The court offered him a choice: going to jail or returning to Arizona. At that, Martin had to admit that Ira had broken her trust and would be better off back in Bapchule with his family. Martin reluctantly paid for his bus ticket back home, despite her willingness to "do anything I can to help him." [31] Betty Martin was torn between her philanthropic feelings and her pragmatic judgment. [32]

Hayes expressed both his remorse and his gratitude to the Martins. "They all liked me out there," he said. "The kids always wanted me to play with them and I used to take them for rides in the car." [33] After his first arrest in Los Angeles, he begged Betty Martin, "Please don't let the children see me." [34] A reporter for the *Tacoma News Tribune* was one of the few who came to Ira's defense, writing, "If his disease were cancer, heart trouble, or tuberculosis, he would be more understood." [35]

Ira boarded the bus back to the reservation. Unlike most true alcoholics, he admitted that he had a problem and that the problem centered on his bingeing. Under the heading "Saddened Ira Hayes Comes Home" in the *Tucson Citizen*, Ira stated to reporters upon his arrival in Phoenix:

> I guess I'm just no good. I've had a lot of chances. But just when things start looking good, I get that craving for whiskey and foul up...Maybe after I'm around my family awhile, I will be able to figure things out. Maybe I'll join Alcoholics Anonymous. [36]

As the article heading indicated, Ira's homecoming was hardly a joyous occasion. The loss of the job in the Martin household affected him deeply. On top of his numerous other emotional and social difficulties, he now thought of himself as a failure. He shouldered the blame, which made his PTSD much worse. Despondency was by then part of his psychological makeup.

The Chicago and Los Angeles arrests and job losses sparked a spate of newspaper articles about Ira's drinking. To his great shame his name was now associated with Iwo Jima *and* alcoholism. On the ninth of November, even before he was sent home from California, the *Akron Beacon Journal* carried a story titled "Reluctant Hero." The writer interviewed Keyes Beech, the Marine who accompanied Bradley, Gagnon, and Ira on the Mighty Seventh Tour in 1945. The article commented on The Photograph and added that it "started Ira Hayes on his slide from hero to Skid Row bum." Beech pronounced that Ira "drank to escape," which was partially correct, and the correspondent asked the question, "Must the story end there—with Hayes continuing on as a drunken bum until he finally drinks himself to death?" Beech was also quoted as saying, "I'll always remember him for being what he was—a damned good Marine," as if Ira were already dead. Finally, the writer ended the story with a plea posed as a question. "Why not," the correspondent wrote, "rehabilitate Hayes and send him back to the job he liked best—that of being a 'damned good Marine.'" [37]

Although the wording of the article was harsh, it made a point. Perhaps Ira should have stayed in the service. He was a corporal and had no doubt had what Marines called a "shipping-over" lecture with his immediate commanding officer. He probably would have been promoted to sergeant, and by the time the

Korean War came five years later he might very well have been a gunnery sergeant. Why he did not "ship over" is a good question. Perhaps he simply wanted to go home to his family. But from another perspective, the commandant's prejudice in removing Ira from the Mighty Seventh Tour could have lingered. Perhaps Ira was discouraged from reenlisting because he was, to quote Commandant Vandegrift in 1945, "your Indian."

A few days later, Dick Spencer, who described himself as a "burned-up ex-Marine," wrote a letter to the editor of the *Beacon Journal* decrying the use of "drunken bum" in its November 9 article. To Spencer, Hayes was "no drunken bum." It was likely that Spencer shared with Ira the memories of combat and the survivor's guilt that tormented the minds of so many Marine veterans of the Pacific war. After recalling Ira's heroics through the war, Spencer called the correspondent a "bum." Spencer's words probably echoed the thoughts of a good number of angry veterans who fought and saw one of their own take the blame for his undeserved downfall. [38]

On the same day that Spencer's letter was published, another rather angry letter concerning Ira appeared in the *Tucson Citizen*. Mrs. Glenn G. Hays, head of the National Women's Christian Temperance Union, was quoted as saying, "The alcoholic plight" that Ira suffered "is symbolic of what is happening to American Indians" since Congress had legalized the sale of alcohol to Native peoples. She stated unequivocally that the government had "handed the Indians bottled suicide." The blame for Ira's problems did not rest on his shoulders. An editorial in the *Tacoma News Tribune* declared that Ira was a "sick man" who would be "pitied" if he were suffering from cancer. Ira, the papers reiterated, was "fighting a constant war against the habit." [39]

Given the publicity of Ira's arrests, it is little wonder that he more or less hid himself away on the reservation. Sadly, he began bingeing again. When he went into Phoenix the police were on the lookout for him. So were the reporters. Between November and the New Year of 1954, he was arrested several times, every one on a drunk-and-disorderly charge. Ira's anger and depression and bingeing continued into the new year. In January and February, he was arrested on two drunk-and-disorderly charges. [40] Both arrests were reported in newspapers across the country. Even when family members did something to attract the attention of the press, Ira's name was mentioned. When his brother was involved in a car wreck, the article automatically announced that Kenneth was the brother of Ira Hayes. Had it not been Kenneth Hayes, the incident probably would not have made the news. [41]

After the February stint in jail, Ira's indulging in alcohol was the subject of a good deal of debate. A Los Angeles man wanted to have Ira "placed in his custody." He would provide a "good home and help him master an inclination to drink." [42] The man, whose name was not given, displayed an almost overwhelming sense of arrogance and privilege that existed in 1950s America in asking that Ira be remanded to his "custody." In any case, after his February arrest, Ira voluntarily joined Alcoholics Anonymous. For doing so, the judge in the case put Ira on probation and under the supervision of the AA organization. [43]

Even though there were no further newspaper columns announcing another arrest, Ira was not forgotten. A few people still remembered Ira with respect and even admiration. In June, the famous syndicated columnist Dorothy Kilgallen devoted an entire editorial to educating Americans about the disastrous effects frontier expansion had had on Native Americans. She singled out Ira Hayes as an American hero to demonstrate that Native cultures were worth more than how they had been depicted in film. Indians were not, in Kilgallen's mind, the incorrigible savages as shown on movie screens but responsible citizens of different, but worthwhile, cultures. [44]

In the same newspaper, the *Arizona Republic*, a letter to the editor pointed out that Ira was a true American hero and merited more than a simple pat on the back. The writer asked whether or not the government and the public had done enough to help Ira. He wrote, "Did we throw in the sponge too quickly?" Moreover, "Should we permit the stigma of his 'sprees' to continue?" The writer was warning readers that the public was attempting to force Ira into obscurity. [45] By the time the Marine Corps War Memorial was dedicated, Ira was employed as a warehouseman with the Bureau of Indian Affairs. Alcoholics Anonymous was apparently working.

But then on November 10, 1954, the Marine Corps birthday, Ira was once again in the news. On that day, Felix de Weldon's gigantic statue of the Rosenthal picture was dedicated as the Marine Corps War Memorial in Arlington, Virginia. Rene Gagnon, Jack Bradley, and Ira were pictured together as they listened to the remarks made by de Weldon, President Dwight D. Eisenhower, and several other dignitaries. The commandant of the Marine Corps officially presented the memorial to the American people and Vice President Richard M. Nixon gave the dedicatory speech. [46]

The three supposed flag raisers were pictured in papers across the country once again. None of the three looked like the men who, ten years before, smiled for the public in the Mighty Seventh War Bond Tour. Rene, once the "poor man's Tyrone Power," seemed dour and withdrawn. Jack Bradley appeared older than his actual age of thirty-two. Ira also looked much older than his real age. His face was puffy and frowning. He bore the scars of his automobile accident on his nose, forehead, and upper lip. He looked much older than his thirty-one years. [47] Within two months, Ira belatedly joined his buddies who wrestled the second flag into position on Suribachi, Harlon Block, Mike Strank, and Franklin Sousley, in death. He was the only true survivor of the photograph out of the three men so honored. Long after Ira's death, diligent researchers would discover that Rene Gagnon and Jack Bradley were not in The Photograph. Two other survivors of that image were unknown and unrecognized by the public. Their identities would not be discovered until much later. And by then, all of those who really pushed that flag erect had passed away. And following Ira's passing, another American tumult would arise over alcoholism, mental health, and the honoring of a hero.

Chapter 9

"He Won't Answer Anymore" [1]

They found Ira, according to his death certificate, a mile west of St. Peter's Mission, near Bapchule. [2] In other accounts he was lying near an abandoned adobe house and in a creek bed. His death was announced in newspapers from coast to coast, and he lay in state in the Arizona capitol rotunda. He was in uniform with his corporal's stripes, parachutist's badge, sharpshooter's medal, and ribbons pinned on his chest.

Almost immediately after his body was discovered there arose a controversy over the cause of Ira's death. Most of the newspapers that announced his death as front-page news recounted that his autopsy report stated that he had died of exposure and alcohol poisoning. [3] Today, hypothermia would replace exposure as a cause of death. The *Arizona Republic* reported that the low temperature for January 24, the day of Ira's death, was twenty-nine degrees, or three degrees below freezing. [4] It might very well have been a few degrees lower out on the desert near Bapchule.

As a cause of death, hypothermia means that the body's core temperature drops below ninety-five degrees Fahrenheit. The victim first feels cold and shivers in the effort to raise his or her

197

internal temperature. Shortly thereafter, the sufferer becomes disoriented and even feels hot. The body attempts to protect the brain, heart, and lungs and draws blood from the extremities, causing numbness in the arms and legs. Sometimes, the feeling of being hot causes the victim to remove clothing. Once under the ninety-five-degree core temperature, though, the victim soon falls into a coma, and death eventually follows unless some kind of treatment against the cold is rendered. A person can die within minutes if the temperature is extreme or if certain other factors are involved in the process of hypothermia. Water also can exacerbate the chilling effect because it tends to disperse the body's heat faster than air. Strangely enough, alcohol poisoning has almost the same symptoms. The body loses heat and confusion sets in, followed by coma and death. Alcohol in the system also quickens the effects of hypothermia. Ira probably did not die in pain. After he left a card game, he may have simply lain down to sleep off the effects of the cheap wine all the card-players had drunk, and died in a hypothermic coma.

Apparently, the physician who wrote up the death certificate had a very different idea about why Ira had died than he led the newspapers to believe. Dr. John Parks, who filled out the death certificate, told the *Arizona Daily Star* reporter that Ira had indeed died of exposure and the "over-consumption" of alcohol. On the death certificate, Parks had written that the cause of death was "asphyxia from aspiration of stomach contents into trachea and bronchi" due to "acute alcoholism." In other words, Dr. Parks clearly specified that Ira's death was accidental and was caused by choking on or drowning in his own vomit. He also indicated that Ira vomited while "comatosed" (*sic*). Likely, the doctor was also reading into the death that Ira was an alcoholic because of the recent news coverage of his public drunkenness. An autopsy was supposedly performed but must have been most perfunctory in that Ira's body was discovered in the early morning hours of the twenty-fourth of February and the death certificate was signed on the twenty-seventh. That did not allow much time for a toxicology screening, although presumably Parks had examined Ira's trachea and lungs. Again, Dr. Parks might well have been influenced by Ira's reported alcoholism. In his statement to the press, John Parks had it reasonably correct. Ira died of "exposure" or hypothermia complicated by alcohol consumption, although just how much alcohol was in Ira's system was never determined. [5]

At first, Ira's brothers Kenneth and Vernon had a different idea regarding their brother's death. They asserted that Ira attended a card game and drank some cheap muscatel wine, which has a relatively low alcohol content compared to other alcoholic beverages like tequila, bourbon, or vodka. Ira became engaged in an altercation with Henry Setoyant, another Akimel O'odham citizen. As Kenneth and Vernon saw it, the fight led to a battered Ira wandering off into the night and eventually becoming disoriented. He fell, went to sleep, and died. The Hayes brothers' allegations of manslaughter came to nothing. Ira's death was ruled accidental. [6]

Betty Binner Nash, a Native American writer from Great Falls, Montana, stated boldly that "Ira Hayes was murdered." His death was the result of the white man plying him with liquor in celebration of Ira's heroism. Nash evidently supported some level of temperance for Native peoples. She wrote that because the Akimel O'odham made a saguaro wine, they were "not tee-totalers." But there was a law against selling Indians alcohol that the white people consistently ignored and the PXs on military installations disregarded. Ira attended dinners and parties in his honor where he was offered drinks, and when he was in Hollywood making *The Sands of Iwo Jima* there were even more parties and even more drinks. "We know," she wrote, "alcoholics are sick mentally. They are escaping from life." Nash made a final assertion that Ira's drinking was more or less a way to escape and sleep the drunkenness off. She wrote, "He was a soft spoken, sleepy Indian. He died in one of those drunken sleeps. That is why I say he was murdered." [7] Betty Nash was probably correct in saying that Ira died in his sleep. The Women's Christian Temperance Union even invoked Ira's name in an advertisement taken out in the *Wakefield* (NE) *Republican* that ended in the call to "Support Total Abstinence." [8]

In Hayes' death, the media saw a story of both triumph and tragedy. It was a triumph in Ira's participation in the Iwo Jima campaign and a tragedy that he brought upon himself. It was also a message of human frailty. Ira even testified to that frailty. He testified that he seemed drawn to the bottle, despite all the help he had been given. [9] Ironically, Ira had taken the first step in Alcoholics Anonymous' twelve-step program by the admission that he needed alcohol to get through his mental state. He had stated over and over again that the war had affected him deeply. He once said, "We hit the beach with 250 men in my company and left with 27 a month and a half later...I still think about those things all the time." [10] That declaration alone served to reveal his state of mind, and his "combat neurosis" or PTSD.

A good deal of guilt and verbal breast-beating over Ira's death filled the newspapers of the day. One editorial from a New York paper was especially interested in spreading the blame to the general public. The government and public had blithely ignored their "obligation to a war hero, that through callous treatment of Indians or through plain neglect or social indifference they did not come to Ira Hayes' help when he needed it." Native Americans "regarded him as the modern example of their races' legendary warrior virtues." On the other hand, the white world asks veterans to put away thoughts about what they had been through. That was why, the columnist explained, "the history of Ira Hayes may explain why so many decorated veterans put away their medals and do not encourage conversation about them." [11]

Another column in another newspaper stated unequivocally that the public and government officials only "cared about the symbol" that was Rosenthal's photograph. Ira and his fellow Marines were secondary to the overwhelming symbolism of the photograph, for it depicted not only victory in war but also unity of purpose that overshadowed ethnic and social differences. [12]

In the same vein another reporter, Charles Lucey, thought of Ira's death as a cost of warfare. War was "a maiming of human souls." According to Lucey, Ira was, quoting another source, "a hero to everyone but himself," and "maybe we need to look harder on what is done on the human and spiritual side for the young men who come back from the foxholes." [13] To Lucey, the war was left unfinished—it was not over until those who fought it were healed of the trauma along with the social problems they had acquired in deadly combat. What went unrecognized was that while the emotional damages were not as bad as the physical wounds the veterans received, they were both serious and long-lasting nonetheless.

These editorials summed up the angst over Ira's untimely death. The public reaction to the accusation that Ira had been let down in his time of need led to the renewal of an effort to push a serious anti-alcoholism bill through the Arizona state senate. It likely stemmed from a need to assuage the white man's guilt as well.

Within a few days of Ira's death, Arizona state senator William A. Sullivan of Gila County announced that he was introducing Senate Bill 78 to establish an "Alcoholic Commission" ostensibly to fight "one of the most vicious diseases that afflicts mankind." He called for an initial appropriation of $30,000, a fair sum in those days, to use science to determine the causes and treatments for alcoholism. It was to be less a religious cause than one that would, in theory, treat alcoholism as a disease. [14]

On January 30, 1955, columnist Clayborne Nuckolls wrote an extensive review of Sullivan's proposed Alcoholic Commission. Sullivan was a Democrat, likely of the New Deal persuasion, who believed that government on some level could indeed provide answers to social and economic problems. The senator was very clear that had the state "had such a bill two years ago or even a year ago, I am confident that Ira Hayes would be with us today." [15]

Sullivan wanted to title his bill the Ira Hayes Memorial Act, should it be passed. At the time, two other bills that invoked Ira's name were under consideration in the Arizona legislature. One was a resolution to permit Ira's body to lie in state in the capitol. It passed easily. The other was a bill that would appropriate the funds to erect a copy of the sculpture of the Iwo Jima flag raising that had just been dedicated in Washington two months previously. It was to be called "The Ira Hayes Memorial." According to columnist Clayborne Nuckolls, "All Arizona and the nation was saddened last week at the tragic death of Ira Hayes...and the...sad part about it was that these gestures came only after his death." Nuckolls favored the notion that an agency should be created to diagnose, cure, rehabilitate, and offer guidance to those afflicted with the disease. But he appeared to be somewhat critical of a certain amount of political cynicism calculated to produce an outcome based on the national shame over Ira's death. [16]

Sullivan had introduced the idea twice before, but he felt that Ira's story could be used to "pinpoint what a real problem alcoholism poses." But Sullivan's bill and the resolution to build a replica of the Marine Corps War Memorial ultimately failed. The Sullivan bill was likely doomed from its very introduction even though it was decidedly within the public good. Sullivan argued that there were twelve thousand "confirmed" alcoholics in Maricopa County alone. The state capital and Arizona's largest city, Phoenix, was located in Maricopa County. Not only that, but the plan had been "well-thought-out" and designed to save lives and "make useful, self-respecting citizens who are now burdens on society." The foretold failure of Sullivan's Ira Hayes Memorial Bill came because of a "natural reluctance" to spend money and a "disinclination" to add to the already established government agencies. Taxpayer groups, according to the newspapers, would surely oppose the plan. [17]

The Sullivan bill was more or less a temperance measure with an overlay of science rather than moralism. The notion that alcoholism could or should be handled by an agency of its own, rather than charging law enforcement with rounding up drunks and throwing them in jail, was quite innovative for the time. But in the mid-twentieth century, alcoholism was still considered a problem of individual responsibility and moral rectitude. It was easier to think of it as a problem of the degenerate few who could not control their desires, so a way of handling the problem was not clearly thought out. As such, people with alcohol addiction were threats to society and not worth spending vast amounts of money on. It was considered a problem of law enforcement. Even the building of free flophouses for the addicted would have been less expensive than locking up chronic alcoholics and binge drinkers. What seems to be involved in the thinking on the matter was the fear that brown and black people might create mayhem when white drunks would not.

Meanwhile, it was time to bury Ira Hayes. The first leg of Ira's last journey began at the Presbyterian church in Sacaton. Around two thousand people crowded into and around the small church. There were American flags hung from the altar. At two p.m. the church bell rang, and six Marine reservists carried in Ira's casket. A color guard from the Mathew Juan American Legion post of Chandler followed. When the casket was placed in front of the altar, the choir sang two hymns, and the Reverend Roe B. Lewis of the Phoenix Indian Presbyterian Church gave the opening prayer. After that, Reverend Esau Joseph gave the eulogy. He spoke in both Akimel O'odham and English. "On foreign soil," he said, "Ira Hayes bravely performed his duty. When he enlisted, he told his parents he was fighting for them—to insure their freedom...But he fought for all of us. He battled on our behalf." [18]

As was customary, the congregation inched forward to express their condolences to the family, passed by the open casket, and filed outside. The pallbearers carried Ira's casket outside to a waiting hearse to be taken to the Arizona capitol in Phoenix. The newly sworn-in governor, Ernest W. McFarland, was there to meet the cortege.

The ceremony at the capitol rotunda was appropriately solemn and rigidly timed. Several veterans' organization representatives and color guards had already formed on the capitol lawn. Ira's body was brought under the dome, Governor McFarland laid a wreath, and Reverend Lewis gave the benediction. Outside, a rifle squad stood ready to fire the salute. Governor

McFarland had requested that all Arizonans observe a moment of silence at precisely 3:15 p.m. At that moment, the squad fired the salute, the colors were retired, and taps was sounded. [19] Hundreds of Arizonans passed by the open casket, and someone surreptitiously snapped a photograph of Ira's body from the upper level of the building. [20]

Ira was taken by train to Washington, D.C., for interment in Arlington National Cemetery. A fund to help the family defray the cost of the trip was established. On February 2, the body bearers, color guard, and rifle squad from the Marine barracks took over the rites for Ira's burial. The weather was fitting that day: cold wind, sleet, and snow on the ground. The burial detail wore their green uniforms with raincoats. They slipped in the icy snow because of the metal cleats on their shoes. [21]

The funeral first took place at the Fort Myer chapel. The casket was carried to the burial site. Ira's mother and father watched the precision with which the body bearers, as they are called, made the twelve folds in the flag that covered Ira's casket. The officer in charge took the folded flag and handed it off to the then commandant of the Marine Corps, General Lemuel Shepherd Jr. The general slowly walked to Nancy Hayes, gave her Ira's flag, and said in an undertone, "You have every reason to be justly proud of your son who is immortalized in the great statue that stands close by." [22] Shepherd, of course, was referring to the Marine Corps War Memorial that had been dedicated just a few months before. Rene Gagnon was present at the funeral along with the secretary of the interior and his assistant secretary. The commissioner of the Bureau of Indian Affairs, Glenn L. Emmons, was also present. Ira's death and interment also provoked a renewed call for a probe into Indian policy, which would have meant that Emmons would be under scrutiny as well. [23]

After the Arlington ceremonies, the use of Ira's name to promote causes arose a few more times. An organization that went by the name Arrow, Inc. hoped to raise money and awareness of Native issues. Among its board of directors were Thomas Segundo, a former tribal chair of the Tohono O'odham Nation, then called the Papago Tribe, Will Rogers Jr., actor and son of the Cherokee humorist Will Rogers, and Ernest L. Wilkinson, then president of Brigham Young University and legal advocate for Native American tribes and nations. Arrow, Inc. called itself "a charitable organization in using the death of Ira Hayes, the Arizona Indian hero, to keynote a fund drive for Indian reservations." The group worked with the National Congress of American Indians to "train Indian leaders and improve conditions on the more backward reservations." According to a *New York Times* article that ran the story of Arrow, Inc., and quoted in the *Arizona Republic*, there was a decided need for improved education and health conditions on the reservations. "Ira Hayes," the *Times* concluded, "is not an isolated case among American Indians. He was one of almost half-million first Americans in our country today. They have been dispossessed, exploited, neglected, and forgotten." [24]

In May, a veterans' organization made up of World War II and Korean War veterans renamed their Phoenix post in honor of Ira. In 1944, veterans formed the World War II American Veterans organization to aid returning servicemen in securing benefits from the federal government. Korean War veterans were later added to the membership, and the organization grew in size and in influence. Chapters were started up, and each of them attempted to aid their members, other veterans, and their dependents in gaining benefits guaranteed under the G.I. Bill of Rights. The Phoenix chapter adopted Ira's name to promote the notion that it was a self-help, nonpartisan organization rather than a type of veterans' club. [25]

In Los Angeles, a citizens' committee led by Princess Tsianina, described in the news as the daughter of a Cherokee chief, was organized to establish the Ira Hayes Foundation. The board of the new association promised "a new approach to the American Indian problem." The foundation was to be built on a one-off and off-the-wall form of funding. On occasion, Princess Tsianina had been able to raise funds for a different organization by asking for donations in Indian head nickels. It worked well at the time, and she began asking for the same kind of donation. She promised that the Ira Hayes Foundation funding would be a voluntary enterprise rather than "government paternalism." She hoped to make Iwo Jima Day every February 23 a recurring tribute to "Ira's willingness to serve the United States." The column also mentioned Kenneth Hayes, Ira's younger brother, who was wounded in Korea. Princess Tsianina also envisaged that the foundation would acquire enough funds to buy property in Arizona or New Mexico to establish a trade school for Ira's people to open on the next Iwo Jima Day in 1956. "Let's start," she stated, "a different trend on the Indian question, on the basis of humanity." Sadly, she was unable to realize her dreams for a "different trend" in Native American affairs. [26]

The honors and monuments continued to come, and the exploitation of Ira's name to promote events, organizations, and credos lasted for months after his death. Since his death, a number of Christian groups, especially women's clubs and service organizations, took up the cause of improving Native American conditions. It appeared that Ira's story was an integral part of each of these meetings because it tended to demonstrate that no matter how many honors a person received, there was always the possibility of a tragic turn of fortune. Organizations like the Christian Women's Fellowship, the Wesleyan Service Guild, the Women's Society of Christian Service, and the Presbyterian Women's Association were affiliated with particular Protestant sects. Much like the Christian reformers of nearly one hundred years before, they advocated education, sobriety, and fundamental Christian teachings to solve the "Indian problem."

In their righteous passion to "uplift the Indian," Ira Hayes' name was invoked many times. As a speaker at a meeting of the Presbyterian Women's group in August of 1955 stated emphatically, "Ira Hayes, hero of Iwo Jima, died an alcoholic because he could not understand being made a hero one day and being discriminated against on another." Another rose to say, "The only hope for the Indian is the church...Jesus can make up for the deceit and broken promises made by our government to our Indian brothers." [27] Little was offered at any of these meetings in terms of policy direction or economic relief for impoverished tribes like the Akimel O'odham, who were still seeking to regain their water rights.

The Christian zeal in trying to pursue an Indian policy based on their interpretation of the Bible made the news all over the U.S. It was, for the most part, a very religious period in American history. The rhetoric at the meetings of the Christian Women's Fellowship, the Women's Christian Temperance Union (WCTU), and the Women's Society of Christian Service was pitched upward from a message of hope to a righteous crusade. In June of 1956, Nettie Griswold conducted a meeting of the WCTU in Canton, Pennsylvania, and reviewed positively a piece about Ira entitled "From Glory to the Gutter." [28] Although perhaps moving to the members of the WCTU, Griswold's talk presented an image of the "drunken Indian" that had yet to be cast away.

While the Christian groups were waging a futile and stereotypical campaign to reform Indian policy, a meeting of Akimel
O'odham mothers of veterans took place to establish a service
organization of their own. They met in October of 1955 and
decided to become a part of the national Blue Star Mothers of
America. Founded in 1942, the association was made up of mothers and grandmothers of sons and daughters serving in the military during the war. The "Blue Star" was based on the small flag
that families of servicemen hung in their windows to demonstrate
their patriotism and contributions to the war effort. The Blue
Star Mothers continued after the war to serve returning veterans
and aid them in securing their rights under the G.I. Bill. Because
there were so many Akimel O'odham mothers of service members, a chapter of the Blue Star Mothers on the reservation was
thought to be a practical way to present a united voice in service
to their sons and daughters. Ira Hayes' death actually impelled
the mothers to organize. They named their group the Ira Hayes
Chapter. Their group was recognized by the national organization and Nellie Leonhard, the national Blue Star Mothers president, came to Sacaton to install the Ira Hayes Chapter's fourteen
officers and grant the chapter national recognition. [29]

A few days after the anniversary of Ira's passing, the Akimel
O'odham gathered at Bapchule to honor his memory. They
erected a flagpole and set up a plaque in front of the Presbyterian church aided by the Marine Corps Reserve's color guard. In
October, a larger ceremony was held at the church to present a
flag to Nancy Hayes by the mayor of Chandler, Bert Lewis, and
the Matthew B. Juan American Legion Post. At that ceremony,
the Reverend Ralph Wheeler, chaplain of the post, announced
that they were completing a project that would establish a veterans' cemetery named after Ira. Nancy thanked the American

Legion post and the mayor, and said that her son "never felt worthy of the national recognition, insisting that all the boys serving at all the fronts of the world were the real heroes." [30]

As with just about everything that Ira faced in life after climbing Mount Suribachi, and even after his death, the Rosenthal picture overshadowed it all. His death brought about a renewed interest in The Photograph. No one could possibly have missed seeing it. It had turned into a gigantic monument, rivaling in size and artistry nearly every statue in the environs of Washington, D.C., at the time. But there was still something troubling about it. Some people still questioned whether or not it was staged. And Ira himself had questioned the identification of one member of the team who lifted the flag into place. As it turned out, he likely could have questioned the identity of others in the picture.

Despite the widespread acceptance of Rosenthal's picture, there were obviously questions still left. Columnist Westbrook Pegler went looking for a story and found Jack Bradley. Pegler's column made papers all over the U.S. In Tucson, his headline read, "Flag Raising Was a Retake," and in Shreveport, Louisiana, the headline stated, "Famed Picture of Iwo Jima Flag Raising Was Framed by Photographer." The meaning of the headline could have been interpreted in two ways. In the first, Rosenthal set the whole thing up and staged the picture. The other idea was that Rosenthal took the picture of the second flag raising and more or less took away the heroic meaning of the first. [31]

Rosenthal never tried to promote the picture as *the* flag raising and had actually taken the picture on the spur of the moment. But Pegler's interview with Bradley did raise another doubt about who was actually part of the party that raised the flag. Bradley denied taking part in the first flag raising. He did name the six men. According to Bradley, they were Henry Hansen, Franklin

Sousley, Mike Strank, Rene Gagnon, Ira Hayes, and himself. By 1956, though, Harlon Block, as Ira indicated in 1945, had replaced Hansen as the Marine guiding the pole among the rocks on the mountain's summit. The truth about the Rosenthal photograph was settled by Bill Genaust's film of the flag raising. In it, Ira can be seen as coming forth, gripping the long pole with both hands, putting his weight on it so as to drive it into the ground, and smiling as others held it in place with him. Other Marines were seen in the film gathering rocks to place at the base of the flagpole to steady it. It was not until 2019 that it was discovered that Bradley and Gagnon were not in The Photograph. They had been replaced officially by Harold Schultz and Harold Keller, both members of Easy Company who had been unsung for so many years. [32] Ira knew but kept mum, except in the case of his good friend Harlon Block. He was either silenced by higher authorities, as he was in the case of Harlon, or he simply did not want to expose Rene or Jack. Whatever the case, Ira was loyal to the end.

There was another secret that few knew about surrounding Ira's death. At the time Ira's body was being prepared for his funeral, a woman named Hortense Johnson surreptitiously entered the funeral home and took a plaster cast of Ira's face. She told her immediate family and friends that she wanted to create a bust of Ira in his memory. She did not follow through with her plan. After her death, her husband passed the mask along to a family friend name Shirley Nelson in Yuma. Nelson, in turn, gave it to Navajo artist Robert Yellowhair in the 1980s. Yellowhair turned the mask over to a Native art and jewelry dealer named Gilbert Ortega Sr., who installed it in what became the Ortega Museum in Scottsdale, Arizona. Yellowhair claimed that he gave the mask to the senior Ortega on consignment and that it was therefore his to use as he saw fit. Gilbert Ortega Jr. inherited the museum and its contents. Gilbert Jr. finally gave it to Kenneth Hayes, Ira's brother, in 2009.

Larry Cook, Ira's great-nephew, and his wife, Sharon, explained that the mask was an object that should have been buried with their relative. Sharon Cook indicated that in Akimel O'odham traditions something that close or representative of Ira should be treated as part of him. "Ira's body was never sent to rest," she said. Larry Cook reiterated his wife's feelings. "Ira's spirit is not totally rested," he stated. The family thanked Ortega and took the mask to the graveyard where Ira's parents were interred. Kenneth broke it into several pieces and buried it in an unmarked place. Ira's spirit could finally rest after fifty-four years. [33]

Chapter 10

Hollywood Calls Again

Ira had been interred for less than a month when well-known author William Bradford Huie came to the reservation to ask the Hayes family for access to Ira's letters. [1] Huie had several books under his belt, including *The Revolt of Mamie Stover* (1951) and *The Execution of Private Slovik* (1954), and many articles in major journals and magazines. He wrote about military matters and history and was doing some investigative reporting on the need for social and civil justice for African Americans. At the time he was visiting the reservation, he had written a manuscript that would be published the next year about the injustice suffered by Ruby McCollum, an African American woman who shot and killed her white rapist, for which she was convicted of murder and sentenced to death. Later, several of Huie's books would be made into films, including his biography of Ira.

Huie has been called a "checkbook" journalist. In other words, he paid for his access to those who had actually been part of or had seen a newsworthy event. In the 1950s it was sort of a derogatory term, implying that a journalist was paying for a story rather than doing his or her investigating homework. The stories that Huie wrote, on the other hand, were all about society's injustice to human beings, in particular people of color. He also wrote about war and the human cost of war. His writings were critical of the military and of the bigotry in American society. So if he paid people to tell their stories, he was doing some service to social justice. [2]

Ira's story was printed in Huie's 1959 book *Wolf Whistle*. The lead story in that particular volume was about the lynching of Emmett Till by members of the Ku Klux Klan. Huie died in 1985. In 2021, Jill Collen Jefferson, writing for the *Mississippi Free Press* blog, indicated that Huie could possibly have been prosecuted as an accessory after the fact in Emmett Till's murder. Huie had interviewed the killers and concealed, Jefferson argued, the identities of some of those who took part in the crime. [3]

Whether or not he was a conspirator or criminal or just sloppy, Huie's writings covered many years and many subjects. He became linked to writings on the civil rights movement beginning with his book on Ruby McCollum and continuing through his works on the murders of Emmett Till, Martin Luther King Jr., and James Chaney, Andrew Goodman, and Michael Schwerner in Mississippi.

The Execution of Private Slovik was Huie's study of bureaucratic injustice in the United States military. The book was to be made into a film in the 1950s but was shelved for a time because it was thought to be too controversial. Huie made an enemy of President Dwight Eisenhower because he confirmed, as the commander of the Allied Forces in Europe, the order to execute by firing squad Private Eddie Slovik. Frank Sinatra, who held the rights to the book, later sold them to Universal Television productions. The book was picked up as a made-for-television movie. It aired on March 13, 1974, on NBC.

By the time Huie's *Wolf Whistle* was published in 1959, he was well known in Hollywood. His book *The Revolt of Mamie Stover* was made into a film in 1956 and enjoyed solid reviews and was a top box office hit, largely because of its famous director, Raoul Walsh, and its star, Jane Russell. Apparently, Hollywood at the time would not touch his story about the lynching of Emmett Till, but Ira's biography was something else. Huie's version of Ira's story, then titled "Our Torture Execution of Marine Hero Ira Hayes," was picked up by a major studio within two years after its publication in *Cavalier*, a magazine that began in 1952 to publish various kinds of stories and would later turn into one of the numerous *Playboy* imitators. After the story was printed in *Wolf Whistle*, it captured the attention of Hollywood. Universal-International took up the distribution rights and hired Delbert Mann to direct the film. Tony Curtis was selected to play Ira. [4] It is interesting to note that while Hollywood would not touch the Emmett Till or the Ruby McCollum stories, studio executives wanted a story about a Native American. Of course, to them the Hayes story was about a fall from grace and not about equality in the justice system.

Huie's story of Ira's life actually set the tone of later books about Ira. It also set the tone for the film. Huie's book, although it managed to depict Ira as a sympathetic figure, was an attempt to get at the heart of his biography. It must be remembered that in Huie's time, PTSD was not really a known condition as much as it was an outcome of grief. Alcoholism was a known disorder, but its origins in individual people were generally thought to be either a result of a genetic predisposition to drink or the outcome of personal emotional problem like grief, isolation, anger, or a need to forget the tragedies and calumnies in an individual's life. Social drinking was considered almost harmless. Most everyone could agree that it was a disease, but whether of moral turpitude or of physical addiction was not all that well recognized at the time. After all, the failure of Prohibition had happened only about twenty years before. Up until then, people in law enforcement were trying to keep alcohol under control.

Huie was certain that alcoholism was an addiction of both the mind and the body, or at least that is what his biography of Ira indicated. In opening Ira's story, Huie wrote:

> The Japanese didn't kill Ira Hayes. We killed him. We didn't intend to kill him. We tried to help him. How we killed our Indian hero of Iwo Jima is one of the meaningful stories of our time. [5]

Ultimately, Ira was a victim of wrongful government policies, rapacious white settlers stealing Akimel O'odham water, and ignorance of Native cultures.

Huie had free access to Ira's letters. Huie tells a story of an intelligent young man, born and raised in the poverty of the reservation, who goes to war with a good heart and an indomitable spirit. Huie found that Ira was not really the introvert and loner that the press and subsequent biographies had painted him to be. In one letter, Ira wrote, "Our drill instructors are swell," meaning that he must have been doing something right and was capable of the physical training he was going through. His athleticism and his lighthearted, self-deprecating humor came through in another letter asking his mother to "tell Leonard [his brother] to take my place on the football team" and "tell Kenny not to hang around girls like I did." [6] The tough fighting of Bougainville and Iwo Jima did not break his sense of duty and of integrity. According to Huie, Ira did not participate in the mutilation of Japanese corpses or any one of a number of gruesome battlefield practices that the whites took part in, like putting enemy skulls on stakes or popping out gold teeth from the dead Japanese soldiers that seemed to pile up wherever Ira fought. Huie explained that an Akimel O'odham elder told Ira personally that the white people were "movers." That was to say they, unlike the Akimel O'odham, did not love the place where they lived and wanted to move constantly. The elder equated "mover" with conqueror, because a conqueror had to displace the peoples whose territories they coveted for themselves. Conquest, by its very nature, to the Akimel O'odham was evil. Evil was in the hearts of movers and so they could commit evil deeds like the mutilation and the decapitation of other people. War happened, but true warriors had to maintain virtuous behavior. [7]

Ira's battle with alcohol was very different. He became fast friends with several fellow Marines. He was proud to be a Marine. But according to Huie, Ira missed the friends that he made in boot camp when he went to parachutist training. He became part of an elite unit and got an extra fifty dollars a month for hazardous duty. After Bougainville, the parachute battalions were disbanded, and he lost the extra pay that was part of the funds he sent home to his parents. After Ira became an Iwo Jima flag raiser and an American hero, it seemed that the most important way of showing appreciation for his valor was to give him a watch and drink a toast to him. In American culture, toasting went along with drinking alcohol. And it appeared that drinking followed the "the hero of Iwo Jima" around like a stalking panther. Even the young men back home on the reservation, according to Huie, called anyone who declined a drink a "chicken." [8]

Huie's analysis of Ira's drinking, although inaccurate to a

certain extent, nevertheless contributed to the overall feeling that Ira was completely helpless. But Huie also indicated that the theft of Akimel O'odham water was the real underlying culprit in Ira's decline. If he had had the means to become a well-off grower of wheat and cotton, perhaps Ira would not have fallen into what became a wino culture. In fact, Huie stated unequivocally that Phoenix and its environs was the "winter wino capital." [9] Wino culture essentially meant binge drinking after a grueling week in the fields or performing odd, low-paying, and tedious jobs. The fact that Phoenix wino culture mostly encompassed migrant workers and indigenous people cast a racist pall over it. The police were, from all accounts of the time, simply looking for brown and black bodies to put into jail on drunk-and-disorderly charges. At the same time, white drunks were handed citations and set free.

Pitifully, Ira wrote in December 1954 to his benefactor Betty Martin that he had been in the Phoenix "brig" (the Marine Corps term for "jail") three time since he left Los Angeles. In the letter Ira wrote about a Maricopa County "rest home" Huie called the "Camino de Winos" run by a recovering alcoholic and county supervisor named Tom Sullivan. Sullivan got Ira a job as a laborer that held the promise of his becoming a truck driver with a steady income. Ira stated flatly to Martin that he was trying to "stop being a drunken slop." While in Camino de Winos, he was beaten and scarred by a fellow inmate who was African American, indicating the racial makeup of the camp. The letter was written a little over one month before Ira's death. Ira had tried, over and over, to stop drinking. Betty Martin, Tom Sullivan, the *Chicago Sun-Times*, the various courts, and Alcoholics Anonymous had tried to help him. All had made their mark, but none found the right formula to cure his overindulging and eventual addiction. Huie felt that Ira was a prisoner of cheap wine and the practice of arresting brown and black people. Ira continually felt that he had betrayed his white friends, and the guilt fueled his drinking. Death was the inevitable outcome. That was the tone of Huie's story of Ira Hayes. [10]

By the time the book using Ira's story as the lead was printed, Hollywood had already begun to distribute the film. The story of Ira Hayes went through two changes in title. In 1961, the title was *The Outsider and Other Stories*, probably to market both itself and the movie. The next year it was called *The Hero of Iwo Jima and Other Stories*, its original title. The book's publishing dates range from 1959 to 1962.

In the preface to the 1962 edition of *The Hero of Iwo Jima*, Huie promoted *The Outsider* without critical analysis or, for that matter, scruple. The film had many flaws that Huie refused to acknowledge. Tone aside, the film turned out to be only an apparition of Huie's story. *The Outsider*, as Hollywood films tended to do, compressed several characters into one, or perhaps two, and portrayed Ira as a rather naïve (to the point of stupidity) and physically awkward young man. Nevertheless, Huie advised his readers that:

> "The Outsider" is a brave new film about Indians, about Marines, about war. It will move you to feel and to think. And when you watch the film, I want you to know that many Americans tried to keep you from seeing it.

Huie paid Ira's family $5,000 for the movie rights. They had no objections to the film, but editors kept throwing up objections to the project. Huie wrote that they found the movie script "too depressing...too real...too downbeat...too offbeat." Not only that, but most of the Hollywood producers wanted an "upbeat" ending to Ira's story. [11]

Although Huie fought for the story's major theme of how racism essentially caused the death of Ira Hayes, he apparently went along with another flaw. As was Hollywood's custom, the filmmakers cast whites as Native Americans.

"Redface," as the practice of using Euro-Americans in the roles of Native Americans has been called, was very old in the 1960s. As Philip J. Deloria writes in his 1998 book *Playing Indian*, white people have been dressing up as Indians since at least the mid-eighteenth century. [12] They did so for a variety of reasons: to mimic the Boston Tea Party or to indulge in fraternal and political rituals. In film, white people have been "playing Indian" practically from the beginning of the cinema itself. Of course, whites have been in "blackface" from the minstrel shows of the 1800s and in film just as long. Whites playing Mexicans (brownface) and Asians have not been around quite as long as white depictions of Native and African Americans but have nevertheless been a part of cinematic tradition for one hundred or so years.

Several of the earliest American movies in the Western genre actually employed Native actors. Between 1910 and 1920 there was an American mania for frontier, conservation, and Western movies, and Native American cultures were seemingly "close to nature." Hundreds of "Indian movies" were produced in the period that used Native actors, largely those who were in Wild West shows and could provide their own clothing. That particular craze for "real" Indians soon fell out of popularity, especially among producers and directors. Alan Hale Sr., director of the 1925 film *Braveheart*, candidly defended his use of an all-white cast to make an "Indian movie." The lead roles in the film were Braveheart, played by heartthrob Rod La Rocque, and Standing

Rock, played by Tyrone Power Sr. Hale, according to Native actor the late Will Sampson, was stating a "widespread Hollywood belief" when the director said, "White men make better motion picture actors than the red men themselves." Moreover, he stated, "A white man with strong features resembles the Indian more than the Indian does himself." [13]

In the same year that *Braveheart* was released, Paramount Pictures distributed *The Vanishing American*, which could be called the first modern Native American war film. Richard Dix, a leading man from the 1920s through the 1940s, played Nophaie, the lead Native American character. Following Dix was a spate of non-Native leading men playing indigenous chiefs, warriors, World War II soldiers and Marines, and Jim Thorpe. Henry Brandon played blue-eyed Comanche chief Scar in *The Searchers* (1956). Equally blue-eyed Chuck Connors played Geronimo in the film of the same name (1962). Jeff Chandler played Cochise in *Broken Arrow* (1954). Burt Lancaster, another blue-eyed Apache, starred as Massai in *Apache* (1954). Lancaster also was cast as Jim Thorpe, in *Jim Thorpe—All American* (1951).

Consequently, when it came to filming *The Outsider*, Tony Curtis exactly fit the mold of the blue-eyed heartthrob as Native American war hero. Vivian Nathan, known primarily as a stage actor and leader of the Actors Studio, played Ira's mother, Nancy. Most of the picture was filmed in the Gila River community, a sign that the movie had the approval of the Hayes family and of their tribal government.

Universal-International announced that it had reached agreement with Huie and that a film about Ira was being prepared. The first operating title for the film was *The Sixth Man*, in reference to Ira being identified as the last man in Rosenthal's photograph. As the script was developed, the theme emerged that Ira had been marginalized by his admirers, the Marine Corps, and his own people. Hence, the title, *The Outsider.*

The film unfortunately reverted to the pathetic Ira depicted in the newspapers rather than the good-hearted and outgoing young man whom Huie discovered in his letters and interviews with Ira's friends. Although Curtis did a credible job acting the part, the Ira he portrayed was not the real Ira. The Hollywood Ira is overwhelmed by the white man's society. He sits stiff and grim in the company of white women, hardly the person who warned his brother not to "hang around the girls like I did." He goes on liberty with white friends but cannot seem to understand why they joke and drink to entertain themselves. In the film, his buddies literally pour whiskey down his throat.

The boot camp scenes are preposterous. Curtis, while being berated by the Marine NCO who initiated the new recruits, tries to hold back laughter and is punished by being forced to duckwalk back and forth in front of the rest of the recruits with his hands clasped behind his head. In real life, the punishment would have been far worse, especially during the war, when the drill instructors were attempting to prepare the "boots" for combat. In reality, Ira's experience in the Phoenix Indian School and with the Civilian Conservation Corps–Indian Division, if nothing else, taught him how to deal with teachers, bosses, and coaches.

When the recruits are being taught to swim, "drown-proofing" in Marine parlance, Curtis as Ira jumps into the pool and nearly drowns because he can't swim or even float. This act seems to categorize Ira as a thoughtless simpleton. Instead of drowning, Curtis as Ira is rescued by James Sorenson, played by James Franciscus. At that point, the drill instructor places Ira/Curtis in Sorenson's care. Sorenson helps Ira through boot camp, coaches him over the obstacle course, and teaches him how to adjust himself to the rigors of basic training. The bumbling, stumbling Ira as Curtis portrayed him had nothing to do with the real Ira. The real Ira was athletic, smart, and disciplined. Even though the Phoenix Indian School had more or less dropped its militaristic curriculum, a student there had to follow instructions and keep himself immaculately clean and orderly. In the CCC-ID, Ira was taught carpentry and to show up at work on time. Moreover, after recruit training, Ira was sent to parachute school. In order to qualify to become part of this elite Marine parachutist unit, he had to have gotten through boot camp with a clean record. He had to be disciplined, intelligent, and physically prepared to graduate from the rigorous training of jump school.

Curiously, another Marine Corps film imitated the boot camp Ira/Curtis portrayal in *The Outsider*. In Stanley Kubrick's 1987 epic *Full Metal Jacket*, Private Joker (Matthew Modine) is ordered to help Private Gomer Pyle (Vincent D'Onofrio) get through the grueling Marine Corps boot camp. D'Onofrio's Private Pyle does everything wrong and often gets the entire recruit platoon in trouble. The platoon retaliates by holding Private Pyle down and beating him with soap bars wrapped in towels. Joker hesitantly participates in the beating. At the same time, Private Joker begins to help Private Pyle with shining shoes, cleaning his rifle, drill, and on the obstacle course, reminiscent of Sorenson taking care of the bad film version of Ira Hayes.

Ira and Sorenson are shipped to the Pacific to fight the Japanese. The film does not go into any detail about Ira's service in the Marine Parachute Battalion. Together, the two fight their way up Mount Suribachi, and both Ira and Sorenson take part in the flag raising. Not long afterward, Sorenson is killed beside Ira. After the fight for the island is over, Ira visits his friend's grave. Along with the other surviving flag raisers, Ira is sent back to the

U.S. to take part in the bond tour. He is despondent over the loss of Sorenson and hates being called a hero and thrust into the spotlight. He is often handed drinks and becomes addicted to alcohol.

Determined to rid himself of his addiction, Ira/Curtis returns to the reservation. In the film, he lives once again within the loving acceptance of home and family. He is asked to use his celebrity status to petition for the tribe's water rights. He fails but becomes interested in tribal politics. He runs for office and, unfortunately, is rejected. Once again, Ira begins to mourn the loss of Sorenson and descend into melancholy. He takes up the bottle once again, resulting in his death. The story line is straightforward and nowhere near as complex as Ira's life was in reality.

While Universal-International was negotiating with Huie for the rights to his story, another Ira Hayes melodrama was in the planning stages. In the 1950s and early 1960s, the three television networks developed anthology series like the *United States Steel Hour*, *Playhouse 90*, and *Sunday Showcase*. Once a week these shows presented one-hour dramas that were, in fact, often written by noted playwrights and sometimes writers who had been blacklisted in the Red Scare. In the case of the Ira Hayes videoplay, Merle Miller and renowned young director John Frankenheimer were hired respectively to write and direct the story for the National Broadcast Company. It was to be filmed in and around Tucson, Arizona, and on the Tohono O'odham (then Papago) reservation west of the city. Lee Marvin, a Marine veteran of the Saipan invasion, was tapped to play Ira. Like many of the other "Redface" actors, Marvin had blue eyes.

The producers of *The Outsider* and NBC executives clashed in early 1960. The NBC film began shooting in February amidst vigorous opposition from the Akimel O'odham. The tribal government got wind of the NBC production in December of 1959, when writer Merle Miller showed up in Tucson to do research. The Akimel O'odham tribal council had made a verbal agreement to cooperate in the production of *The American*, as the melodrama had been titled, but after a preliminary reading of the draft of the script withdrew tribal government support. The drama was, in the minds of the Akimel O'odham council members, to be about the people and the reservation and Ira was to be an "incidental" part of the show. In short, a "drawing card." "Instead," said tribal chairman Jay R. Morago Jr., "they're shooting the story of a drunken bum."

Morago's comment was not intended to be a dart thrown at Ira but at the way the script appeared to emphasize the "drunken Indian" stereotype. Robert Piser, a reporter who published a story on the controversy over the film said, after reading the script, "This reporter can see why tribal leaders don't like it." In response to the controversy, NBC executives essentially wrote off the opposition as being woefully ignorant of the intent of *The American*. The NBC brain trust announced, "The script represents Hayes as a victim of society." Consequently, NBC was going to go forward with the production. "We don't care," said the executives, "whether the Pimas like it or not. We're going ahead with it." Once again, white corporate privilege won out.

The Akimel O'odham council nevertheless continued their protest. They had the support of the local Presbyterian church council and the Bureau of Indian Affairs. The National Congress of American Indians also expressed support of the protest and stopping the airing of *The American*. Vern Stephens, the assistant to the commissioner of Indian affairs, said that the bureau would "fight NBC all the way." [14] Finally, Jay Morongo and Akimel O'odham tribal attorney Z. Simpson Cox flew to

Washington to carry their message of opposition to the production to Congress. [15] Their mission ultimately failed. Congress was not about to intercede in the freedom of corporations to produce what they liked. This was the period in American history when any questioning of corporate rights was labeled communism. NBC had greater political influence than Native American governments.

The *Sunday Showcase* production was aired in March 1960 as an hour-long drama featuring stock footage of the Iwo Jima battle and an emphasis on Ira's rounds of drinking and attempts at sobriety. Lee Marvin, who made his reputation as a "tough guy" in films, plays Ira as a weepy, marginalized man trying to avoid contact with anybody and everybody. He is more or less pressured to act in support of his people's water rights but is rejected by government officials. At one point, Ira/Marvin kneels in prayer in a reservation chapel, presumably asking God to intervene on behalf of his people. As Ira/Marvin prays, "the camera cuts to a shot of sand blowing across a dry desert." [16] The symbolism is not subtle. Even God can't help the loss of the people's water rights. Overcome by the rejection of Ira's good intentions, his heroic status disregarded, Ira sinks into alcohol abuse. To make his death even worse than it really was, Ira/Marvin drunkenly stumbles into a creek bed and drowns in a couple of inches of water. The idea of drowning in the desert in a small puddle of water was pathetic to say the least, the irony lost on no one. In this aspect of the NBC production, Merle Miller outdid himself as a scriptwriter.

Even before NBC began filming *The American* there were hints that a lawsuit was brewing. In November 1959, an *Arizona Daily Star* article stated that NBC could be charged with "piracy" in stealing the plot of the Huie story. [17] Huie had already sold the rights to the story to Universal-International. And the story ran much the same as the NBC plotline. NBC had possibly pirated the story line or, unlikely as it sounds, conjured up the tale of Ira Hayes out of the ether.

Huie filed suit. The court case was an attempt to enjoin NBC from broadcasting *The American*. In essence the case came down to whether or not a writer can copyright facts. There is a body of law that more or less indicates that facts can be collected by anyone and they cannot therefore belong exclusively to a single person. [18]

The lawsuit made national news. The *Miami Herald* quoted Huie as saying that "the only true and complete Hayes story is copyrighted by me and in my name." He had consulted the Marine Corps, the Akimel O'odham, and the Hayes family before filing for the injunction. Huie argued that "the NBC effort is a crass and cynical move to defraud the Indian family and to violate my copyrights." [19] Although the tribe remained neutral in the case, they later protested the content of NBC's script for *The American*. In March 1960, the court ruled in favor of NBC. [20] Huie's original story, "Our Torture Execution of Marine Hero Ira Hayes," was not plagiarized. The scriptwriter, Merle Miller, had proved that his script was the result of original research. The fact that he reached a similar conclusion about those facts was not proof of plagiarism.

Huie let the anger of his loss flow in the foreword to the 1962 re-release of *The Outsider* under the new title of *The Hero of Iwo Jima and Other Stories*. According to Huie, the broadcast network "rushed to capitalize on a 'quickie' version of the story." The Akimel O'odham of Gila River embraced the production of *The Outsider*, and the Hayes family accepted $5,000 for their cooperation in both the book and the movie. Tony Curtis was pictured with the family, and the Pimas "would not allow the NBC production to be filmed on the reservation." Admitting that his suit had failed, Huie went on to describe the *Sunday Showcase* broadcast as little else but "dreary snatches of film sandwiched between commercials for Sweetheart Soap and Beads o' Bleach." [21] The film was, as Huie indicated, pieced together from newly shot film, newsreel stock footage, and even scenes borrowed from *The Sands of Iwo Jima*.

Aired a year and a half before *The Outsider* was released, *The American* received good reviews on the whole and Marvin was praised for his acting and versatility. He was not the "bad guy" after all. After its release in December 1961, *The Outsider* was given solid reviews as well. Tony Curtis was praised for his acting skills, and the movie itself was considered compelling. The movie-length version of Ira's story came to be the better known of the two. Television in 1961 was considered a very different kind of entertainment. Cinema was worth a night out and paying a sum of money at the box office. *The American* was TV; *The Outsider* was cinema.

The public would have to wait quite a few more years before Hollywood would return and retell the Ira Hayes story. And in this case, it was not strictly about Ira. James Bradley, son of John "Jack" Bradley, had always wondered about the hushed stories about his father's heroism and his service on Iwo Jima. His father, although he spent moments in silence and woke up at night with nightmares, rarely spoke of his experiences as a corpsman. It was only after his father's death that James rummaged through some stowed-away boxes and discovered some letters and several medals, including the Navy Cross, the second-highest medal for valor that the United States Navy can bestow on a sailor. Later, James and his family would visit Iwo Jima. That visit inspired him, along with co-author Ron Powers, to seek out veterans of Iwo Jima and interview them for a book about the flag raisers, who at that time were thought to be Rene Gagnon, Harlon Block, Mike Strank, Franklin Sousley, Ira Hayes, and Bradley's father, Jack. [22]

Bradley and Powers' book was a hit, showing up on the *New York Times* bestseller list for several months. It was a paean to Jack Bradley's courage, tenacity, and basic love of family. At the same time Jack Bradley and his wife were raising eight children and running a hometown funeral home, Jack himself was a haunted man. He saved lives but felt deeply that he had not done enough to stop the horrific bloodletting. Like many combat veterans, he somehow blamed himself for not doing enough. To many people, that sort of notion seems incongruous and even cognitively dissonant, given that Jack Bradley attended the wounded even while badly wounded himself. The day he was wounded, Bradley crawled for several yards while suffering shrapnel wounds in his leg and foot to tend to a Marine whose wounds were probably not as bad as his own. That kind of dedication, professionalism, valor, and sacrifice is truly without equal. But John Bradley nevertheless thought that the "real heroes" of Iwo Jima were those buried in its soil. Bradley could not bring himself to talk about the experience of that kind of combat. Again, he likely thought that it was much too terrible to relate to someone who had not actually been there, combat being a personal reality as well as an experience shared by only a few others.

What makes the Bradley and Powers book memorable, unique, and a great story is that it is less a history than it is a memoir and a detective story. Bradley and Powers pieced together a manuscript that reflected not simply James Bradley's memories of his father but also what could be called the memories of Jack Bradley himself. Clearly brought to life in the book is the history of the terrible price the Marines paid to take the island through the eyes of Jack Bradley. Bradley the son was able to interview several of the veterans of the Iwo Jima battle, who have unfortunately passed on. Those veterans, who apparently knew that it might be their last chance to tell their story, told Bradley and Powers what combat was really about—in all of its gruesome detail. The authors genuinely outdid themselves in that regard.

While dramatic and well worth reading, *Flags of Our Fathers* does not delve into explaining the emotional disorder that caused his father to stay silent about his service or his father's nightmares. In essence, the book pointed out the symptoms of war-related trauma but did not explain their origins. Of course, the book likely was not intended to do so. The book did take a dive into how public adulation works in the United States. Heroes, it seems, are soon forgotten or, at minimum, not seen as deserving of any more than the praise they have received at the moment. The stories of Ira and of Rene Gagnon are examples. Bradley and Powers point out that Rene, while trying to cash in on his celebrity status and the (in the moment) interest shown in assisting him in some kind of lucrative position, failed because his heroic status waned. The promises of businessmen who had not served in battle were broken, and Rene ended up in low-paying and low-status jobs. The adulation was ephemeral. Ira's expectations of rewards probably were not as high as Rene's. But Ira returned to an impoverished reservation that his service, and that of the many other Akimel O'odham veterans, did nothing to change in terms of economic, social, and civil justice. Although the book assumes that Ira's alcohol abuse is related to the loss of his friends and the hypocrisy of the war bond tour and his own status as a hero, there is the strong suggestion that Ira feels the effects of American racism.

Jack Bradley, on the other hand, simply put his energy into job security and attempted to put the hero worship and the war behind him. He often refused, unlike Rene and Ira, to be a part of the almost continual celebration of the Iwo Jima campaign and especially of the Rosenthal picture. He could not put away his PTSD. Jack Bradley's devotion to his profession and his family might have dulled some of the pain. And his dedicated wife provided the stability that helped him in the long run. Jack Bradley nonetheless died with the nightmares and flashbacks and feelings of depression his son described in the book. In the long run the Bradley and Powers book is a significant addition to the literature on World War II and the survivors of that terrible conflict.

The film made from the Bradley and Powers book is, once again, told from James Bradley's perspective. Steven Spielberg's DreamWorks production company purchased the rights to the book in the same year as its publication. Spielberg assigned William Broyles Jr. to write the script. Production was then turned over to Clint Eastwood and his Malpaso production company. Eastwood had Paul Haggis rewrite the script and then decided that he would actually film a joint production of *Flags of Our Fathers* and *Letters from Iwo Jima*. The latter film was to be the story of the battle for the island from the Japanese point of view. Indeed, Eastwood filmed the picture in Japanese and gave General Kuribayashi his due as a military commander.

The Eastwood version of *Flags* was a rumination on the horror of warfare and how it affected those who experienced it firsthand. It follows Bradley through Iwo Jima and the Mighty Seventh War Bond Tour. The battle scenes were shot in muted tones, making the landscape look somewhat like a newsreel. The explosions are flashes of bright colors on a background of grays and blacks. Bradley is continually on the move, tending to the many wounded men on the beach. When moving inland, he is attacked by a Japanese soldier while bandaging a bleeding Marine. He is forced to kill the soldier with his knife. At night, Bradley is in a fighting hole with his friend Ralph "Iggy" Ignatowsky when he hears an American call for help. Bradley leaves the hole against Iggy's advice to find the wounded Marine. When Bradley returns, Iggy has been carried off by the Japanese. Later, Bradley identifies Iggy's body in a cave. The act of leaving Iggy in the fighting hole alone haunts Bradley perhaps more than any of the other horrors he has seen.

The film also picks up on the animosity that presumably developed between Ira and Rene after Ira threatened to kill Rene if he exposed Ira as one of the flag raisers. Rene chastises Ira for getting drunk and threatening the tour, which Rene believes will lead to connections that would land him a high-paying job. The movie paints Rene's future wife, Pauline, as a kind of fortune hunter ready to cash in on Rene's fame. The dislike between Rene and Ira was palpable. Jack Bradley is depicted as the stabilizing force interceding between the two and keeping track of Ira. Rene's ambition also leads him to ask Jack if he would be the best man at Rene and Pauline's wedding. The scene depicts Rene's purpose in asking Jack to participate in his wedding ceremony as an attempt to keep up the pretense of a heroic brotherhood in order to stay in the limelight. Apparently, in Rene's mind the wedding would attract even more media coverage.

Bradley agrees to Rene's request but is more drawn toward helping Ira. In one scene, Bradley gets Ira out of trouble and helps him back to a reenactment of the flag raising at Soldier Field in Chicago. Ira was drunk and threatening to break up a local bar with a chair because the bartender would not serve an Indian. This scene is a piece of Hollywood fiction. Before the reenactment at Soldier Field, Ira had been rescued by Keyes Beech, who frequently drank with Ira and declared him to be an "amiable drunk." Ira is obviously drunk and vomits in front of the commandant of the Marine Corps, who, in turn, takes Ira off the tour, saying, "Goddamn Indian." Eastwood's depiction of the racism involved in removing Ira from the Mighty Seventh Tour is accurate. There is nothing about Ira returning to the 5th Marine Division, preparing for the invasion of the Japanese homelands, and taking part in the occupation of Japan after the surrender. That aspect of Ira's life was not dealt with in either *The American*, *The Outsider*, or *Flags of Our Fathers*. Neither did the films mention his service in the Parachute Regiment or his participation in the Bougainville campaign. Both of these features of Ira's life would have helped to portray Ira as a seasoned veteran of the Pacific war.

Ira's character, played by Adam Beach in a solid performance, is in several of the battle scenes. In one, he, like Bradley with a knife, kills an attacking Japanese with a bayonet. The soldier actually impales himself on Ira's bayonet while jumping into Ira's fighting hole. That particular incident actually occurred during the fighting on Bougainville. Ira is there when Strank, Hansen, Block, and Sousley are killed, adding to his own trauma. Rene, because he is a battalion runner, is left out of the battle scenes almost entirely. During an exchange of harsh words with Rene, Ira says something on the order of "at least I fired my weapon," implying that Rene did not see "real" combat. The animosity between the two was likely overblown in the film. At least Rene attended Ira's funeral; Jack Bradley did not.

Ira/Beach has two very compelling scenes. The first is when, at a reception, he meets Mike Strank's mother, holds her close, and begins to cry. The second is when he leaves Arizona and hitchhikes to Texas to tell Harlon Block's father that Harlon, not Hank Hansen, was in the picture guiding the flagpole into the earth. He walks most of the way and then, after talking to the elder Block, turns around and walks back home. Harlon's mother had picked out her son upon first seeing Rosenthal's photograph. Ira/Beach's self-sacrifice to confirm Harlon's mother's belief is sad and moving. Marine officials finally confirm Harlon's participation and callously and unexpectedly inform Hank Hansen's mother that her son has been removed from the list of flag raisers.

The film *Flags of Our Fathers* follows *The Outsider* and *The American* in focusing on Ira's alcohol addiction. The film overlooks Ira's relocation to Chicago and Los Angeles and the policies that took him to those cities. The film does depict a newspaper photographer snapping a picture of Ira sitting behind bars. Eastwood's film follows Huie's story in one important but quickly passed-over aspect. In the scene when the three flag raisers and the Keyes Beech character meet Bud Gerber, the Treasury Department's supervisor of the Mighty Seventh Tour, Gerber casually offers drinks to the party. In this one scene, Eastwood subtly depicts how much alcohol was consumed in almost every social gathering at that time in America.

But most revealing was the way in which Ira was constantly stereotyped and subjected to casual racism. He was asked if he killed "Japs" with his tomahawk, referred to as "Chief," and questioned about taking scalps. One encounter in the film was almost outlandish in its cruel irony and portrayal of the attitude of white supremacy. A government official speaks a few words that cannot be comprehended by anyone in the scene. When Ira has a look of incomprehension on his face, the official asks him if he did not understand his own language. Instead of telling the white man that he was not speaking the Akimel O'odham language but rather gibberish, Ira courteously tells the man that he has not been on the reservation for some time. Adam Beach plays the scene well and even leaves the impression that anger underlies his outward civility.

The film establishes the idea that Ira's battles with alcohol are the direct result of seeing the horrors of war and being subjected to the flagrant racism of the era in which he lived. But the story of Ira's life is not seen as being a compound of numerous outrages, horrors, policies, poverty, and perfidy. Ira displays no other symptoms of post-traumatic stress other than alcoholism. Keyes Beech, who was an alcoholic, is depicted as a social drinker, as is every other white man in the motion picture. Ira is still the "drunken Indian" of American lore.

Ira's degradation moves from one step downward to another. He is thrown in jail. Shamed by a newspaper photographer, he exits the courthouse looking disheveled and broken. A poignant scene in the middle of a field takes place. A tourist family stops and asks him if he was the Indian in the photograph. With a look of unutterable suffering and what might be interpreted as being in a state of drunken incomprehension, Ira/Beach pulls a tiny American flag from his pocket and smiles an agonized smile. The family takes a picture with Ira and the father hands Ira some change as if he were nothing else but a tourist attraction or a prop. One of Ira's fellow workers in the field makes a derogatory remark. Ira's shame is complete. He is the object of scorn to his own people. In actuality, the opposite is true.

Despite a great deal of sympathy toward Ira, all three films, *The American, The Outsider,* and *Flags of Our Fathers,* see Ira as a victim of alcoholism without explaining PTSD. Of course, moviemaking is really shortcut storytelling and imagery rather than documentation of the complexity of the emotional and social problems involved in surviving combat. Eastwood saw war as the problem but could not tell the whole story of its consequences, especially in Ira's case.

Eastwood did, thankfully, deviate from both the "gung-ho" war film and the pontificating antiwar picture. And his film also departed from the stereotypes of the war film with an Indian character that almost became a cinema subgenre in and of itself. Since the 1925 film *The Vanishing American,* war movies have, more than any other genre save Western shoot-'em-ups, featured Native Americans as enemies. In 1970, the late Vine Deloria Jr., easily the most prolific and acerbic Native American writer of the twentieth century, pointed out an unrecognized occurrence in American war films he called "the All-American Platoon." This fighting unit, he wrote, was made up of "red-blooded White American boys with its own set of Indians." When the platoon got in trouble, Deloria contended, Indians used their "inscrutable phraseology" to call in the artillery or warn the platoon leader of an impending enemy attack. After saving the platoon, the Native American Code Talkers drifted into the background only to be called upon again if, and only if, the enemy was planning another attack. [23]

The Rosenthal photograph was instantly used to promote the imagery of Deloria's All-American platoon. Just as *True Comics* in 1945 listed the ethnic backgrounds of the Iwo Jima flag raisers to prove the existence of the American melting pot, the war movies of the 1940s and 1950s used the trope over and over again.

Many of the dark-skin roles were written as being Mexican American, such as Rodrigo in *Wake Island* (1942), Alvarez in *Guadalcanal Diary* (1943), Lopez in *The Story of G.I. Joe* (1945), and

Roderigues in *Battleground* (1949). Of course, Mexican Americans are actually indigenous people without tribal treaty relations with the United States.

Some films of the period did have Native American characters. In *Pride of the Marines* (1945), the character Al Schmid takes over a machine gun from the dead gunner, a Native American played by a white man, and, although blinded, wins the Navy Cross for halting a Japanese banzai attack on Guadalcanal. Navajo Code Talkers are seen for a few seconds in *Battle Cry* (1955). And Ira himself had a bit part in *The Sands of Iwo Jima* (1949).

Perhaps the most prominent Native American character in any of the war movies in the 1950s was in *To Hell and Back* (1955). The film was a biography of Audie Murphy, the most decorated soldier in World War II. Murphy played himself in the movie and with director Jesse Hibbs attempted to drive home the terrible cost of the war in terms of lives lost and the emotional problems it created. Felix Noriego played "Swope," a cigar-chomping Indian buddy of Murphy's who is stoic through most of his time on-screen but finally has an emotional breakdown as a result of seeing and taking part in the carnage of the battlefield. Swope might have been a major character in the film, but the role is really peripheral to that of Murphy's other white friends. Noriego/Swope disappears after his psychological collapse. [24]

Eastwood's *Flags of Our Fathers* received good reviews but did not cover its budget at the box office. Eastwood's companion film, *Letters From Iwo Jima*, did better critically and financially. A minor controversy over *Flags of Our Fathers* occurred when filmmaker Spike Lee criticized Eastwood for not depicting African American Marines in the Iwo Jima campaign. There were segregated African American units that served in the battle, and they were seen in some shots that Eastwood made of the troops aboard the ships prior to the landings. Lee later apologized. [25]

The depiction of Ira Hayes in American popular culture is woefully lacking despite the great performance of Adam Beach. He captured the emotional pain, depression, rage, nightmares, heightened startle responses, and isolation that veterans who are sufferers of PTSD are plagued with. In many ways too, Beach demonstrated the connection between PTSD and Ira's alcohol abuse. Unlike Tony Curtis, for example, Beach looked pained rather than pitiful. For his efforts he was nominated for two acting awards. He was an indigenous person in a Native American role.

Because Eastwood's film, like the book, centers on Jack Bradley, it ultimately moves Ira's story to its margins. It presents Ira again as the loner, an outsider, even while on his own reservation. There are no family members present, except perhaps for the person who was supposed to pick Ira up when he is released from jail and whom Ira ignores before going his own way. Ira is depicted as fighting his demons by himself for himself. There is no mention of Alcoholics Anonymous or of the fact that he tried over and over again to stop drinking. Even in *The Outsider*, Ira/Curtis has a mother and an uncle. In *Flags of Our Fathers*, Ira is alone. Although the film does indeed depict Ira's pain at being called a hero and his consequent bouts with alcohol abuse, it emphasizes his isolation. The last shot of Ira is of him lying facedown dead in a tiny shed with children climbing up on fence rails to see his disheveled, solitary corpse.

In short, nothing in the movie shows how Ira was part of a living though poverty-stricken society. Nothing in the film hints of the way in which his people have honored his memory over time. There was nothing in the film to suggest that people tried to help him and that he was buried with full military honors in Arlington National Cemetery.

The film ends with the James Bradley character's thoughts on the nature of heroism. "Heroes," the narrator recites, "are something we create...They may have fought for our country, but they died for their friends...If we wish to truly honor these men, we should remember them as they really were." These words best reflect Ira's rejection of his heroic status.

When Hollywood called upon Ira once again, his life had already ended. And so Hollywood pictured his life in any way it desired. He became the outsider, the loner, the wino, the poor Indian, the bum. American popular culture framed Ira in the trope of "Behold, the poor Indian," and as an example of the "plight" that Native Americans suffered. Vine Deloria Jr., ever the acerbic genius, once commented that Indians were, by birth, automatically enrolled in "plight" school. The movies about Ira, although their directors tried hard to sympathize with him, still could not or did not break away from the stereotypes that the public was familiar with. The script required them to condense biographies into two-hour movie formats.

Ira's story has been the inspiration for art forms other than biographies and films. Hollywood, in short, was not the only one to call upon Ira's image and melancholy history. The late Ai, a poet of no mean talent, wrote a curious poem in the late 1990s entitled "I Can't Get Started, for Ira Hayes." The poem appeared in her book *Vice: New and Selected Poems*, for which she won a National Book Award for Poetry in 1999. Ai was of Japanese, Chickasaw, Choctaw, and African American heritage and held a professorship at Oklahoma State University. She died in 2010.

Loren Webster, in his blog "In a Dark Time...the Eye Begins to See," introduced Ai's poem in this way:

Her [Ai's] poetry…seems to see life from the perspective of those who've been maimed by life, maimed in ways
most of us never directly experienced…Here's a poem
about a marine who is portrayed in the famous picture of
American marines raising the flag on Iwo Jima. [26]

Ai is writing about a war-maimed figure in Ira Hayes:

1. SATURDAY NIGHT
                      A coyote eats chunks of the moon…
                      while I lie drunk, in a ditch…

2. SUNDAY MORNING
                      …I remember raising that rag…
                      The bullets never touched me.

Ai ends the poem with Ira's confession of passing "gin and
excuses from hand to mouth" and, moreover, saying, "I'm the
one dirty habit / I just can't break." It was as if Ai felt Ira's earlier
shame at being unable to stop bingeing on alcohol and his guilt
for being alive when others lie dead in the rocks, sand, scrub
brush, dirt, and sulfury smell of Iwo Jima. She did indeed write
as one "maimed by life." [27]

Ai was not the only poet who wrote of Ira Hayes. One, posted
online after 9/11, is a flag-waving burst of American patriotism
in which the poet Marsha Burks Megehee exploits the spirit of
Ira Hayes:

A spirit hand reached out to them
The hand…of Ira Hayes

The poem goes on to speak of the dead of Iwo Jima as being true heroes just as those buried "at Ground Zero." [28] Once again, Ira, in this case his spirit, is used in the moment to exploit his name to convey the image of American unity and steadfast patriotism.

In essence Ira moves people in different ways. He seems to be looked upon generally with pity infused with a certain amount of contempt. On one end of the spectrum, Ira is the quintessential hero who sinks into a mire of shame, guilt, and rage. Ira has been abandoned by society but lives as a symbol of those "maimed by life." On the other side is an image of Ira as the spirit of American virtue and patriotism. Raising the flag on Iwo Jima still symbolizes victory, unity, and an indomitable spirit. Ira would probably have scratched his head in amazement and amusement at the divergent ways he has been portrayed through time. If anything, he felt, as he always did, that those he left behind on both Bougainville and Iwo Jima were the real heroes.

But long before Ai or Megehee touched pen to paper, another poet of note wrote a song about Ira that was perhaps as popular as his Hollywood images. The artist was folksinger and songwriter Peter LaFarge. His father, Oliver LaFarge, was a Harvard-trained anthropologist who studied Native American peoples of the Southwest. The senior LaFarge wrote a novel entitled *Laughing Boy* that won the Pulitzer Prize for fiction in 1929. The setting of *Laughing Boy* was in the Southwest among the Diné or Navajo people.

Peter, who was born Oliver Albee LaFarge in 1931, became estranged from his father and changed his name perhaps to distance himself from LaFarge senior. Peter maintained an interest in the Southwestern Native peoples. When he became a folksinger-songwriter, LaFarge chose as his subject matter Native Americans and subsequently wrote songs such as "As Long as the Grass Shall Grow," "Custer," "Drums," "White Girl," and "The Ballad of Ira Hayes." All of these songs were recorded by Johnny Cash in his album *Bitter Tears*.

According to scholar Keith Cook, LaFarge "unimaginatively" titled the track "The Ballad of Ira Hayes." The Cash version had a flute playing in the background apparently to emphasize the "Indianness" of the piece. The recording trails off at its conclusion with a muffled snare drum quietly beating out a retreat or funeral dirge. The drum was used "as if to give Cash a military sendoff." It was a sendoff for Ira as well. [29]

There are two key lines in the song that encapsulated two ideas about Ira and the dominant white society. The lines were: "When war came he [Ira] volunteered / And forgot the white man's greed." There was no explanation for Ira joining the Marines so it could be assumed that he was simply trying to be a good American citizen whose patriotic duty it was to fight against the Japanese. The line "And forgot the white man's greed" insinuates that Ira had a "childlike" quality that easily brushed off the effects that colonialism had on his people. [30] This supposed simplicity of mind and culture is a very old theme in Native-white relations. It rested on the idea that Indians were and are "children of nature," both unsophisticated and dependent on the forests, rivers, seas, deserts, and plains to provide a rudimentary hand-to-mouth existence. LaFarge's song simply reiterated the notion that Ira was indeed an outsider who, although pitied, could not live in either the white or the Indian world. He had no one to blame but himself for his degradation. It might be noted that on Cash's album cover, the singer is raising his fist above his right eye. Is he blocking out the shining rays of the sun, or raising his fist in a gesture of solidarity with the Native American cause, or is he doing his best imitation of the Indian scout looking into the distance for signs of an enemy attack? Whatever the case, Cash wore a leather headband to accentuate the Indian theme of the album. Several other artists have recorded LaFarge's song, including Bob Dylan, Joan Baez, and Kris Kristofferson.

When Hollywood called after Ira's death it was ultimately for profit in its appeal to the non-Native movie-goer. In all of the books and films with Ira as a character, or caricature, he is portrayed as a pathetic figure but a victim of his own making. The portrayals were sympathetic, to be sure, but they supported the notion of white supremacy. Ira was "racialized" for his alcoholic binges and arrests for public drunkenness and disorderly conduct. In its obituary for Ira, *Time* magazine asserted that Ira had been arrested more than fifty times in the ten years between the war's end and his death in 1955. [31] That would work out to an average of being locked in the drunk tank or in "Camino de Winos" at minimum five times a year. And if Ira had been arrested more than fifty times in less than ten years, that seemed to mean the police were looking for Ira specifically.

All of the poets, filmmakers, and writers simply portrayed Ira as being unable to cope with life on the reservation and in the white man's world. Stuck in between these different societies, he lost his sense of identity, became depressed, and took up the bottle. The blame is nonetheless placed on the individual rather than on a history of traumatic events like warfare, colonialism, and the loss of culture.

Another portrayal of Ira looms large in his story. The portrayal of Ira as a hopeless wino appears to harken back to the idea of racial, rather than self-determination. The Native American has been seen as genetically inclined to drink, just as the Irish have been so depicted in years past. This is an even more insidious portrayal because it stems from the old eugenics notions that the Nazis espoused in the 1930s. The main point of eugenics was to distinguish lower and higher races based on genetic attributes. This pseudoscience was simply racist mythology disguised as fact and was still around after the fall of Nazism. Racial segregation and miscegenation laws were in place in the 1960s and beyond. It was a method that colonizers and settlers could use to displace indigenous peoples, maintain systemic racism, and establish state sponsored class-caste systems. It has lived in a great deal of the rhetoric that has fueled the recent mass murders of African Americans in Charleston, South Carolina, and Hispanic Americans in El Paso, Texas.

The artists who wrote the songs, poems, books, and scripts could not apparently think past these old and tired ideas that underpinned the stereotypes like the "drunken Indian" and the "stoic Indian." Although they all wrote about Ira's depression, anxiety, and sense of isolation, they ignored the very real psychological disorder of PTSD. And, for that matter, they ignored or had no idea about the very real historical intergenerational trauma he experienced. Clearly, Ira's image was fixed in the American mind long before Hollywood and the literary community took up his story. He was stereotyped soon after it was revealed that he was one of the flag raisers. The trope of the Indian scout as a super warrior who could see and hear beyond the white soldiers' abilities was exploited in a comic book in 1945. The drunken Indian stereotype was employed to explain where Ira had gone "wrong" in the early 1950s. Art followed a certain perception of reality in Ira's case rather than the other way around. Instead of changing ideas, art followed preconceived images. It made a great story. But it was a fairy tale nonetheless.

Afterword

The second I took on the task of writing about Ira Hamilton Hayes I knew I was going to find it difficult to maintain some kind of scholarly detachment from the subject matter. The more I found out about him, the more I identified with his life story. I am a citizen of the Cherokee Nation, born in a rural area of Oklahoma that lies in the western part of the Cherokee Nation. I have done the farm labor of picking strawberries and hauling hay and worked in a machine shop and a gas station. I've gathered wild onions, hickory nuts, walnuts, and pecans and hunted and fished in my homeland. Additionally, I served as a Marine in Vietnam, shared symptoms of post-traumatic stress disorder with my fellow Vietnam veterans, and, at one point in time, drank heavily. I've seen combat. I have seen bodies of both my friends and my enemies. I have even seen the bodies of neutral or non-combatant Vietnamese people. Later in life, I was also part of a powwow drum group, the Panther Creek Singers, that served as host drum for the Ira Hayes powwow in Sacaton, Arizona, the place of Ira's birth. I have also sung in Bapchule, his hometown. During my long tenure as a faculty member at the University of Arizona, I wrote several articles and a book on Native veterans of the Vietnam War. Ira's life represents all of us. All Native American veterans can identify with him. The hatred and fear I felt during the war can only be understood by other veterans. I've only begun to talk about these things in recent years, and only with my old friends and relatives and those who served in a war. Too many people would not understand.

Still, I did not experience the intensity of warfare that my fellow Marine Ira Hayes did. I can only imagine the perils of fighting in the Bougainville jungles or the horrors of Iwo Jima. Ira survived and was left with truly terrible memories that were more than difficult to discuss. Unlike Ira, I was given several opportunities to further my education and take part in various tribal ceremonies that aided me in healing the trauma of war.

Also, unlike most people who have written about him, I am amazed that Ira lived until the age of thirty-two. Given the history of colonization and exploitation of the Gila River Reservation on which he was born and the war he lived through, it is a wonder that he survived as long as he did. He had, after all, a brother and a sister who died as small children and two brothers who died in their twenties. Life on the Gila River Reservation at the time of his birth was incredibly hard. Ira was only a generation away from a full-blown famine that took place among his people. For all Native Americans at the time, life expectancy was only in the mid-forties.

Ira is revered on the reservation, as he should be. A road, a school, a park, and a library are named after him. Unfortunately, the school was closed. A monument is dedicated to his memory and that of another Akimel O'odham soldier, Mathew B. Juan, who was killed in action in 1918. In fact, the place in Sacaton known as the Veterans' Memorial Park has several plaques dedicated to women veterans and those who served in several wars. The Akimel O'odham and Piipaash tribes who live in the Native communities of the area have a high regard, indeed a reverence, for their warriors, male and female.

For the most part, the media attention on Ira's life was laser-focused on his drinking and the literary angle of his sadly killing himself by way of alcohol abuse. Because of a taboo the larger society places on the issue of mental health, few journalists at the time put combat neurosis together with alcohol addiction. Drinking was thought of as an escape or even a cure for emotional problems. In fact, the print coverage of Ira's life reads like a tragedy that was inevitable. The stories always hinted that his degradation was self-imposed because he could not deal with the horrors of war and the values of the dominant society. It is the contemptuous retelling of the mythology of how marginalized and racialized people are prone to immoral behavior, self-loathing, and ruination. They are thus to be pitied or treated as inferior beings. To the storytellers Ira was simply a poor Indian gone wrong despite being applauded by mainstream society as a hero. He fitted into a long-standing stereotype of the degraded Native American who had been caught between two worlds and could no longer make sense of either. Of course, the stereotype is wrong. Native Americans, including Ira, have been subject to colonization for more than five hundred years. His people had their water stolen, which, in sequence, undermined their economy, their political structures, their ceremonial practices, and their relationships within and without their culture. Colonization also wreaked havoc with their environment and their connection with the spirit world, their religion that is many centuries older than Christianity. The late scholar Robert K. Thomas once said that colonization was the deprivation of experience. By that he meant that colonized people have not been allowed to experience change on their own terms. In the case of the Akimel O'odham change was forced down their throats, and Ira was one generation from a horrific famine that happened because his people's water supply was stolen by those who professed to be Christians.

I have tried with this book to put Ira's life into the context of his times and historical circumstance, as well as a more recent understanding of how and why PTSD affects human behavior. Ira was not a tragic victim of his own making. He was, like every other member of a marginalized group in the U.S., a product of limited choices and the processes of colonization.

Ira's story is about the sting of events that made him who he was. He was the "man in the maze." PTSD was a circumstance of war, and binge drinking was a self-medicating response to PTSD. Ira lived in a kind of rondo of linkages from extreme poverty on the reservation, to war, to heroic status, and back to poverty on the reservation. He could be called a victim of circumstance. But at the same time, he did not take a single step into the realm of victimhood. He simply lived life as it came. And the story of his life encompassed a significant change in Native American history and the relations of his and other tribes' interactions with white Americans. Ira was caught up in those changing times.

In many ways, Ira was the personification of Native warrior-hood. He was honest, brave, humble, and generous. In 1996, I published a book about Native veterans of the Vietnam War. Its title, *Strong Hearts, Wounded Souls*, embodied the character, virtue, and melancholy facts of fighting in and surviving combat and returning home to poverty and oppression. Ira had a strong heart and a damaged but giving, honorable spirit. His kind of courage and unassuming nature epitomized the Native warrior. Warfare and an uninterested larger society, not his culture or his bingeing on alcohol, caused him pain.

He should be remembered for who he was rather than for what the dominant society has been led to believe about him.

Acknowledgments

First and foremost, I would like to thank my friend and colleague over the years, Professor Matthew Sakiestewa Gilbert, the director of American Indian Studies at the University of Arizona. Years ago, I voted to hire him as a young Native scholar in the program. Unfortunately, it didn't work out. But now he's heading the program and has taken it into the direction that Vine Deloria Jr. attempted to take it in the 1980s.

Fortunately, Matt put me in touch with Sean Desmond and Zohal Karimy at Twelve. Sean and Zoe have been encouraging, challenging, and focused on producing this book. I hope that it meets their expectations. I've thoroughly enjoyed working with them.

Robert A. Williams of the James E. Rogers College of Law at the University of Arizona gave me some insight into the Isabel Crocker case and on restricted neighborhoods during the late 1940s. I thank him for his knowledge and his willingness to share it with me.

I want to acknowledge my old friend, Professor Don Fixico of Arizona State University. Don is easily the finest Native American historian around. He shared with me his understanding of how and why Native peoples have migrated to urban areas since the 1930s. His perceptiveness of the history of the factors involved in the relocation and termination policies is more than remarkable and more than appreciated.

I cannot forget to acknowledge my friends Bill Meadows, Richard Allen, Jerry C. Bread, Franci Washburn, and David Wilkins, all of whom have contributed to this effort without realizing it. Over the years, I have absorbed their ideas and understanding of Native American cultures, politics, and military service. I'm grateful for their friendship and knowledge.

I also have to pay tribute to my colleagues and mentors at the University of Arizona, the late Vine Deloria Jr. and the late Robert K. Thomas. They were among the most intelligent and discerning persons I've ever known.

I want to express my appreciation to my sons, Garett and Michael, their wives, Andrea and Sandra, and my grandchildren, Zeke, Joaquin, Sadie Grace, and Eli, for always being there for me. Finally, to my wife of over half a century and to whom I have dedicated this book, thank you for saving my life.

Bibliography

U.S. Government Publications

Bureau of Indian Affairs, Department of the Interior. *Indians at Work.* Washington, D.C.: Bureau of Indian Affairs, 1933. https://library.si.edu/digital-library/book/indians-work.

Chapin, John C. *Top of the Ladder: Marine Operations in the Northern Solomons.* Marines in World War II Commemorative Series. Washington, D.C., Marine Corps Historical Center, 1997.

Condit, Kenneth W., Gerald Diamond, and Edwin T. Turnblad. *Marine Corps Ground Training in World War II.* Washington, D.C.: U.S. Marine Corps, 1956.

Garand, George W., and Truman R. Strobridge. *Western Pacific Operations and History of U.S. Marine Corps Operations in World War II, Vol. 4.* Washington, D.C.: U.S. Marine Corps, 1971.

Hoffman, Lt. Col. Jon T. *Silk Chutes and Hard Fighting: U.S. Marine Corps Parachute Units in World War II.* Washington, D.C.: U.S. Marine Corps, 1999.

Marine Corps University. *Corporal Ira Hamilton Hayes, USMCR (Deceased).* https://www.usmcu.edu/Research/Marine-Corps-History-Division/People/Whos-Who-in-Marine-Corps-History/Gagnon-Ingram/Corporal-Ira-Hamilton-Hayes/.

Nalty, Barand C., and Danny J. Crawford. *United States Marines on Iwo Jima: The Battle and the Flag Raisings.* Washington, D.C. U.S. Marine Corps, 1995.

National Park Service. "History of the Marine Corps War Memorial." nps.gov/gwmp/learn/historyculture/usmcwarmemorial .htm.

Naval History and Heritage Command. *Amphibious Operations, Capture of Iwo Jima, 16 February to 16 March 1945.* https://www .history.navy.mil/research/library/online-reading-room/title -list-alphabetically/a/amphibious-operations-capture-iwo -jima.html.

Office of Indian Affairs. *Indians in the War.* Chicago: U.S. Department of the Interior, 1945.

Office of Veterans Affairs. *Legacies of Vietnam: Comparative Adjustment of Veterans and Their Peers.* Washington, D.C.: Government Printing Office, 1981.

Robertson, Breanne, ed. *Investigating Iwo: The Flag Raising in Myth, Memory and Esprit de Corps.* Quantico, VA: Marine Corps History Division, 2019.

Russell, Frank. "The Pima Indians." *Twenty-Sixth Annual Report of the Bureau of American Ethnology, 1904–1905.* Washington, D.C.: Government Printing Office, 1908.

Shaw, Jr., Henry I. *The United States Marine Corps in the Occupation of Japan.* Washington, D.C.: Historical Branch, U.S. Marine Corps, 1969.

Updegraph, Charles L., *Special Marine Corps Units of World War II.* Washington, D.C.: U.S. Marine Corps, 1977.

U.S. Army. *Japanese Mortars and Grenade Dischargers.* Washington, D.C.: Government Printing Office, 1945.

U.S. Department of War. *Annual Report of the Secretary of War.* Washington, D.C.: Government Printing Office, 1891.

U.S. Marine Corps. "Marine Corps Updates Its Official Records of First Flag Raising over Iwo Jima." https://www.marines.mil /News/Press-Releases/Press-Release-Display/Article /924206/marine-corps-updates-its-official-records-of-first -flag-raising-over-iwo-jima/.

War Department, Division of Military Intelligence. *Japanese Mortars and Grenade Launchers.* Washington, D.C.: Government Printing Office, 1945.

Newspapers

Akron (Ohio) *Beacon Journal*
Arizona Daily Star
Arizona Republic
Atlanta Constitution
Baltimore Sun
Birmingham News
Boston Globe
California Eagle
Canton (Ohio) *Independent-Sentinel*
Casa Grande (Arizona) *Dispatch*
Chicago Tribune
Corpus Christi Times
Daily News (New York, New York)
Democrat and Chronicle (Rochester, New York)
Des Moines Post-Star
Detroit Free Press
East Valley (Arizona) *Tribune*
Evening Star (Washington, D.C.)
Fort Collins Coloradoan
Fort Worth Star-Telegram
Glens Falls (New York) *Post-Star*

Great Falls (Montana) *Tribune*

Hagerstown (Maryland) *Daily Mail*

Honolulu Advertiser

Kansas City Star

Knoxville (Tennessee) *News Sentinel*

Long Beach (California) *Press-Telegram*

Los Angeles Daily News

Los Angeles Evening Citizen News

Los Angeles Times

Louisville (Kentucky) *Courier-Journal*

Messenger (Catholic News)

Messenger-Inquirer (Owensboro, Kentucky)

Miami Herald

News Journal (Wilmington, Delaware)

News Tribune (Tacoma, Washington)

Pike County (Pennsylvania) *Dispatch*

Pomona (California) *Daily Progress*

Sacramento Bee

San Pedro (California) *News Pilot*

Shreveport Times

St. Louis Star-Times

Tucson Citizen

Valley Times (Hollywood, California)

Vidette-Messenger (Valparaiso, Indiana)

Visalia Times-Delta (Tulare County, California)

Wakefield (Nebraska) *Republican*

Washington Post

Wichita Falls (Texas) *Times*

Wichita Falls (Texas) *Times Record News*

Record Album

Cash, Johnny, "The Ballad of Ira Hayes," track 5 on *Bitter Tears: Ballads of the American Indian.* Columbia-Legacy, n.d., first recorded in 1961. Compact disc.

Books and Articles

Abbott, Patrick J. "American Indian and Alaska Native Aboriginal Use of Alcohol in the United States." *American Indians and Alaska Native Mental Health Research* 7, no. 2 (1996).

Ai. *Vice: New and Selected Poems.* New York: W. W. Norton and Company, 1999.

Allen, Nathan. "O'odham Himdag: The O'odham Way." *Wicazo Sa Review* 11, no. 2 (1995).

American Psychiatric Association. *Diagnostic and Statistical Manual of Mental Disorders*, 3rd Edition. Washington, D.C.: American Psychiatric Association, 1980.

———. *Diagnostic and Statistical Manual of Mental Disorders*, 3rd Edition (revised). Washington, D.C.: American Psychiatric Association, 1987.

———. *Diagnostic and Statistical Manual of Mental Disorders*, 5th Edition. Washington, D.C.: American Psychiatric Association, 2013.

Anderson-Colon, Jessica. "Marine Corps Boot Camp During World War II: The Gateway to the Corps' Success at Iwo Jima." *Marine Corps History* 7, no. 1 (Summer 2021).

Andreas, Peter. *Killer High: A History of War in Six Drugs.* New York: Oxford University Press, 2020.

Babor, Thomas F. "Classification of Alcoholics: Typology Theories from the 19th Century to the Present." *Alcohol Health and Research World* 20 (1996).

Baker, Brian. *Masculinity in Fiction and Film: Representing Men in Popular Genres, 1945–2000*. London: Bloomsbury Publishing, 2008.

Baragona, Justin. "Fox News Host: Native Americans Are Alcoholics Hooked on the Government." *Daily Beast*, October 14, 2021. https://www.thedailybeast.com/fox-news-host-rachel-campos -duffy-says-native-americans-are-alcoholics-hooked-on-the -government.

Basso, Keith, ed. *Western Apache Raiding and Warfare from the Notes of Greenville Goodwin*. Tucson: University of Arizona Press, 1998.

Bee, Robert L. "Quechan." In *Handbook of North American Indians*, vol. 10, edited by Alfonso Ortiz. Washington, D.C.: Smithsonian Institution, 1983.

Berkhofer, Robert F., Jr. *The White Man's Indian: Images of the American Indian from Columbus to the Present*. New York: Alfred A. Knopf, 1978.

Billington, Ray Allen. *Westward Expansion*, 3rd ed. New York: Macmillan, 1971.

Bourne, Peter G. *Men, Stress and Vietnam*. New York: Little, Brown and Company, 1970.

Bradley, James, and Ron Powers. *Flags of Our Fathers*. New York: Bantam Books, 2016.

Brave Heart, Maria Yellow Horse. "Integrating Trauma: Informed and Historical Trauma Informed Care." *Interventions with American Indians and Alaska Natives, 2017*. His.gov/sites /historicaltrauma 0617.pdf.

Brave Heart, Maria Yellow Horse, Josephine Chase, Jennifer Elkins, and Deborah B. Altschul. "Historical Trauma Among Indigenous Peoples of the Americas: Concepts, Research and Clinical Considerations." *Journal of Psychoactive Drugs*. https//doi.org/10.1080/02791072.2011.628913.

Brave Heart, Maria Yellow Horse, and Lemyra M. DeBruyn. "The American Indian Holocaust: Healing Historical Unresolved Grief." *American Indian and Alaska Native Mental Health Research* 8, no. 2 (1998).

Britten, Thomas A. *American Indians in World War I: At War and at Home.* Albuquerque: University of New Mexico Press, 1997.

Brown, Dee. *Bury My Heart at Wounded Knee: An Indian History of the American West.* New York: Holt, Rinehart and Winston, 1971.

Brown-Rice, Kathleen. "Examining the Theory of Historical Trauma Among Native Americans." *The Professional Counselor* (n.d.). tpcjournal.nbcc.org.

Broyles, William, Jr. "Why Men Love War." In *The Vietnam Reader*, edited by Walter Capps. New York: Routledge, 1990.

Carroll, Al. *Medicine Bags and Dog Tags: American Indian Veterans from Colonial Times to the Second Iraq War.* Lincoln: University of Nebraska Press, 2008.

Dejong, David H. *Stealing the Gila: The Pima Agricultural Economy and Water Deprivation, 1848–1921.* Tucson: University of Arizona Press, 2009.

Deloria, Philip, J. *Playing Indian.* New Haven: Yale University Press, 1998.

Deloria, Vine, Jr. *We Talk, You Listen: New Tribes, New Turf.* Lincoln: University of Nebraska Press, 1970.

Denicola, Robert C. "Copyright in Collection of Facts: A Theory of the Protection of Nonfiction Works." *Columbia Law Review* 81, No. 3 (April 1981).

Dippie, Brian W. *The Vanishing Indian: White Attitudes and U.S. Indian Policy.* Lawrence: University Press of Kansas, 1982.

Dobyns, Henry F. *The Pima-Maricopa.* Indians of North American Series. New York: Chelsea House, 1989.

Drinnon, Richard. *Facing West: The Metaphysics of Indian Hating and Empire Building.* New York: New American Library, 1980.

Dunbar-Ortiz, Roxanne, and Dina Gilio-Whitaker. *All the Real Indians Died Off and 20 Other Myths about Native Americans.* Boston: Beacon Press, 2016.

Dunlay, Thomas W. *Wolves for the Blue Soldiers: Indian Scouts and Auxiliaries with the United States Army.* Lincoln: University of Nebraska Press, 1982.

Dunnigan, James F., and Albert A. Nofi. *Victory at Sea: World War II in the Pacific.* New York: William Morrow and Company, 1995.

Dupuy, T.N. *The Evolution of Weapons and Warfare.* New York: Bobbs-Merrill, 1980.

Enloe, Cynthia H. *Ethnic Soldiers: State Security in a Divided Society.* New York: Penguin Books, 1980.

Feldstein, Sarah W., Kamilla L. Nenner, and Philip A. May. "American Indian and Alaska Native Alcohol-Related Incarceration and Treatment." *American Indian and Alaska Native Mental Health Research* 13, no. 3 (2006).

Ferguson, R. Brian. "Masculinity and War." *Current Anthropology* 62, no. 23 (2021).

Fernandez-Santamaria, Jose A. "Juan Ginés de Sepúlveda on the Nature of the American Indians." *The Americas* 31 (April 1974).

Fernandez-Santamaria, Jose A., Juan Fide, and Benjamin Keen. "Bartolome de las Casas in History: Toward an Understanding of the Man and His Work." *Hispanic American Historical Review* 53, no. 1 (1973).

Figley, Charles R., ed. *Stress Disorders Among Vietnam Veterans: Theory, Research and Treatments.* New York: Brunner/Mazel Publishers, 1978.

Fixico, Donald L. *Termination and Relocation: Federal Indian Policy, 1945–1960*. Albuquerque: University of New Mexico Press, 1990.

Flynn, Hannah. "More Evidence That Stress Accelerates Biological Aging." *Medical News Today*, December 10, 2021. medicalnewstoday.com/articles/more-evidence-that-stress-accelerates-biological-aging.

Forbes, Jack D., and Howard Adams. *A Model of "Grass Roots" Community Development: The D-Q University Native American Language Education Project*. Davis: University of California-Davis Tecumseh Center, 1976.

Franco, Jeré. *Crossing the Pond: The Native American Effort in World War II*. Denton: University of North Texas Press, 1999.

Frisk, Kristian. "What Makes a Hero: Theorizing the Social Structuring of Heroism." *Sociology* 53, no. 1 (2018).

Gailey, Harry A. *Bougainville, 1943–1945: The Forgotten Campaign*. Lexington: University Press of Kentucky, 1991.

Garland, Brock, ed. *War Movies*. New York: Facts on File, 1987.

Gibson, Arrell M. *America's Exiles: Indian Colonization in Oklahoma*. Oklahoma City: Oklahoma Historical Society, 1976.

Goodnow, Trischa, and James J. Kimble, eds. *The 10 Cent War: Comic Books, Propaganda and World War II*. Jackson: University Press of Mississippi, 2017.

Grossman, Lt. Col. Dave, ret. *On Killing: The Psychological Cost of Learning to Kill in War and Society*. Boston: Little, Brown and Company, 1995.

Harjo, Joy. *Crazy Brave: A Memoir*. New York: W. W. Norton and Company, 2013.

Hemingway, Albert. *Ira Hayes: Pima Marine*. Lanham, MD: University Press of America, 1988.

————. "Pete Ellis, Father of Amphibious Warfare." *Warfare History Network.* https://warfarehistorynetwork.com/pete-ellis -father-of-amphibious-warfare/#:~:text=Pete%20Ellis%3A%20 Prophet%20of%20Amphibious,Island%2C%20from%20 1911%20until%201913.

Henri, Cpt. Raymond, 1Lt. Jim G. Lucas, T-Sgt. David K. Demsey, T-Sgt. W. Keyes Beech, and T-Sgt. Alvin M. Josephy. *The U.S. Marines on Iwo Jima.* Uncommon Valor Press, 2014. First published: Dial Press, 1945.

"Heroes: Then There Were Two." *Time,* February 7, 1955.

Hertzberg, Hazel W. *The Search for an American Indian Identity: Modern Pan-Indian Movements.* Syracuse, NY: Syracuse University Press, 1971.

Hierholzer, R., T. Munson, C. Peabody, and J. Rosenberg. "Clinical Presentation of PTSD in World War II Combat Veterans." *Hospital Community Psychiatry* 43, no. 8 (1992).

Hines, Anthony. "Marine Corps Cultural Similarities to Native Americans." *Spectrum* 7, no. 1 (Spring 2018).

Hirsch, Paul. "This Is Our Enemy: The Writers' War Board and Representation of Race in Comic Books, 1942–1945." *Pacific Historical Review* 83, no. 3 (August 2014).

Hirschberger, Gilad. "Collective Trauma and the Social Construction of Meaning." *Frontiers in Psychology* 9 (2018). https:// www.frontiersin.org/articles/10.3389/fpsyg.2018.01441/full.

"History of PTSD and Trauma Diagnoses," Trauma Dissociation, March 8, 2022. http://traumadissociation.com/ptsd/history.

Holm, Tom. "Fighting a White Man's War: The Extent and Legacy of American Indian Participation in World War II." *Journal of Ethnic Studies* 9, no. 2 (Summer 1981).

————. *Strong Hearts, Wounded Souls: Native American Veterans of the Vietnam War.* Austin: University of Texas Press, 1996.

————. *The Great Confusion in Indian Affairs: Native Americans and Whites in the Progressive Era.* Austin: University of Texas Press, 2005.

Hoxie, Frederick E. *A Final Promise: The Campaign to Assimilate the Indians, 1880–1920.* Lincoln: University of Nebraska Press, 1984.

Huie, William Bradford. *The Hero of Iwo Jima and Other Stories.* New York: Signet, 1962.

Innes, Robert Alexander, and Kim Alexander, eds. *Indigenous Men and Masculinities: Legacies, Identities, Regeneration.* Winnipeg, Canada: University of Manitoba Press, 2015.

Janssen, J. Scott. "Locked in the Vault: Survivor Guilt in Combat Veterans." *Social Work Today.* https://www.socialworktoday.com/news/enews_0713_1.shtml.

Jefferson, Jill Colleen. "Journalist William Huie Concealed Lynchers in Emmett Till Case and Got Away with It." *Mississippi Free Press* (2021). https://www.mississippifreepress.org/15462/journalist-william-huie-concealed-lynchers-in-emmett-till-case-and-got-away-with-it.

Jones, Edgar, and Nicola T. Fear. "Alcohol Use and Misuse Within the Military: A Review." *International Review of Psychiatry* 23 (April 2011).

Jones, James. *WWII: A Chronicle of Soldiering.* New York: Ballantine Books, 1975.

Junger, Sebastian. *Tribe: On Homecoming and Belonging.* New York: Twelve, 2016.

Keegan, John. *The Second World War.* New York: Penguin Books, 1989.

Krause, Susan Applegate. *North American Indians in the Great War.* Lincoln: University of Nebraska Press, 2007.

Kroeber, Clifton B., and Bernard L. Fontana. *Massacre on the Gila: An Account of the Last Major Battle Between American Indians with Reflections on the Origin of War.* Tucson: University of Arizona Press, 1992.

Lackenbauer, P. Whitney, R. Scott Sheffield, and Craig Leslie Mantle, eds. *Aboriginal People and Military Participation: Canadian and International Perspectives.* Kingston: Canadian Defense Academy Press, 2007.

Langer, Ron. "Combat Trauma, Memory and the World War II Veteran." *Literature and the Arts: An International Journal of the Humanities* 23, no. 1 (2011).

Maguen, S., T.J. Metzler, B.T. Litz, S.J. Knight, and C.R. Marmar. "The Impact of Killing in War on Mental Health: Symptoms and Related Functions." *Journal of Traumatic Stress Studies* 22, no. 5 (October 2009).

Marling, Karal, and John Wetenhall. *Iwo Jima: Monuments, Memories and the American Hero.* Cambridge, MA: Harvard University Press, 1991.

Marshall, S.L.A. *Men Against Fire: The Problem of Battle Command.* Norman: University of Oklahoma Press, 2000. First published in 1947.

Martinez, David. "Elder Brother Lives Here: How the Man-in-the-Maze, I'itoi Ki, Became a Symbol of the O'odham Himdag." *Southwest Symposium Proceedings* (2020). Academia.edu/44234972.

Martinez, Luis. "Marine Corps Again Correct Who Was in Iconic Iwo Jima Flag Raising Photo." ABC News, October 17, 2019. abcnews.go.com/us/marines-correct-identity-member-raising-flag-iconic-iwo/story?id=66348494.

Marubbio, M. Elise, and Eric L. Buffalohead, eds. *Native Americans on Film: Conversations, Teaching and Theory.* Lexington: University Press of Kentucky, 2013.

Meadows, William C. *The Comanche Code Talkers of World War II.* Austin: University of Texas Press, 2002.

Megehee, Marsha Burks. "(The Ghost of) Ira Hayes." 2021. http://www.wrensworld.com/irahayes.htm.

Military.com. "Force Recon: Mission and History." N.d. https://www.military.com/special-operations/force-recon-missions-and-history.html.

Neuberger, Richard L. "On the Warpath." *Saturday Evening Post,* October 24, 1942.

———. "The American Indian Enlists." *Asia and the Americas* 42 (November 1942).

Orr, Scott P., Roger K. Pitman, Natasha B. Lasko, and Lawrence R. Hertz. "Psychophysiological Assessment of Posttraumatic Stress Disorder Imagery in World War II and Korean Combat Veterans." *Journal of Abnormal Psychology* 102 (1993–02).

Parker, Dorothy R. *The Phoenix Indian School: The Second Half Century.* Tucson: University of Arizona Press, 1996.

Parman, Donald L. "The Indian and the Civilian Conservation Corps." *Pacific Historical Review* 40 (January 1971).

Paul, Doris. *The Navajo Code Talkers.* Philadelphia: Dorrance and Company, 1973.

Pavlik, Steve, M. Elise Marubbio, and Tom Holm. *Native Apparitions: Critical Perspectives on Hollywood's Indians.* Tucson: University of Arizona Press, 2017.

Pearce, Roy Harvey. *Savagism and Civilization: A Study of the Indian and the American Mind.* Berkeley: University of California Press, 1988.

Philip, Kenneth R. *John Collier's Crusade for Indian Reform, 1920–1954.* Tucson: University of Arizona Press, 1977.

Polich, A. E. "Epidemiology of Alcohol Abuse in Military and Civilian Populations." *American Journal of Public Health* 71 (1981).

Prat, N.S., J.L. Daban, E.J. Voiglio, and F. Rongieras. "Wound Ballistics and Blast Injuries." *Journal of Visceral Surgery* 154, Supp. 1 (December 2017).

Prucha, Francis Paul, S.J. *American Indian Policy in Crisis: Christian Reformers and the Indian, 1865–1900.* Norman: University of Oklahoma Press, 1976.

Rentería-Valencia, Rodrigo F. "Colonial Tensions in the Governance of Indigenous Authorities and the Pima Uprising of 1751." *Journal of the Southwest* 56, no. 2 (Summer 2014).

Reuters Life. "Eastwood Rejects Lee's Criticism of His WW2 Films." Reuters (May 28, 2008).

Reyhner, Jon, and Jeanne Eder. *American Indian Education: A History.* Norman: University of Oklahoma Press, 2006.

Robinette, C. Dennis, Zdeneck Hrubec, and Joseph T. Fraumeni, Jr. "Chronic Alcoholism and Subsequent Mortality in World War II Veterans." *American Journal of Epidemiology* 109, no. 6 (June 1979).

Rollins, Peter C., and John E. O'Connor, eds. *Why We Fought: America's Wars in Film and History.* Lexington: University Press of Kentucky, 2008.

Rosenthal, Joe, and W. C. Heinz. "The Picture That Will Live Forever." *Collier's,* February 18, 1955.

Rosenthal, Nicolas G. *Reimagining Indian Country: Native American Migration and Identity in Twentieth-Century Los Angeles.* Chapel Hill: University of North Carolina Press, 2012.

Rosier, Paul C. *Serving Their Country.* Cambridge, MA: Harvard University Press, 2009.

Saiassi, I., G. Crocetti, and H.R. Spiro. "Drinking Patterns in a Blue-Collar Population." *Quarterly Journal of Studies on Alcohol* 34, no. 3 (1973).

Schumm, Jeremiah A., and Kathleen M. Chard. "Alcohol and Stress in the Military." National Institute on Alcohol Abuse and Alcoholism, *Alcohol Research and Current Review* 34, no. 4 (2012).

Scott, Wilbur J. "PTSD in DSM III: A Case in the Politics of Diagnosis and Disease." *Social Problems* 37, no. 3 (August 1990).

Sefa, Bulut. "Classification of Posttraumatic Stress Disorder and Its Evolution in *Diagnostic and Statistical Manual of Mental Disorders* (DSM) Criteria." *International Journal of Psychology and Counseling* 12, no. 4 (October–December 2020).

Severo, Richard, and Lewis Milford. *The Wages of War: When America's Soldiers Came Home—From Valley Forge to Vietnam.* New York: Simon & Schuster, 1989.

Shaw, Anna Moore. *A Pima Past.* Tucson: University of Arizona Press, 1974.

Slotkin, Richard. *Regeneration Through Violence: The Mythology of the American Frontier, 1600–1860.* Middleton, CT: Wesleyan University Press, 1973.

Stahre, Mandy A., Robert D. Brewer, Vincent P. Fonseca, and Timothy S. Naimi. "Binge Drinking Among U.S. Active-Duty Military Personnel." *American Journal of Preventive Medicine* 36, no. 3 (2009).

Steiner, Stan. *The New Indians.* New York: Delta Books, 1968.

Stouffer, Samuel A., Arthur A. Lumsdaine, Robin M. Williams, Jr., M. Brewster Smith, Irving L. Janis, Shirley A. Star, and Leonard S. Cottrell, Jr. *The American Soldier: Combat and Its Aftermath,* Vol. II. New York: John Wiley and Sons, 1965. First published: 1949.

Sun Tzu. *The Art of War.* Oxford, UK: University of Oxford Press, 1971. Edited and translated by Samuel B. Griffith.

Szasz, Margaret Connell. *Education and the American Indian: The Road to Self-Determination.* Albuquerque: University of New Mexico Press, 1999.

Taylor, Graham D. *The New Deal and American Indian Tribalism: The Administration of the Indian Reorganization Act, 1934–45.* Lincoln: University of Nebraska Press, 1980.

Townsend, Kenneth William. *World War II and the American Indian.* Albuquerque: University of New Mexico Press, 2000.

Usbek, Frank. "Fighting Like Indians, the 'Indian Scout Syndrome' in American and German War Reports of World War II." In *Visual Representations of Native Americans: Transnational Contexts and Perspectives, American Studies, a Monograph Series,* Vol. 186, edited by Karsten Fitz. Heidelberg, Germany (Winter 2012).

Verhoeven, J.E., R. Yang, O.M. Wolkowitz, F.S. Bernani, D. Linquist, S.H. Mellon, R. Yehuda, J.D. Flory, D. Abu-Amara, I. Makotine, C. Marmar, M. Jett, and R. Hanimameh. "Epigenic Age in Combat-Exposed War Veterans: Associations with Posttraumatic Stress Disorder Status." *Molecular Neuropsychiatry* 4 (2018).

Webb, George. *A Pima Remembers.* Tucson: University of Arizona Press, 1959.

Webster, Loren. "Ai's 'I Can't Get Started.'" February 19, 2008. https://www.lorenwebster.net/In_a_Dark_Time/2008/02/19/ais-i-cant-get-started/.

Wheal, Elizabeth-Anne, and Stephan Pope, eds. *The Macmillan Dictionary of the Second World War,* 2nd Edition. London: Macmillan, 1997.

Wolf, Erika J. "PTSD and Accelerated Aging." *PTSD Research Quarterly* 28, no. 3 (2016).

Woods, Teri Knutson, Karen Blaine, and Lauri Francisco. "O'odham Himdag as a Source of Strength and Wellness Among the Tohono O'odham of Southern Arizona and Northern Sonora." *Journal of Sociology and Social Work* 29 (March 2002).

Woodun, JoAnn. "Gender and Sexuality in Native American Societies: A Bibliography." *American Indian Quarterly* 19, no. 4
(Autumn 1995).

Theses and Dissertations

Cook, Keith. "The Indian Who Raised the Flag: An Examination
of the Legacy of Ira Hayes, 1945–Present" (master's thesis,
University of Arizona, 2020).
Scott, Cord. "Comic and Conflict: War and Patriotically Themed
Comics in American Cultural History from World War I
Through the Iraq War" (Ph.D. diss., University of Loyola-
Chicago, 2011).
Seviertson, B. L. "Historical/Cultural Etiology of the Tohono
O'odham Nation" (Ph.D. diss., University of Arizona, 1999).

Notes

Introduction

1. Justin Baragona, "Fox News Host: Native Americans Are Alcoholics Hooked on the Government," *Daily Beast*, October 14, 2021, https://www.thedailybeast.com/fox-news-host-rachel-campos-duffy-says-native-americans-are-alcoholics-hooked-on-the-government.

Chapter 1. Mount Suribachi and the Price of Combat

1. The official history of the Iwo Jima battle is Henri et al., *The U.S. Marines on Iwo Jima* (Uncommon Valor Press, 2013; first published: Dial Press, 1945), p. vii.
2. Henri et al., *The U.S. Marines on Iwo Jima*, p. 125.
3. Sun Tzu, *The Art of War*, p. 85.
4. Perhaps the most comprehensive narrative of the 2nd Battalion, 28th Marines' fight on Iwo Jima is Hemingway, *Ira Hayes: Pima Marine*. Also see Nalty and Crawford, *The United States Marines on Iwo Jima: The Battle and the Flag Raisings*, p. 1, and James F. Dunnigan and Albert A. Nofi, *Victory at Sea: World War II in the Pacific* (New York: William Morrow and Company, 1995), p. 68.
5. Henri et al., *The U.S. Marines on Iwo Jima*, pp. 3–9.
6. Naval History and Heritage Command, *Amphibious Operations*, p. 6-1. Also see Prat et al., "Wound Ballistics and Blast Injuries," pp. S9–S12.
7. Henri et al., *The U.S. Marines on Iwo Jima*, pp. 6–12.
8. U.S. Army, *Wound Ballistics in World War II* (Washington, D.C.: Government Printing Office, 1962), pp. 6–12. Also War Department, *Japanese Mortars and Grenade Dischargers*.
9. Hayes' account appeared in "Hayes Left Own Account of Historic Flag Raising," *Knoxville News Sentinel*, p. 13.

10. Naval History and Heritage Command, *Amphibious Operations, Capture of Iwo Jima*, pp. 1–15.
11. Henri et al., *The U.S. Marines on Iwo Jima*, pp. 47–48. Most of these weapons—satchel charges, hand grenades, and flamethrowers—are curiously personal and impersonal at one and the same time. Unless a Marine was an Olympic hammer thrower, he or she had to get close to the bunker or cave target so as not to endanger him or herself. The same with a flamethrower. To get within range of a target, one must put him or herself in a dangerous position. These weapons, however, killed and maimed indifferently. Personal and impersonal.
12. Hemingway, *Ira Hayes*, pp. 73–76.
13. Henri et al., *The U.S. Marines on Iwo Jima*, p. 48.
14. Hemingway, *Ira Hayes*, pp. 73–74.
15. Henri et al., *The U.S. Marines on Iwo Jima*, p. 50.
16. Hemingway, *Ira Hayes*, p. 83.
17. "Hayes Left Own Account of Historic Flag Raising," *Knoxville News Sentinel*, p. 13.

Chapter 2. Ira Hayes' People: War, Water, and the Collective Ordeal of the Akimel O'odham

1. Kroeber and Fontana, *Massacre on the Gila*, p. 22.
2. Holm, *Strong Hearts, Wounded Souls*. A significant percentage of Native Vietnam veterans surveyed for the study said that participation in tribal ceremonies either to honor or purify them helped in their healing. Basically, the ceremonies could be called the social absorption of war trauma.
3. There are many books that deal with the false and often harmful stereotypes of Native North Americans. Among the best are: Robert F. Berkhofer Jr., *The White Man's Indian*; Brian W. Dippie, *The Vanishing Indian*; Richard Drinnon, *Facing West*; and Roy Harvey Pearce, *Savagism and Civilization*.
4. See especially Richard Slotkin, *Regeneration Through Violence*.
5. Allen, "O'odham Himdag: The O'odham Way," pp. 87–89; Woods, Blaine, and Francisco, "O'odham Himdag as a Source of Strength and Wellness"; and Seviertson, "Historical/Cultural Etiology of the Tohono O'odham Nation." See also David Martinez's important piece entitled "Elder Brother Lives Here."
6. Frank Russell, *The Pima Indians*, pp. 200–204.
7. Basso, *Western Apache Raiding and Warfare*. See especially the narrative of John Rope.
8. Rodrigo F. Rentería-Valencia, "Colonial Tensions," pp. 345–364.

9. Rentería-Valencia, "Colonial Tensions," pp. 347–348.

10. "The *Relectios* of Francisco de Vitoria of Salamanca University," typescript in English. Collection of the author.

11. Fernández-Santamaria, "Juan Ginés de Sepúlveda on the Nature of the American Indians," pp. 434–451. Fernández-Santamaria, Fide, and Keen, "Bartolomé de las Casas in History," p. 122.

12. Rentería-Valencia, "Colonial Tensions," p. 358.

13. Dobyns, *The Pima-Maricopa*, p. 23.

14. Dobyns, *The Pima-Maricopa*, p. 29.

15. Basso, *Western Apache Raiding and Warfare*, p. 16.

16. Bee, "Quechan," p. 93.

17. Dupuy, *The Evolution of Weapons and Warfare*, p. 2.

18. Russell, *The Pima Indians*, pp. 95–96.

19. Russell, *The Pima Indians*, pp. 120–121.

20. Russell, *The Pima Indians*, p. 96.

21. Webb, *A Pima Remembers*, pp. 39–40.

22. Russell, *The Pima Indians*, p. 203. Also see Dobyns, *The Pima-Maricopa*, pp. 47–59.

23. Dobyns, *The Pima-Maricopa*, p. 32.

24. Dobyns, *The Pima-Maricopa*, p. 14.

25. Billington, *Westward Expansion*, p. 587.

26. Dobyns, *The Pima-Maricopa*, p. 40.

27. Kroeber and Fontana, *Massacre on the Gila*, pp. 18–19; Enloe, *Ethnic Soldiers*, pp. 23–49; Tom Holm, "Strong Hearts: Native Service in the U.S. Armed Forces," in Lackenbauer et al., *Aboriginal Peoples and Military Participation*, pp. 127–152.

28. Dobyns, *The Pima-Maricopa*, p. 43.

29. Dobyns, *The Pima-Maricopa*, pp. 47–48. Also see Dunlay, *Wolves for the Blue Soldiers*, pp. 30–31, 103.

30. Dunlay, *Wolves for the Blue Soldiers*, p. 50.

31. Dunlay, *Wolves for the Blue Soldiers*, pp. 50, 64.

32. Hemingway, *Ira Hayes*, p. 45.

33. Vine Deloria Jr. and Raymond J. DeMallie, *Documents of American Indian Diplomacy: Treaties, Agreements, and Conventions, 1775–1979*, vol. I (Norman: University of Oklahoma Press, 1999), pp. 711–712.

34. Quoted in Dobyns, *The Pima-Maricopa*, p. 16.

35. DeJong, *Stealing the Gila*, p. 70.

36. DeJong, *Stealing the Gila*, pp. 72–73, 83.

37. There are numerous studies of the policy of Indian removal. Most focus on individual tribes or peoples from specific regions that were transported to

the Indian Territory. Arrell Morgan Gibson, in *America's Exiles*, attempts to cover relocated groups by the area in the Indian Territory where they were eventually settled. Gibson's book was at least a novel approach to the issue of Indian removal. Also see Gary Clayton Anderson, *Ethnic Cleansing and the Indian: The Crime That Should Haunt America* (Norman: University of Oklahoma Press, 2015), and Angie Debo, *A History of the Indians of the United States* (Norman: University of Oklahoma Press, 1970).

38. DeJong, *Stealing the Gila*, pp. 76–82.
39. DeJong, *Stealing the Gila*, p. 90.
40. DeJong, *Stealing the Gila*, Table 6.1, p. 93.
41. DeJong, *Stealing the Gila*, pp. 98–99, 102–107.
42. "Indian Fruit Pickers," *Los Angeles Times*, p. 16.
43. "The Starving Pimas," *Chicago Tribune*, p. 6.
44. "Indians Starving," *Pomona* (California) *Daily Progress*, p. 1.
45. Hirschberger, "Collective Trauma."
46. "Test of Indians' Right to Vote," *Tucson Citizen*, p. 1; Smith, "State Supreme Court Rules Indians May Vote If Able to Read," p. 6.
47. Brave Heart and DeBruyn, "The American Indian Holocaust," pp. 60–82; Brave Heart et al., "Historical Trauma among Indigenous Peoples of the Americas," pp. 43–44, 282–290; Brave Heart, "Integrating Trauma"; Brown-Rice, "Examining the Theory of Historical Trauma among Native Americans."
48. Quoted in Hemingway, *Ira Hayes*, p. 151.

Chapter 3. The Education of Ira H. Hayes

1. Russell, *The Pima Indians*, p. 32.
2. See especially Prucha, *American Indian Policy in Crisis*; Prucha, *Americanizing the American Indian*; Holm, *The Great Confusion in Indian Affairs*; and Hoxie, *A Final Promise*.
3. Hertzberg, *The Search for an American Indian Identity*, pp. 38–42; Holm, *The Great Confusion*, pp. 56–58; Doctor Charles Eastman Obituary, *Detroit Free Press*, p. 19.
4. Hertzberg, *American Indian Identity*, pp. 138–139; Holm, *The Great Confusion*, pp. 116–117; "Mrs. Bonnin Dies," *Evening Star*, p. 12.
5. "The Pima Mission," *Arizona Republic*, p. 4; "Mortuary, Reverend Charles H. Cook," Arizona *Daily Star*, p. 8; "Apostle to the Pimas Is Dead," *Arizona Republic*, p. 10.
6. Shaw, *A Pima Past*, p. 92.

7. Webb, *A Pima Remembers*, p. 86.
8. See http://thefamouspeople.com/profiles/ira-hayes-9341.php.
9. Prucha, *American Indian Policy in Crisis*, pp. 272–280.
10. Holm, *The Great Confusion*, pp. 88–92. For a general look at Indian education, see especially Jon Reyhner and Jeanne Eder, *American Indian Education* and Szasz, *Education and the American Indian*.
11. Meadows, *The Comanche Code Talkers of World War II*, pp. 87–88; Shaw, *A Pima Past*, pp. 143–144.
12. Britten, *American Indians in World War I*, pp. 66–67.
13. Krouse, *North American Indians in the Great War*, p. 20.
14. Shaw, *A Pima Past*, pp. 142–145.
15. See https://legion.org/honor/photos/214575/veterans-memorial-park-sacaton-az; see also https://honorstates.org/index.php? id_366328.
16. Holm, *Strong Hearts, Wounded Souls*, pp. 151–152; Carroll, *Medicine Bags and Dog Tags*, pp. 86–113.
17. "Indians in the War," *The Indian's Friend*, p. 1.
18. Department of War, *Annual Report of the Secretary of War*, p. 14.
19. "Ira Hayes: Immortal Flag Raiser at Iwo Jima," https://news.va.gov/68545/ira-hayes-immortal-flag-raiser-iwo-jima/.
20. Holm, *The Great Confusion*, pp. 113–114.
21. Shaw, *A Pima Past*, p. 85.
22. Shaw, *A Pima Past*, p. 121.
23. Webb, *A Pima Remembers*, pp. 42–44.
24. Bradley, *Flags of Our Fathers*, p. 41.
25. Rogers, "A Fading Picture from Iwo Jima," p. 4.
26. "In Continuum Ira Hamilton Hayes," *Arizona Republic*, p. 77.
27. Carroll, *Medicine Bags and Dog Tags*, p. 131; Also see Hemingway, *Ira Hayes*. Examples of Hayes' fun-loving demeanor and willingness to share his thoughts exist in many places in Hemingway's short but excellent book.
28. Bradley, *Flags of Our Fathers*, pp. 41–42. For more on Indian education in the 1930s and beyond, see Szasz, *Education and the American Indian*, and Parker, *The Phoenix Indian School*.
29. Philip, *John Collier's Crusade for Indian Reform*, pp. 17–18.
30. Philip, *John Collier's Crusade for Indian Reform*, p. 24.
31. The history of the Roosevelt administration's American Indian policies is detailed in Taylor, *The New Deal American Indian Tribalism*.
32. Parman, "The Indian and the Civilian Conservation Corps," pp. 39–46.
33. Parman, "The Indian and the Civilian Conservation Corps," p. 50.

NOTES

34. Parman, "The Indian and the Civilian Conservation Corps," pp. 52–53. See also Bureau of Indian Affairs, *Indians at Work*, Vols. 1–13, https://library.si.edu/digital-library/book/indians-work.
35. Bradley, *Flags of Our Fathers*, p. 42.
36. See Neuberger, "On the Warpath," p. 79 and his "The American Indian Enlists," *Asia and the Americas*.
37. Holm, "Fighting a White Man's War," pp. 69–81; Enloe, *Ethnic Soldiers*, pp. 192–193.
38. Frank Usbeck, "Fighting like Indians, the 'Indian Scout Syndrome' in American and German War Reports of World War II," in Karsten Fitz (ed.), *Visual Representations of Native Americans: Transnational Contexts and Perspectives*, American Studies, A Monograph Series, Vol. 186, Heidelberg (Winter 2012), pp. 125–143.
39. Holm, "Strong Hearts: Native Service in the U.S. Armed Forces," in Lackenbauer et al., *Aboriginal Peoples and Military Participation*," pp. 127–151.
40. Hines, "Marine Corps Cultural Similarities to Native Americans," pp. 1–6.
41. Anderson-Colon, "Marine Corps Boot Camp During World War II," pp. 46–63.

Chapter 4. From Boot Camp to Bougainville

1. Condit, Diamond, and Turnblad, *Marine Corps Ground Training in World War II*, pp. 18–20.
2. Anderson-Colon, "Marine Corps Boot Camp," pp. 47–50.
3. Anderson-Colon, "Marine Corps Boot Camp," pp. 62–63.
4. Huie, *Hero of Iwo Jima*, pp. 14–18.
5. Condit et al., *Marine Corps Ground Training*, p. 22.
6. Bradley and Powers, *Flags of Our Fathers*, pp. 77–78.
7. Condit et al., *Marine Corps Ground Training*, pp. 175–177.
8. Hemingway, "Pete Ellis, Father of Amphibious Warfare." Also see Robert Pearman, "Mystery of a U.S. Spy Who Was 20 Years Ahead of History," *Louisville Courier-Journal*, November 30, 1962, p. 10.
9. Doris Paul's *The Navajo Code Talkers* still stands out among the many books on the Navajo Code Talkers.
10. Military.com, "Force Recon: Mission and History."
11. Updegraph, *Special Marine Corps Units*, p. 39.
12. Huie, *Hero of Iwo Jima*, p. 23.
13. Hoffman, *Silk Chutes*, pp. 12–13.
14. Updegraph, *Special Marine Corps Units*, p. 38.
15. Updegraph, *Special Marine Corps Units*, pp. 38–40; Hoffman, *Silk Chutes*, p. 13.

16. Hoffman, *Silk Chutes*, p. 7.

17. Bradley and Powers, *Flags of Our Fathers*, p. 79; Marine Corps University, "Corporal Ira Hamilton Hayes."

18. Dunnigan and Nofi, *Victory at Sea*, pp. 283, 297–302.

19. Marine Corps University, "Corporal Ira Hamilton Hayes," p. 1.

20. Dunnigan and Nofi, *Victory at Sea*, pp. 30–33, 316–318.

21. Hoffman, *Silk Chutes*, pp. 8–19.

22. Keegan, *Second World War*, pp. 297–307; Dunnigan and Nofi, *Victory at Sea*, pp. 39–40.

23. The idea of being "tribal" in war was part and parcel of basic training. In my study of Native Vietnam veterans, I found that the veterans often emphasized "taking care of each other." When they returned home, several of them depended on their tribal traditions to help them heal. They gained status by participating in tribal ceremonies. Native veterans seem to understand the meaning of mutual aid in the tribal sense of the words. Holm, *Strong Hearts*, pp. 165–168, 183–197. Also see Anderson-Colon's conclusion to her "Marine Corps Boot Camp," p. 63; and Sebastian Junger, *Tribe*. Junger seemed to confirm the hypothesis. Boot camp instilled in Marine Corps recruits the notion of teamwork and a tribal-like, to quote Anderson-Colon, p. 63, "dedication to each other."

24. Keegan, *Second World War*, p. 297.

25. Chapin, *Top of the Ladder*, pp. 6, 11.

26. Gailey, *Bougainville*, pp. 20–21.

27. Dunnigan and Nofi, *Victory at Sea*, p. 546.

28. Dunnigan and Nofi, *Victory at Sea*, p. 54.

29. Gailey, *Bougainville*, pp. 22–38.

30. Chapin, *Top of the Ladder*, pp. 7–8.

31. Chapin, *Top of the Ladder*, pp. 9–11; Gailey, *Bougainville*, pp. 40–59.

32. Gailey, *Bougainville*, pp. 52–53; also see Hoffman, *Silk Chutes*, pp. 22–28.

33. Gailey, *Bougainville*, p. 54; Hoffman, *Silk Chutes*, p. 26.

34. Updegraph, *Special Marine Corps Units*, p. 44; Chapin, *Top of the Ladder*, p. 10.

35. Office of Indian Affairs, *Indians in the War*, p. 28; Marine Corps University, "Corporal Ira Hamilton Hayes," p. 1; Townsend, *World War II and the American Indian*, p. 130.

36. Chapin, *Top of the Ladder*, p. 3.

37. Gailey, *Bougainville*, pp. 96–100.

38. Chapin, *Top of the Ladder*, pp. 19–20.

39. Gailey, *Bougainville*, p. 95.

40. Gailey, *Bougainville*, pp. 75, 130–131.

41. Gailey, *Bougainville*, pp. 116–117.

42. Gailey, *Bougainville*, p. 117.
43. Hemingway, *Ira Hayes*, p. 28.
44. Hemingway, *Ira Hayes*, p. 29.
45. Hemingway, *Ira Hayes*, pp. 30–32.
46. Chapin, *Top of the Ladder*, p. 14.
47. Hemingway, *Ira Hayes*, p. 32.
48. Bradley and Powers, *Flags of Our Fathers*, p. 86.
49. Hoffman, *Silk Chutes*, p. 36.
50. Bradley and Powers, *Flags of Our Fathers*, pp. 86–87.
51. Hemingway, *Ira Hayes*, p. 33.
52. Bradley and Powers, *Flags of Our Fathers*, p. 87.
53. Stouffer et al., *American Soldier.*
54. Grossman, *On Killing.*
55. Marshal, *Men Against Fire.*
56. Grossman, *On Killing*, pp. 149–170.
57. Niraj Warikoo, "Controversial Speaker Canceled," *Detroit Free Press*, April 28, 2021, p. A4.
58. Ron Langer, "Combat Trauma," pp. 50–58; Maguen et al., "The Impact of Killing," pp. 435–443.

Chapter 5. The Photograph *and Its Immediate Aftermath*

1. Quoted in Marling and Wetenhall, *Iwo Jima*, p. 121.
2. Henri et al., *Marines on Iwo Jima*, p. 73; Garand and Strobridge, *Western Pacific Operations*, pp. 616–617.
3. Garand and Strobridge, *Western Pacific Operations*, pp. 548, 616–620.
4. Garand and Strobridge, *Western Pacific Operations*, pp. 620–621.
5. See especially Paul, *The Navajo Code Talkers*, pp. 52–53.
6. Garand and Strobridge, *Western Pacific Operations*, p. 625.
7. Bradley and Powers, *Flags of Our Fathers*, p. 231.
8. Bradley and Powers, *Flags of Our Fathers*, pp. 232–233.
9. Hoffman, *Silk Chutes*, p. 38.
10. Garand and Strobridge, *Western Pacific Operations*, pp. 628–629.
11. Bradley and Powers, *Flags of Our Fathers*, p. 234.
12. Garand and Strobridge, *Western Pacific Operations*, pp. 630–642.
13. Henri et al., *Marines on Iwo Jima*, p. 173.
14. Bradley and Powers, *Flags of Our Fathers*, pp. 244–245.
15. Hemingway, *Ira Hayes*, p. 127.
16. Henri et al., *Marines on Iwo Jima*, p. 173; Garand and Strobridge, *Western Pacific Operations*, p. 710.

17. Keegan, *The Second World War*, p. 566; Garand and Strobridge, *Western Pacific Operations*, pp. 711, 797.

18. Henri et al., *Marines on Iwo Jima*, pp. 179–180; Bradley, *Flags of Our Fathers*, p. 246. Chaplain Gettelsohn's words are quoted in Hemingway, *Ira Hayes*, p. 126.

19. See Rosenthal and Heinz, "The Picture That Will Live Forever," pp. 65–70; Fred H. Allison, "Oral History: Interview with Joseph Rosenthal," in Robertson, *Investigating Iwo*, pp. 313–321; "Joe Rosenthal: Shot Flag Raising at Iwo Jima," *Washington Post*, August 22, 2006, p. BO6.

20. Marling and Wetenhall, *Iwo Jima*, pp. 102–104.

21. Marling and Wetenhall, *Iwo Jima*, p. 113.

22. Henri et al., *Marines on Iwo Jima*, p. 23.

23. Jones, *WWII: A Chronicle of Soldiering*, p. 122.

24. Bradley and Powers, *Flags of Our Fathers*, p. 268.

25. Bradley and Powers, *Flags of Our Fathers*, pp. 268–269.

26. Bradley and Powers, *Flags of Our Fathers*, p. 269.

27. Marling and Wetenhall, *Iwo Jima*, p. 111.

28. Michael Landesberg, "Disputed Image of Victory," *Wichita Falls Times Record News*, February 12, 1995, p. 35. Also see Melissa Renn, "*Time, Life* and the Flag Raisings on Iwo Jima," in Robertson, *Investigating Iwo*, pp. 45–62.

29. U.S. Marine Corps, "Marine Corps Updates Its Official Records."

30. Marling and Wetenhall, *Iwo Jima*, p. 104.

31. Marling and Wetenhall, *Iwo Jima*, p. 104.

32. "Iwo Photo Not Posed, Says Rosenthal," *Los Angeles Times*, June 15, 1945, p. 13.

33. Bradley and Powers, *Flags of Our Fathers*, pp. 196–197.

34. "Iwo Jima Flag Will Fly over Capitol," *Los Angeles Times*, May 9, 1945, p. 4.

35. See Bradley and Powers, *Flags of Our Fathers*, pp. 281–295, for details of the Seventh War Bond Tour.

36. Huie, *Hero of Iwo Jima*, p. 38.

37. For the references to Vandegrift's "your Indian" quote, see Marling and Wetenhall, *Iwo Jima*, pp. 119–120.

38. Jones and Fear, "Alcohol Use and Misuse within the Military," pp. 168–169; Robinette et al., "Chronic Alcoholism," pp. 687–700; Peter Andreas, "The Untold Story of How Booze Soaked the Battlefields of World War II," 2020 (https://taskandpurpose.com/history/killer-high-war-drugs-excerpt/), excerpted from his book *Killer High*.

39. The quote is in Marling and Wetenhall, *Iwo Jima*, p. 119; regarding Keyes Beech's alcoholism and his nightly drinking with Hayes, see Bradley and Powers, *Flags of Our Fathers*, pp. 284, 286.

40. See Dunbar-Ortiz and Gilio-Whitaker, *All the Real Indians Died Off*, pp. 130–136, about the myths and images of Native American alcoholism.

41. Marling and Wetenhall, *Iwo Jima*, p. 111.

42. Hy Hurwitz, "Hayes, Iwo Jima Hero, Wants to Return to Battle," *Boston Globe*, May 16, 1945, p. 6.

43. "Iwo Hero Prefers Action to Steak Feasts," *Democrat and Chronicle* (Rochester, New York), May 17, 1945, p. 1.

44. "Flag-Raising Hero Visits Arizona Home," *Arizona Republic*, April 29, 1945, p. 6.

45. "Ira Hayes, Iwo Flag Raiser, Is Honored," *Tucson Citizen*, May 2, 1945, p. 9.

46. George E. McKinnon, "Vets Stage Thrilling 'Battle' on Commons for Bond Drive," *Boston Globe*, May 15, 1945, p. 6.

47. "Hayes Abandons Bond Sales Tour to Fight War," *Arizona Republic*, May 26, 1945, p. 1.

48. Ray Coll, Jr., "Couldn't Take Hero Worship," *Honolulu Advertiser*, July 23, 1945, p. 12.

49. "Good Luck Private Hayes," *Tucson Citizen*, June 2, 1945, p. 12.

50. "Good Luck Private Hayes," *Tucson Citizen*, June 2, 1945, p. 12.

51. "Indians Turn Out to Honor Their Own Ira Hayes," *Tucson Citizen*, June 25, 1945, p. 5.

52. Quoted in Bradley and Powers, *Flags of Our Fathers*, p. 291.

53. Marling and Wetenhall, *Iwo Jima*, p. 102.

54. Marling and Wetenhall, *Iwo Jima*, p. 116.

55. "Iwo Heroes Speak at Rally Here," *Arizona Republic*, June 8, 1945, p. 1.

56. "Indian Hero Prefers Duty on War Front," *Tucson Citizen*, June 2, 1945, p. 1.

57. A concise picture of the Olympic operation is found in Jones, *WWII: A Chronicle of Soldiering*, pp. 242–245.

58. Wheal and Pope, *Macmillan Dictionary*, pp. 35–36.

59. Shaw, *The United States Marine Corps in the Occupation of Japan*.

60. Flynn, "Stress Accelerates Biological Aging"; Verhoeven et al., "Epigenic Age in Combat-Exposed War Veterans," pp. 90–99; Wolf, "PTSD and Accelerated Aging."

61. Quoted in Holm, *Strong Hearts, Wounded Souls*, p. 192.

62. Russell, *The Pima Indians*, p. 193.

63. Kroeber and Fontana, *Massacre on the Gila*, pp. 94–100.

64. Russell, *The Pima Indians*, pp. 204–205.

65. National Park Service, "History of the Marine Corps War Memorial."

66. Frisk, "What Makes a Hero," pp. 87–103.

67. Holm, "Fighting a White Man's War," pp. 78–79.

68. *True Comics*, Winter Issue, no. 46, 1945.

69. See Scott, "Comic and Conflict"; Hirsch, "This Is Our Enemy," pp. 448–456; Goodnow and Kimble, *The 10 Cent War*.

70. *True Comics*, Winter Issue, no. 46, 1945.

Chapter 6. Heroism and Hollywood

1. Harjo, *Crazy Brave*.
2. Hemingway, *Ira Hayes*, p. 42.
3. Marling and Wetenhall, *Iwo Jima*, p. 119.
4. Quoted in Brown, *Bury My Heart at Wounded Knee*, pp. 86, 90.
5. "Wins Further Honors," *Casa Grande Dispatch*, June 29, 1945, p. 5.
6. Bradley and Powers, *Flags of Our Fathers*, p. 307.
7. Marling and Wetenhall, *Iwo Jima*, p. 119.
8. Fixico, *Termination and Relocation*, p. 22.
9. Dobyns, *The Pima-Maricopa*, pp. 81, 90.
10. During my studies of Native American Vietnam veterans, I talked not only to many veterans but also with our Native medicine people and elders. These four virtues—honesty, courage, generosity, and humility—to which I allude are shared almost universally among Native peoples.
11. "Names of Iwo Flag Raisers Not Certain," *Corpus Christi Times*, December 17, 1946, p. 21.
12. "Ousted 'Indian' Family Plans Appeal for Home," *Los Angeles Times*, February 8, 1947, p. 9.
13. "Schmidt, 20 Years on LA Bench, Dies," *Los Angeles Daily News*, February 24, 1947, p. 2.
14. "Indians Fight Eviction of Mother and Girls," *Los Angeles Times*, February 14, 1947, p. 1.
15. "L.A. Indians on Warpath over Eviction," *Los Angeles Daily News*, February 14, 1947, p. 33.
16. "Schmidt, 20 Years on LA Bench, Dies," *Los Angeles Daily News*, February 24, 1947, p. 2.
17. "16 Indian Tribe Chiefs Beat War Drums over Eviction," *Los Angeles Daily News*, February 17, 1947, p. 8; "Indians Open Fight for Racial Equality," *Los Angeles Times*, February 17, 1947, p. 12.
18. "Indians Launch Fight on Covenants," *California Eagle*, March 13, 1947, p. 9.
19. "Warhoop Sounds: Indian War Heroes Protest Unfairness," *Valley Times* (Hollywood, California), March 22, 1947, p. 1; "Help Pledged Indian Evictees," *Los Angeles Times*, March 25, 1947, p. 9.
20. "Indian Uprising in Hollywood," *Visalia Times-Delta* (Tulare County, California), March 26, 1947, p. 9.
21. "Showbiz Imagery and Forgotten History," https://oldshowbiz.tumblr.com/post/187940222694/1947-will-rogers-jr-inadvertently-became-an.
22. "Notables to Attend Indian Mass Meeting," *Los Angeles Evening Citizen News*, March 19, 1947, p. 22; "Msg. O'Dwyer, Kersey on Program Asking

Equal Rights for Indians," *Los Angeles Evening Citizen News,* March 24, 1947, p. 7; "Meeting Underscores Indian's Right to Live Where He Chooses," *Los Angeles Evening Citizen News,* March 25, 1947, p. 5.

23. Aline Mosley, "Hollywood Indians Are on Warpath," *Honolulu Advertiser,* March 16, 1947, p. 30.

24. "Indian Heroes Visit City Hall," *Los Angeles Times,* March 23, 1947, p. 4.

25. "Asserts She and Husband Had No Idea of Fight That Was Coming When They Bought House After Seeking Better Neighborhood," *St. Louis Star and Times,* May 4, 1948, p. 4.

26. Louella Parsons, "Hollywood," *Sacramento Bee,* February 3, 1948, p. 14.

27. Henry Fuller, "Phoenix Pays Famed Train Due Respect," *Arizona Republic,* February 21, 1948, pp. 1–2.

28. Michael T. Isenberg, "The Great War Viewed from the 1920s: *The Big Parade,*" in Rollins and O'Connor, *Why We Fought,* pp. 144–145. Isenberg's chapter was previously published in the journal *Film and History.*

29. Garland, *War Movies,* pp. 20–22. Brock's encyclopedic volume needs to be updated.

30. Richard Allen and Tom Holm, "Fighting the White Man's Wars (On the Silver Screen)," in Pavlik, Marubbio, and Holm, *Native Apparitions,* pp. 558–59.

31. Allen and Holm, "Fighting the White Man's Wars (on the Silver Screen)," in Pavlik, Marubbio, and Holm, *Native Apparitions,* pp. 62–65.

32. M. Elise Marubbio, "Look at the Heart of *The Searchers,*" in Pavlik, Marubbio, and Holm, *Native Apparitions,* p. 111.

33. Bradley and Powers, *Flags of Our Fathers,* p. 322.

34. See especially Baker, *Masculinity in Fiction and Film,* and Ferguson, "Masculinity and War," pp. s108–s120.

35. See Kroeber and Fontana, *Massacre on the Gila,* pp. 165–174, on the sexual difference in labor. Innes and Alexander, *Indigenous Men and Masculinities;* JoAnn Woodsum, "Gender and Sexuality in Native American Societies: A Bibliography," *American Indian Quarterly* 19, no. 4 (Autumn 1995), pp. 527–554.

36. Bradley and Powers, *Flags of Our Fathers,* p. 318.

Chapter 7. "Call Him Drunken Ira Hayes"

1. Peter LaFarge, "The Ballad of Ira Hayes," sung by Johnny Cash, *Bitter Tears: Ballads of the American Indian.* First recorded in 1961.

2. American Psychiatric Association, *Diagnostic and Statistical Manual of Mental Disorders,* pp. 236–238; American Psychiatric Association, *Diagnostic and Statistical Manual of Mental Disorders,* 3rd Edition, Revised, pp. 247–251; Sefa, "Classification of Postraumatic Stress Disorder," pp. 105–108;

"History of PTSD and Trauma Diagnoses." Also see Figley, *Stress Disorders among Vietnam Veterans*, pp. viii–xvii.

3. American Psychiatric Association, https://psychiatry.org/patients-families /ptsd/what-is-ptsd. See also Scott, "PTSD in DSM-III," p. 295.

4. Scott, "PTSD in DSM-III," pp. 294–310; Bourne, *Men, Stress, and Vietnam.*

5. Harry R. Kormos, "The Nature of Combat Stress," in Figley, *Stress Disorders among Vietnam Veterans*, pp. 5–7.

6. American Psychiatric Association, *Diagnostic and Statistical Manual of Mental Disorders*, 5th Edition, pp. 270–281.

7. See Severo and Milford, *The Wages of War*, pp. 283–297; "History of PTSD and Trauma Diagnoses."

8. Orr et al., "Psychophysiological Assessment," pp. 152–159.

9. Langer, "Combat Trauma," pp. 50–58.

10. Janssen, "Locked in the Vault"; "History of PTSD and Trauma Diagnoses," p. 6; Magnen et al., "The Impact of Killing," pp. 435–443; Hierholzer et al., "Clinical Presentation of PTSD in World War II Combat Veterans," pp. 816–820; Scott, "PTSD in DSM-III," p. 297. Also see Office of Veterans Affairs, *Legacies of Vietnam*, and Chaim F. Shatan, "Stress Disorders Among Vietnam Veterans: The Emotional Content of Combat Continues," in Figley, *Stress Disorders among Vietnam Veterans*, p. 47.

11. Broyles, "Why Men Love War," p. 75.

12. Holm, *Strong Hearts, Wounded Souls*, p. 186.

13. Steiner, *The New Indians*, p. 19.

14. Jones, *WWII: A Chronicle of Soldiering*, pp. 122–124, 196–198.

15. Russell, *The Pima Indians*, pp. 193–195.

16. "Ira Hayes Dead; His Act Lives Forever," *Daily Times* (Davenport, Iowa), January 26, 1955, p. 14.

17. Dunbar-Ortiz and Gilio-Whitaker take on and expose all of these myths in *All the Real Indians Died Off.* In the first chapter of *Termination and Relocation*, Fixico explains that American policymakers believed in the idea that Native veterans would want to break away from the reservations and lead their people into mainstream white society.

18. Schumm and Chard, "Alcohol and Stress in the Military"; Jones and Fear, "Alcohol Use and Misuse within the Military," pp. 166–172; Polich, "Epidemiology of Alcohol Abuse," pp. 1125–1132; Robinette et al., "Chronic Alcoholism," pp. 687–700.

19. Coyhis and White, *Alcohol Problems in Native America*, pp. 18–21.

20. Patrick J. Abbott, "American Indian and Alaska Native Aboriginal Use of Alcohol in the United States," p. 3.

21. Coyhis and White, *Alcohol Problems in Native America*, p. 21.

22. Forbes and Adams, *A Model of "Grass-Roots" Community Development*, p. 16.
23. Russell, *The Pima Indians*, p. 32.
24. Russell, *The Pima Indians*, p. 32.
25. Forbes and Adams, *A Model of "Grass-Roots" Community Development*, p. 16.
26. Russell, *The Pima Indians*, p. 32.
27. Dunbar-Ortiz and Gilio-Whitaker, *All the Real Indians Died Off*, p. 130.
28. Coylis and White, *Alcohol Problems in Native America*, p. 1.
29. See Peter Andreas, *Killer High: A History of War in Six Drugs*.
30. Stahre et al., "Binge Drinking among U.S. Active-Duty Military Personnel," pp. 208–217; Babor, "Classification of Alcoholics."
31. Andreas, "The Untold Story of How Booze Soaked the Battlefields of World War II," excerpted from Andreas' *Killer High*.
32. Stahre et al., "Binge Drinking Among U.S. Active-Duty Military Personnel," pp. 208–217; Saiassi et al., "Drinking Patterns in a Blue-Collar Population," pp. 917–926; Schumm and Chard, "Alcohol and Stress in the Military"; Babor, "Classification of Alcoholics."
33. Huie, *Hero of Iwo Jima*, pp. 23–24.

Chapter 8. Ira Hayes and the Failure of Relocation

1. Fixico, *Termination and Relocation*, p. 9. Also see Rosier, *Serving Their Country* for an astute interpretation of Termination as part of an American Cold War mentality that immediately followed World War II.
2. Fixico, *Termination and Relocation*, p. 11.
3. Fixico, *Termination and Relocation*, pp. 17–18.
4. See especially Franco, *Crossing the Pond*, and Townsend, *World War II and the American Indian*.
5. Townsend, *World II and the American Indian*, pp. 104–106.
6. Franco, *Crossing the Pond*, p. 67.
7. Fixico, *Termination and Relocation*, pp. 25–29.
8. Fixico, *Termination and Relocation*, p. 40.
9. Fixico, *Termination and Relocation*, p. 35.
10. Fixico, *Termination and Relocation*, p. 36.
11. Fixico, *Termination and Relocation*, pp. 94–110,
12. Fixico, *Termination and Relocation*, pp. 183.
13. Louella Parsons, "Hollywood," *Sacramento Bee*, February 3, 1948, p. 14.
14. Philip Heisler, "Three Men from Suribachi, Where Are They Now?" *Baltimore Sun*, February 22, 1948, pp. 55, 57.
15. Bob Thomas, "Ira Hayes Leaves His Farm to Raise Iwo Flag in Movie," *Tucson Citizen*, July 28, 1949, p. 17.

16. Jime C. Lucas, "Surviving Iwo Flag Raisers Puzzled by Publicity," *Knoxville News Sentinel*, February 19, 1950, p. 23.

17. Jime C. Lucas, "Surviving Iwo Flag Raisers Puzzled by Publicity," *Knoxville News Sentinel*, p. 23.

18. "Free Worship Session Due," *Arizona Republic*, February, 15, 1948, pp. 1, 3; "Phoenix Pays Famed Train Due Respect," *Arizona Republic*, February 21, 1948, p. 2; "Thunderbird Legion Post to Dedicate Home Today," *Arizona Republic*, March 14, 1948, p. 9.

19. "Ira Hayes in Person" (advertisement for *Sands of Iwo Jima*), *Arizona Republic*, March 4, 1950, p. 13; "Mesa Groups Will Honor Iwo Veteran," *Arizona Republic*, March 6, 1950, p. 7; "Ask State Indian Vet to Re-enact Iwo Jima," *Tucson Citizen*, June 29, 1950, p. 23; "Iwo Flag Raising to Be Re-enacted," *Fort Collins Coloradoan*, June 29, 1950, p. 4; "Exposition at Anadarko Will Draw 30,000 Indians," *Wichita Falls Times*, June 10, 1951, p. 43; "Let's Go Marines," *Arizona Republic*, July 15, 1952, p. 17.

20. "Still in the Fight," *Los Angeles Evening Citizen News*, March 8, 1950, p. 19.

21. Feldstein, Nenner, and May, "American Indian and Alaska Native Alcohol-Related Incarceration and Treatment," pp. 1–22.

22. Fixico, *Termination and Relocation*, pp. 134–157; Rosier, *Serving Whose Country?*, pp. 151–152. Also see Rosenthal, *Reimagining Indian Country*.

23. "Welcome Ira Hayes," *Chicago Tribune*, May 19, 1953, p. 31.

24. Henry M'Lemore, "The Lighter Side," *Los Angeles Times*, May 26, 1953, p. 12.

25. Bradley and Powers, *Flags of Our Fathers*, p. 323.

26. "Drive Starts Here to Help Down-and-Out Arizona Hero," *Arizona Daily Star*, October 17, 1953, p. 15.

27. Huie, *Hero of Iwo Jima*, p. 56.

28. "Iwo Jima Hero, Rescued from Skid Row, Finds Job, New Life," *Birmingham News*, October 24, 1953, p. 9; "Iwo Hero Climbs Again—to a Job," New York *Daily News*, October 25, 1953, p. 70.

29. "Iwo Hero Climbs Again—to a Job," New York *Daily News*, October 25, 1953, p. 34.

30. "We Met Briefly Through a Camera Viewfinder," *Los Angeles Evening Citizen News*, October 28, 1953, p. 4.

31. "Marine Hero Can Keep Job in Spite of Arrest," *Long Beach* (California) *Press Telegram*, November 3, 1953, p. 5.

32. Hemingway, *Ira Hayes*, pp. 152–156; Bradley and Powers, *Flags of Our Fathers*, pp. 322–325.

33. "Saddened Ira Hayes Comes Home," *Tucson Citizen*, November 11, 1953, p. 10.

34. Hemingway, *Ira Hayes*, p. 155.

35. George Matthew Adams, "Our Indian Heritage," *News Tribune* (Tacoma, Washington), November 15, 1953, p. 24.

36. "Saddened Ira Hayes Comes Home," *Tucson Citizen*, November 11, 1953, p. 10.

37. "Reluctant Hero," *Akron Beacon Journal*, November 9, 1953, p. 6.

38. "Reluctant Hero," *Akron Beacon Journal*, November 9, 1953, p. 6.

39. "Hayes Again Lands in Jail," *Tucson Citizen*, November 12, 1953, p. 2 and *News Tribune* (Tacoma, Washington), November 15, 1953, p. 24.

40. "Indian Hero Jailed Again," *Arizona Republic*, January 16, p. 3; "Court Places Indian War Hero on Probation," *Arizona Daily Star*, February 12, 1954, p. 17.

41. "Phoenix Area Traffic Brings Injuries to 7," *Arizona Republic*, July 5, 1952, p. 13.

42. "Ira Hayes in Jail Again," *Valley Times* (Hollywood, California), January 16, 1954, p. 12; "Ira Hayes, a Hero of Iwo Jima, Still Being Arrested," *Hagerstown* (Maryland) *Daily Mail*, January 18, 1954, p. 10.

43. "Ira Hayes Joins AA, Granted Probation," *Arizona Daily Sun*, February 12, 1954, p. 6.

44. Dorothy Kilgallen, "Voice of Broadway," *Arizona Republic*, June 26, 1954, p. 18.

45. "Hero of Iwo Jima Deserves a Chance," *Arizona Republic*, September 21, 1954, p. 6.

46. "Statue as U.S. Symbol," *Kansas City Star*, November 10, 1954, p. 38.

47. "Symbol of a Nation's Spirit," New York *Daily News*, November 11, 1954, p. 123.

Chapter 9. *"He Won't Answer Anymore"*

1. Peter LaFarge, "The Ballad of Ira Hayes."

2. I obtained a copy of this death certificate through a site known as "famous-docs" on Ebay.com. Although not an official or certified copy, it appears genuine. The signatures are all there and all the dates are correct. If it is authentic, then Dr. Parks divulged to the newspapers something different from what he wrote on the death certificate. Ira, in fact, died from hypothermia and not from "acute alcoholism," as Parks put it. The papers had labeled Ira as an alcoholic, and it appears that Parks simply used the characterization to declare alcoholism as the cause of death. Hereinafter cited as "Death Certificate."

3. "Arizona's Iwo Flag Raiser Is Dead," *Arizona Daily Star*, January 25, 1955, p. 1; "Iwo Hero Ira Hayes Dies," *Arizona Republic*, January 25, 1955, p. 1; "Lost in 'White Man's World' Indian Survivor of Flag Raising on Jwo Jima Dies on

Reservation," *Fort Worth Star-Telegram*, January 25, 1955, p. 1; Ralph McGill, "He Is the One with Rifle Slung," *Atlanta Constitution*, January 27, 1955, p. 1.

4. "Iwo Hero Ira Hayes Dies," *Arizona Republic*, January 24, 1955, p. 1.

5. Death Certificate.

6. Bradley and Powers, *Flags of Our Fathers*, p. 333; "Heroes: Then There Were Two," *Time*.

7. Betty Binner Nash, "Local Indian Woman Says Hero Murdered," *Great Falls Tribune*, February 4, 1955, p. 6.

8. Advertisement, "Are You Accused? by Ira Hayes," *Wakefield Republican*, February 24, 1955, p. 7.

9. "Arizona's Iwo Flag Raiser Is Dead," *Arizona Republic*, January 25, 1955, p. 1.

10. "Iwo Hero Ira Hayes Dies," *Arizona Daily Star*, January 25, 1955, p. 1.

11. "Death of Ira Hayes," Glens Falls, *New York Post Star*, January 27, 1955, p. 4.

12. "He Found No One Who Could Save Him," *Des Moines Tribune*, February 10, 1955, p. 10.

13. Charles Lucey, "A Cost of War [Ira Hayes]," *The Messenger*, February 11, 1955, p. 4.

14. Claiborne Nuckolls, "Alcoholism Fight Proposed as Memorial for Ira Hayes," *Arizona Republic*, January 30, 1955, p. 13.

15. Claiborne Nuckolls, "Alcoholism Fight Proposed as Memorial for Ira Hayes," *Arizona Republic*, January 30, 1955, p. 18.

16. Claiborne Nuckolls, "Alcoholism Fight Proposed as Memorial for Ira Hayes," *Arizona Republic*, January 30, 1955, p. 18.

17. Claiborne Nuckolls, "Alcoholism Fight Proposed as Memorial for Ira Hayes," *Arizona Republic*, January 30, 1955, p. 18.

18. Don Dedera, "Pima Tribesmen Weep at Farewell to War Hero Brother Ira Hayes," *Arizona Republic*, January 28, 1955, p. 1.

19. Don Dedera, "Pima Tribesmen Weep at Farewell to War Hero Brother Ira Hayes," *Arizona Republic*, January 28, 1955, p. 1.

20. The picture of Ira lying in state can be seen at https://gettyimages.com /detail/news-photo/this-is-an-elevation-view-showing-mourners-as-they -filed-news-photo/515015306.

21. John Leptich, "Ira Hayes Burial Still Vivid in Mind of Scottsdale Man," *East Valley Tribune*, May 30, 2005, updated October 7, 2011, https://east valleytribune.com/social/ira-hayes-burial-still-vivid-in-mind-of-scottsdale -man/article-f264035b-ee59-5640-bec6-f2a16626f8ab.html.

22. Jerry Poole, "Body of Arizona War Hero Rests in Arlington Plot," *Arizona Republic*, February 3, 1955, p. 15.

23. "Inside Washington, Death of Hero Ira Hayes to Spark New Indian Probe?," *Vidette-Messenger*, February 19, 1955, p. 4.

24. "Hayes' Death Stirs National Group," *Arizona Republic*, February 5, 1955, p. 1.

25. "Post Named for Hayes," *Tucson Citizen*, May 14, 1955, p. 8.

26. "Hayes Foundation to Assist Indians," *Messenger Inquirer*, September 21, 1955, p. 2.

27. "Presbyterian Women Meet," *Pike County Dispatch*, August 25, 1955, p. 4.

28. "Mrs. Ethel Russell Entertains WCTU," *Canton Independent-Sentinel*, June 28, 1956, p. 10.

29. "Blue Star Mothers Honor Ira Hayes," *Arizona Republic*, October 10, 1955, p. 16; "Ira Hayes Veterans Service Unit Formed," *Casa Grande Dispatch*, October, 13, 1955, p. 7; "Blue Star Mothers Honor Hayes," *Arizona Republic*, January 31, 1956, p. 4.

30. "Memorial Rites Honor War Hero Ira Hayes," *Tucson Daily Citizen*, February 23, 1956, p. 11; "Flag Presented at Ira Hayes Monument," *Casa Grande Dispatch*, October 25, 1956, pp. 1, 4.

31. "Famed Picture of Iwo Jima Flag Raising Was Framed by Photographer," *Shreveport Times*, June 21, 1956, p. 10; Westbrook Pegler, "Flag Raising Photo Was a Retake," *Arizona Republic*, June 23, 1956, p. 6.

32. Luis Martinez, "Marine Corps Again Correct Who Was in Iconic Iwo Jima Flag Raising Photo," ABC News, October 17, 2019, abcnews.go.com /us/marines-correct-identity-member-raising-flag-iconic-iwo/story ?id=66348494.

33. Dennis Wagner, "War Hero's Death Mask Discovered, Laid to Rest," *Arizona Republic*, December 2, 2009, pp. 1, 14.

Chapter 10. Hollywood Calls Again

1. "Huie to Write Hayes Story," *Tucson Citizen*, February 18, 1955, p. 6.

2. "William Bradford Huie," *Encyclopedia of Alabama*, https://encyclopedia ofalabama.org/article/h-1547.

3. Jill Collen Jefferson, "Journalist William Huie Concealed Lynchers in Emmett Till Case and Got Away with It," *Mississippi Free Press*, 2021.

4. "'Ira Hayes' Heads to Arizona," *Arizona Republic*, November 11, 1959, p. 10; Jack Curtis, "'Sixth Man' Filming Begins," *Arizona Republic*, September 27, 1960, p. 47.

5. Huie, *The Hero of Iwo Jima*, p. 9.

6. Huie, *The Hero of Iwo Jima*, p. 16.

7. Huie, *The Hero of Iwo Jima*, pp. 26–27.

8. Huie, *The Hero of Iwo Jima*, p. 21.

9. Huie, *The Hero of Iwo Jima*, p. 49.

10. Huie, *The Hero of Iwo Jima*, pp. 62–63.
11. Huie, *The Hero of Iwo Jima*, p. vii.
12. See Philip J. Deloria, *Playing Indian*.
13. Marubbio and Buffalohead, *Native Americans on Film*, p. 148.
14. Robert Piser, "Story Sparks Bitter Pima Protest," *Arizona Republic*, February 28, 1960, p. 7.
15. Robert Piser, "Pima's Washington Trip to Get TV Story Changed of Little Avail," *Arizona Republic*, March 14, 1960, p. 39.
16. Robert Piser, "Story Sparks Bitter Pima Protest," *Arizona Republic*, February 28, 1960, p. 7.
17. Erskine Johnson, "'Piracy' Founders...," *Arizona Daily Star*, November 30, 1959, p. 10.
18. Denicola, "Copyright in Collection of Facts," pp. 516–542.
19. Joe Finnigan, "NBC Trying to Beat His Film on Marine Hero, Huie Charges," *Miami Herald*, January 5, 1960, p. 51.
20. "Judge Refuses to Halt TV Show," *Baltimore Sun*, March 26, 1960, p. 6.
21. Huie, *Hero of Iwo Jima*, p. viii.
22. I was able to screen *The Outsider* and *Flags of Our Fathers* but not *The American*. Fortunately, I found several reviews of *The American* while searching the internet.
23. Vine Deloria Jr., *We Talk, You Listen*, pp. 35–37.
24. Allen and Holm, "Fighting the White Man's Wars," in Marubbio, Pavlik, and Holm, *Native Apparitions*, pp. 66–67.
25. "Eastwood Rejects Lee's Criticism of His WW2 Films," Reuters, May 28, 2008, https://reuters.com/article/us-eastwood-lee/eastwood-rejects-lees-criticism-of-his-ww2-films-idUSL2360132920080523; Christy Lemire, "In a Spike Lee War Tale, Restraint Is a Casualty, *News Journal*, September 26, 2008, p. 64.
26. Loren Webster, "Ai's 'I Can't Get Started,'" in *A Dark Time...the Eye Begins to See*, February 19, 2008, http://www.lorenwebster.net/In_a_Dark_Time/2008/02/19/ais-i-cant-get-started/.
27. Ai, *Vice: New and Selected Poems* (New York: W. W. Norton & Company, 1999), pp. 38–39.
28. Marsha Burks Megehee, "(The Ghost of) Ira Hayes," n.d., http://wrensworld.com/irahayes.htm.
29. Cook, "The Indian Who Raised the Flag," pp. 84–94.
30. Cook, "The Indian Who Raised the Flag," pp. 90–91.
31. "Heroes: Then There Were Two," *Time*, February 7, 1955.

Index

INDEX

INDEX

INDEX

Photo Credits

Page 1 (top) Department of Defense (USMC), National Archives, Public Domain; (middle) Navy History and Heritage Command, Gift of Abbot Laboratories. Public Domain; (bottom) Historical Branch, Headquarters, USMC / John M. Rentz, National Archives. Public Domain

Page 2 (top) Department of Defense (USMC), National Archives, Public Domain; (middle) Department of Defense / Joe Rosenthal, National Archives, Public Domain; (bottom) AP/Joe Rosenthal

Page 3 (top) Getty Images; (middle) Harry S. Truman Library / Harris and Ewing Photograph; (bottom) Getty Images

Page 4 (top) Getty Images; (middle) True Comics, 1945 / Ralph O. Ellsworth, Art Director / Author's Collection; (bottom) *Herald Examiner* Collection, Los Angeles Public Library Photo Archive, Tessa Photos and Digital Collection

Page 5 (top) Together We Served, Freedom Train Tour, 1947–49; (middle) AP / Ira Guldner; (bottom) Wisconsin Center for Film and Theater Research Photograph, University of Wisconsin-Madison, and Wisconsin Historical Society

Page 6 (top) Getty Images; (middle) AP / *Los Angeles Mirror*; (bottom) AP

Page 7 (top) Getty Images; (middle) Arizona State Library, Archives, Arizona Memory Project; (bottom) AP

Page 8 (top) AP; (middle) Getty Images; (bottom) Getty Images

About the Author

Tom Holm is a professor emeritus of American Indian Studies at the University of Arizona. Professor Holm has published over fifty articles, books, pamphlets, government reports, book reviews and essays, editorials, and book chapters. An enrolled citizen of the Cherokee Nation with Muskogee Creek ancestry, Holm has served on numerous Native American organization boards, panels, and working groups. He is a US Marine Corps veteran of the Vietnam War and has taken part in several programs dealing with veterans' affairs.